DILEMMAS OF REPRESENTATION

DILEMMAS OF REPRESENTATION

Local Politics, National Factors, and the
Home Styles of Modern U.S. Congress Members

Sally Friedman

STATE UNIVERSITY OF NEW YORK PRESS

Published by
State University of New York Press, Albany

© 2007 State University of New York

For information, address State University of New York Press, Albany, NY
www.sunypress.edu

Production by Kelli W. LeRoux
Marketing by Michael Campochiaro

Library of Congress Cataloging-in-Publication Data
Friedman, Sally, 1950–
Dilemmas of representation : local politics, national factors, and
the home styles of modern U.S. Congress members / Sally Friedman.
Includes bibliographical references and index.
ISBN-13: 978-0-7914-7075-6 (hardcover : alk. paper)
1. State governments—United States.
2. Federal government—United States.
3. Representative government and representation—United States.
I. Title.
JK2408.F75 2007
328.73—dc22   2006023730

10 9 8 7 6 5 4 3 2 1

For Gable

CONTENTS

List of Illustrations ix

Acknowledgments xi

Author's Note xiii

Chapter 1. Introduction 1

Chapter 2. Overview of Theoretical and
Methodological Concerns 13

Chapter 3. Rethinking the Local-National Debate 30
Carolyn Maloney: Getting Involved at Home
and in Washington 35
Amo Houghton: Public Service with a
Business Slant 50
John McHugh: "I Know the Process and
I Know the Players" 64

Chapter 4. National Parties, Individual Choices
(with Christopher Witko) 80
Sue Kelly: Balancing Constituent Interests,
Issues, and Party 86
Michael McNulty: Interactions among Party,
Constituency, and a Changing Political Context 101
Carolyn McCarthy: Politics Made Personal on
Long Island's 4th 116

Chapter 5. The Local-National Connection and the
Representation of Minorities *(with Michael Rogers)* 139
Eliot Engel: Bringing Together Difference 149
Nydia Velazquez: Latino Culture Drives
the Politics of the 12th 160

Chapter 6.   Balancing Constituencies: Fenno's
             Bull's-eye Model in the 1990s   176
             Jack Quinn: Having Your Cake
             and Eating It Too   185
             Maurice Hinchey: Issue Activist
             at Home in his District   202

Chapter 7.   Concluding Perspectives   221

             Postscript   242

             Notes   253

             Works Cited   261

             Index   267

ILLUSTRATIONS

Tables

Table 2.1   Demographic Variation across New York State's
            Congressional Districts   26

Table 2.2   Characteristics of Project Sample versus Entire New York
            State Delegation   27

Table 3.1   Constituency Characteristics and Election Results for Reps.
            Maloney, Houghton, and McHugh   37

Table 4.1   Constituency Characteristics and Election Results for Reps.
            Kelly, McNulty, and McCarthy   88

Table 5.1   Constituency Characteristics and Election Results for Reps.
            Engel and Velazquez   146

Table 6.1   Constituency Characteristics and Election Results for Reps.
            Quinn and Hinchey   183

Table 7.1   Analysis of Local and National References on Legislator
            Web sites   225

Table 7.2   Summary of Home Styles, Constituency Characteristics,
            and Legislator Backgrounds   232

Table 7.3   Types of Home Styles by Constituency Factors and
            Legislator Backgrounds   233

Maps

Map 1   New York State Congressional Districts   14

Map 2   Congressional Districts for Reps. Maloney, Houghton,
        and McHugh   31

Map 3   Congressional Districts for Reps. Kelly, McNulty,
        and McCarthy   81

Map 4   Congressional Districts for Reps. Engel
        and Velazquez   140

Map 5   Congressional Districts for Reps. Quinn
        and Hinchey   177

ACKNOWLEDGMENTS

This project began out of discussions in a graduate seminar on legislative process at the State University of New York at Albany. At the time (1998) of the twentieth anniversary of the publication of Richard Fenno's classic *Home Style,* we were surprised to find how little follow-up had been done to understand constituent representation in the context of the changed political context of the subsequent few decades. Thus, several graduate students—Joe Cavasoz (College of St. Rose), Dave Filbert, Paul Goggi, Krista Ketterer, Leah Murray, Michael Rogers, Christopher Witko—and I engaged in a series of stimulating conversations, consumed an inordinate amount of pizza, and produced several convention papers. We would all like to acknowledge the enthusiasm and support of Dick Fenno, a former undergraduate professor of mine at the University of Rochester, for both the quality of his scholarship and the boost his interest and excitement added particularly at the initial stages of our project. It proved a fun time, and I want to acknowledge with love and gratitude the contributions to the project of those former students, two of whom are co-authors on chapters 4 and 5 and all of whom are productively employed and fully engaged in life after graduate school.

I also want to acknowledge the work of several research assistants over what became a longer than expected seven-year odyssey (no wonder they didn't believe me when I insisted it would be done soon!). In particular, the work of Robert Usinger, Erin Smith, and Cecilia Ferradino went above and beyond the call of duty. I would also like to thank John Majewski, Jordan Wishy, Danielle Croce, Tamara Benson-O'Brien, Shannon Scotece, and Robert Tynes for their research assistance; Dick Irving, Ellie Leggieri, and Lorre Smith from the university staff; and Chuck Anderson for an ongoing set of productive discussions on the writing process. In addition, I appreciate the input and support of colleagues, particularly Anne Hildreth, Michael Malbin, Bruce Miroff, and Joseph Zimmerman at SUNY Albany; Bruce Oppenheimer at Vanderbilt University; and Herbert Weisberg at The Ohio State University. It goes without saying that I also acknowledge the ongoing love of family members including my parents, Manny and Doris Friedman, as well as my Friedman sibling Dan along with his family Irene, Dana, and Rebecca. Finally, this book is dedicated with love (though no food) to Gable, my friend and guide dog. He devoured our pizza crusts, shared in the late night work sessions, and contributed his unique brand of fun, making the process considerably more entertaining and enjoyable.

AUTHOR'S NOTE

- Note that the Congressional redistricting of 2002 led to some changes in the district numbers that appear in this book. Since the research took place prior to the 2002 redistricting, the former numbers are used. The following lists the district numbers described throughout this book along with the new numbers (in parentheses):

Chapter 3
Carolyn Maloney:	14th	(14th)
Amo Houghton:	31st	(29th)
John McHugh:	24th	(23rd)

Chapter 4
Sue Kelly:	19th	(19th)
Michael McNulty:	21st	(21st)
Carolyn McCarthy:	4th	(4th)

Chapter 5
Eliot Engel:	17th	(17th)
Nydia Velazquez:	12th	(12th)

Chapter 6
Jack Quinn:	30th	(27th)
Maurice Hinchey:	26th	(22nd)

- Reps. Quinn and Houghton announced their retirements at the conclusion of the 108th Congress. (see Postscript)

- Partisanship—It will become apparent as one reads these profiles that several of the Democrats described throughout this study use fairly partisan rhetoric, often outdoing their Republican counterparts in that regard. Since the profiles are written to highlight the perceptions of the particular legislators under study, the reader should be clear to distinguish those viewpoints as statements of opinion and perspective.

- Press releases are denoted as "PR" throughout the book.

- Congress members' individual Web sites are abbreviated throughout the text. For instance, http://www.house.gov/maloney is denoted as: (www . . . maloney).

- Newspapers and some references are noted first by their full titles in the beginning of the chapters and abbreviated thereafter. The abbreviations are as follows:

New York State newspapers:
   BN: *Buffalo News*
   SG: *Elmira Star Gazette*
   IJ: *Ithaca Journal*
   KDF: *Kingston Daily Freeman*
   DN: *New York Daily News*
   NYP: *New York Post*
   NYT: *New York Times*
   PJ: *Poughkeepsie Journal*
   PS: *Binghamton Press & Sun-Bulletin*
   TU: *Albany Times Union*
   WDT: *Watertown Daily Times*

National newspapers:
   AP: *The Associated Press State and Local Wire*
   WSJ: *Wall Street Journal*
   WP: *Washington Post*

Reference texts:
   Almanac: *Almanac of American Politics*
   CDs in the 1990s: *Congressional Districts in the 1990s*
   CR: *Congressional Record*
   PIA: *Politics in America*

National media:
   NPR: *National Public Radio*

Chapter 1

INTRODUCTION

Carolyn Maloney, Democrat, New York City
August 20, 2001—Maloney Condemns Violence in Middle East
August 7, 2001—NYC Will Lose Millions of Dollars Because Just Like
Florida the Bush Administration Wants the (census) Count to Stop
August 2, 2001—Maloney Speaks to Breastfeeding Advocates in Washington

Jack Quinn, Republican, Buffalo, New York
September 25, 2002—Rep. Jack Quinn Announces $1.8M in Federal Funds
to the Buffalo Niagara International Airport
September 27, 2001—Rep. Jack Quinn Announces Federal Funds for Local
Crime Fighting Technology
September 25, 2001—Historic Rail Infrastructure Legislation Introduced
in U.S. House

Consider the above quotes, drawn from press releases on the Web sites of two members of the United States House of Representatives. If we take these headlines as indications of legislator behavior, it is clear that there are both similarities and differences in how these two legislators present themselves to constituents. Both Reps. Maloney and Quinn are making constituents aware of their activities on behalf of the local areas they represent—Maloney is highlighting the importance of the census to New York City (headline 2), and Quinn, representing the area in and around Buffalo, New York, is focusing on obtaining funding to assist with the local problems of crime prevention and improved airline facilities (headlines 1 and 3). Both representatives are also associating themselves with the national scene, Maloney by commenting on the Middle East and the need for breastfeeding and Quinn by reference to the "landmark" railroad legislation he has sponsored.

However, it is clear that the balance of "local" and "national" emphasis articulated by each of these Congress members differs significantly. Judging from these headlines, Maloney's focus is more national, and her tone is more partisan. Even when she is advocating for local concerns—the impact of the census—she is reminding the voters of her largely Democratic congressional district of her perceptions of the partisan tactics of the Republican Party during the controversial 2000 presidential election. Though Quinn highlights railroad legislation with clear national implications, the image from these headlines is that he first and foremost is attempting to represent his constituents by boosting the economy and quality of life of the local area. In addition, though in fact a solid Republican, Quinn, in these headlines, is downplaying his partisanship, actually providing no indication of his party affiliation.

These headlines serve as concrete illustrations of some of the key themes and ideas of this project. Though the Founders, via the U.S. Constitution, built a certain degree of ambiguity and tension in delineating the complex role of "legislator" (chapter 3)—should a legislator "represent" the local and potentially parochial interests of his/her constituents, or should he or she focus on a larger and perhaps more comprehensive national picture?—the Congress literature of the 1970s and 1980s has led to the dominant impression that "all politics is local." Members of Congress spend a good deal of time interacting with constituents, providing ombudsperson services, and working in Washington on advancing the concerns of the local folks. Heading into the 1990s and beyond, many elements of politics (partisanship, candidate recruitment practices, voter attitudes, 9/11) have changed, potentially pointing legislative behavior in a more national, and even an international, direction. Does this mean that "modern-day" representatives will bring a more national and partisan flavor as they present themselves to local constituents? What factors account for any variation in the balance of local and national emphasis, and what does this variety of home styles teach us about the concept of representation more generally?

The central question of this work focuses attention on the balance of local and national concerns as legislators present themselves to constituents. Relying on public record sources and legislator Web sites, the argument to be developed through an in-depth examination of the activities of ten legislators from a single state (see below) is severalfold. As was true in the 1970s and 1980s, members of Congress today include strong local components in their home styles. But, for even the most locally oriented legislator, national factors matter as well. The intense partisanship characterizing the Washington scene, major national issues, and other out-of-district factors all contribute to an understanding of local politics. Even more, the worlds of the "local" and the "national" may not be as separate as they are often depicted; there appear today to be any number of, mostly (but not entirely) positive, ways by which representatives have found to connect local and national politics.

Because of this variety, it is equally important to explain why some legislators develop a more "national" focus than others. Despite the dominant trend toward more "national" attention, we need to understand the factors underlying legislator behavior and to appreciate that members of Congress may adopt alternative strategies as to how to present themselves to constituents. Hence, the title of this book, *Dilemmas of Representation,* is intended to engage the reader to think about, on the one hand, the appropriate balance of local and national emphasis in legislator presentations and, on the other, the advantages and disadvantages of the contrasting representational styles utilized by some modern-day representatives, who also turn out to comprise an interesting cast of characters.[1]

Politics in the 1970s and 1990s: Toward More National Home Styles

As might be expected, given the above indications of member presentations of self, the starting point for the present work is Richard Fenno's (1978) seminal book, *Home Style.* As congressional scholars well know, by highlighting the district-oriented aspects of a member's activities, Fenno augmented scholarly conceptions of representation. Through an in-depth and "over-the-shoulder" examination of the legislator as he or she perceives the district, Fenno argued in addition to their often studied activity in Washington that "observing and listening to House members at home makes it clear that each one also pursues a career in the district" (Fenno 1978, 171).

As such, Fenno enriched the conceptualization of constituency to highlight its complexity—his well-known bulls-eye model suggests that the geographic (legal) constituency (e.g., Quinn represents the Buffalo area) that often serves as the focus of political analysis might actually be only the beginning of the story. As legislators interact with their nested sets of constituencies (geographic, reelection, primary, intimate; see chapter 2), and additionally, as they consider their own opinions and experiences, representatives make complex choices about their multifaceted presentations of self to constituents, their home styles.

For the most part, in the 1970s when Fenno wrote, these legislative choices pointed representatives homeward. Based on a qualitative analysis of the strategic situations of eighteen U.S. representatives, Fenno's main conclusion emphasized that representation starts at home. Legislators were generally fairly district focused. They and their contemporaries spent large portions of time in their districts (Fenno 1978, 57) and allocated large proportions of staff time to district-oriented activity. Members felt it necessary to know their constituents personally, to be in touch with constituent concerns and to be available to provide a variety of services. Within the district, visibility, allocation of resources, presentation of self, and continually winning and holding constituent trust were important keys to success.

In fact, Fenno's work is replete with all manner of very human stories highlighting the local: representatives re-traversing fairgrounds to demonstrate accuracy in recalling a constituent's name (Congressman A, 64), appearing before multiple audiences in short time periods (Congressman B, 70), and engaging in an astounding number of almost two hundred town meetings per year so as to interact with constituents in literally every legal jurisdiction within the district (Congressman D, 95). Further, Fenno showed that failure to engage in these kinds of personal interactions could be costly; one legislator (Congressman E), in his zeal to make a personal connection, even shook hands with someone in his own caravan of cars (109)—a faux pas indicative of a somewhat problematic home style.

At a more profound level, the members of Congress Fenno studied had incredibly strong roots in their districts. Three generations of Congressman A's family had held public office (Fenno 1978, 65), Congressman B had been the popular local boy who ran for Congress in the same way he ran for high school class president (Fenno 1978, 74), and Congressman D, who wasn't originally from the district, made it a point to develop a detailed understanding of the area's characteristics by gathering knowledge through his commitment to three district offices, "coffees," and open meetings (Fenno 1978, 93–95).

Fenno highlighted the "local" and the personal: "Viewed from this perspective, the archetypal constituent question is not 'What have you done for me lately?' but 'How have you looked to me lately?'" (Fenno 1978, 56). He adds:

> Constituents may want extra policy behavior from their representatives. They may want good access or the assurance of good access as much as they

want good policy. They may want a "good man" or "a good woman," someone whose assurances they can trust, as much as they want good policy. They may want communication promises as much as they want policy promises. (241)

Subsequent legislative scholarship has elaborated on this local view of representation. The often-documented advantages accruing to incumbents, the exigencies of candidate-centered politics and the reduced nature of presidential coattails over the last few decades all give credence to Fenno's view of home style. For one, incumbents can be secure and safe in their districts because their congressional status gives them increased funds for trips home and expands the communication possibilities with constituents (Jacobson 2001; Mayhew 1973, 1974). The increasing importance of the ombudsperson function provides incumbents an additional set of noncontroversial activities to use as credit-claiming material with constituents (Fiorina 1977). So, the fact that winning elections seems to be due to the efforts of individual candidates and their actions within their districts rather than their partisanship, their party's presidential success, or other national factors, means that even more depends on the representative-constituent connection (Jacobson 2001; Mann and Wolfinger 1981; Parker 1989, 1986; Ragsdale 1980). In short, incumbents have been able to utilize a wide array of resources, the franking privilege, increased staff, committee activities, etc., to cement their relationships with constituents and to secure their congressional seats.

Yet, while many of these phenomena have continued to be influential in American politics over the past two decades, major aspects of society and politics have changed. Despite "localism," national factors are currently quite consequential in legislative life and have the potential to pose new dilemmas and choices for representatives.

At the societal level, increased geographic mobility enhances the potential that new residents to an area would naturally bring the broader perspectives of their prior socialization to their current lives. In addition, a wide variety of major corporations (hotels, restaurants, businesses) have franchises all across the nation, "homogenizing" available options and choices. Sources of nationwide television news (CNN, C-SPAN, etc.) are now available and, of course, the Internet and the World Wide Web have opened up unprecedented new communication tools for citizens and legislators alike, contributing to the potential for national and even international perspectives.

More to the point, some fairly remarkable changes in the political arena have increased the potential for extra-district forces to impact local politics, often in more national and polarizing directions. Events of the 1960s and 1970s—including the civil rights movement, the Vietnam War, and Watergate—contributed toward a dramatic growth in public interest groups of all kinds (the women's movement, consumerism, environmentalism, etc.), and throughout the 1970s and 1980s, a more conservative "backlash" impacted modern politics. Also, it goes without saying that the horrific events surrounding 9/11 have certainly moved politics and legislative behavior in more national directions.

Consequently, the number of viable interest groups around the nation has increased dramatically as has the number of groups led by a centralized leadership originating from a Washington headquarters (Barry 1999; Polsby 2004). These groups have the potential both to nationalize some issues and to provide a training ground for politicians who could ultimately run for Congress providing a national perspective (Ehrenhalt 1991). Also, with the advent of campaign finance regulations, the creation of Political Action Committees (PACs) has meant that interest groups and organized sources of out-of-district money can be raised and spent by legislators within their individual constituencies.

Changing recruitment patterns also point in more national directions. Witness the tendency toward more policy-oriented legislators at the state level (Erhenhalt 1991; Fenno 2000; Fiorina 2005). Witness as well the increased diversity of members of Congress, a diversity that might well point more members toward a national focus. The significant increases in the number of representatives with business backgrounds (Davidson and Oleszek 2002) along with, from a very different perspective, the increased number of women and minorities running for office mean that the makeup of Congress is very different today than it was a few decades ago. Since these members may draw attention from many parts of the country (for example, the excitement in 1992 over the particularly large freshman classes of women [Margolies-Mezvinsky 1994] and minorities [Davidson and Oleszek 2002]), and since the interests of these members and their constituents may reflect broad-based concerns reaching beyond the boundaries of their districts, many such representatives could reasonably be expected to bring a more national perspective to their home styles.

Other trends in recruitment patterns also increase the potential for national perspectives among legislators. Herrnson (1994) has demonstrated that an increasing number of Washington staffers go on to run for congressional office. Perhaps low on local district ties, these staffers may have little choice but to emphasize their national connections.

And within Congress, too, there have been major changes. Over the time Fenno was writing, more opportunities for entrepreneurship by members of Congress (an expanded subcommittee system, a decline of the apprenticeship norm, and large classes of activist members [1974 and 1992 on the Democratic side, 1980 and 1994 for the Republicans]) increased the possibilities for legislators to take initiatives in a variety of ways. While many of these changes were occurring at the very time Fenno was researching home styles, it is certainly possible that most of his work took place prior to the full impact of these changes.

Lastly, but certainly not least, the national parties play an increasing role in the lives of members (Davidson and Oleszek 2002; Jacobson 2001; Sinclair 1998). Party has become more of a force at the Washington level as witnessed by events including developments of the 104th Congress, the impeachment controversy, and the more general increase in the role of party leadership, discipline, and clout (chapter 4) (Bader 1996; Davidson and Oleszek 2002; Gimpel 1996; Rohde 1991). Even more, the national parties have come to play an increasing role in local campaigns, targeting certain congressional races as critical, assisting in the recruitment and training of candidates, and contributing significant financial help (Bullock, Shafer, and Bianco 1999; Davidson and Oleszek 2002; Fowler and McClure 1989; Jacobson 2001). As Uslaner (1993) summarizes, "Politics is now not just a serious business but a highly polarized one. Give and take has given way to non-negotiable demands" (1).

Perhaps as a consequence, recent scholarship (see chapter 2) has documented changing voter attitudes toward the local and the national. Scholars have thus demonstrated both an increasing interest in national concerns when examining voter attitudes (Jacobson 2001) and consequently an increasing "national" component to aggregate congressional election results (Fiorina 2005). The bottom line is that sociopolitical times have changed, and members of Congress are confronted with new opportunities and challenges. The political environment in which members operate includes more national, and in some cases international, elements, so forces outside a member's district have an increased potential to influence legislator district-oriented activities. Much has been learned about how these forces operate at the Washington level. In turn, the questions for this book focus attention on how these changes impact representatives' work in the local districts. What do home styles look like given the current political context? How do members of Congress integrate national level forces into their district-oriented presentations of self?

Project Goals and Contribution

It is the goal of this project then to first describe the home styles of some modern-day members of Congress. Given the recent sociopolitical changes described above, there is a need to think through the ways more national elements impact what members do in their individual districts.

Put another way, current congressional scholarship has tended to focus on the national implications of national trends. Literature with a national focus, including that on responsible parties, has emphasized party leadership activity in Washington (Bader 1996; Davidson and Oleszek 2002; Gimpel 1996; Rohde 1991; Sinclair 1998), roll call votes of members (Ansolabehere, Snyder, and Stewart 2001; Davidson and Oleszek 2002; Smith 2000), or explications of the norms of the Washington scene such as a decline in comity (Uslaner 1993). This body of literature has added enormously to our understanding of Congress, yet there is simply a need to know more about the response of the average member working day-to-day in his or her local district to these important national trends.

The research for this work has implications for a related question: What are the connections for the individual member of Congress between activity at home and in Washington? As will become clear in chapter 2, while scholars agree that such a connection is, of course, critical, they disagree about its nature. For instance, whereas important textbooks sometimes point to very little connection between home and Washington (legislators simply engage in different activities in the diverse arenas [Davidson and Oleszek 2002]), other scholars (Fenno 1978) tend to assume negative connections. In terms of time and energy, members must make tradeoffs, and too much of a Washington focus may hurt at home.

At the same time, given today's politics, we might expect representatives to bring a more national focus to Congress. This book will argue that though in some cases the home-Washington connection may in fact be a negative one (what you do in one arena can hurt you in the other), at least in today's House of Representatives, there are indeed a surprisingly wide variety of strategies representatives can use to develop positive connections between the local and the national. At the very least, the case studies will suggest a more complex and variable home-Washington linkage than has been commonly assumed.

A second goal of this book revolves around understanding and explaining variation. Despite trends toward nationalization, the Maloney and Quinn excerpts above make clear that some members of Congress have become more involved nationally while others have chosen to stay more locally focused. Given the more national environment of modern politics, what opportunities and constraints lead members to make alternative choices? Thus, Fenno has argued that a variety of constituency characteristics and member backgrounds explain variation in home styles. In each of the profiles to follow, I will consider the ways these factors impact each legislator's home style and also how the opportunities and constraints at the national level interact to also shape and define or constrain these presentational strategies.

Given this variation, it makes sense that this book is also about understanding and appreciating the alternative choices modern legislators make as they deal with a changing and more national representational environment. Through in-depth case studies of ten members of Congress, the project seeks to put a human face on how and why legislators make the important choices that shape their behavior. In an environment where national factors are present, how and why do some legislators choose to emphasize local or parochial concerns while others highlight more national concerns, connections, or contributions? Why have some members jumped on the "responsible party" bandwagon that has been so prevalent in the last decade or so while others have purposefully eschewed extreme partisanship? Why have some members chosen to focus on a subgroup of constituents (specific racial minorities, partisan or economic interests) while others develop a more inclusive reelection constituency which they hope will appeal to broad segments of the population?

As will become clear, an examination of each of these questions will enhance and broaden an understanding of the local-national linkage. In turn, as is also clear from these questions, such an understanding touches on many aspects of politics. Indeed, one important virtue of the case study methodology employed by Fenno and throughout this study is to highlight the many roles and activities in which members of Congress engage. That is, it is the contribution of any study of home style to highlight the variety of roles played by representatives. Legislators are busy people. Not only do they focus on policy, but they also serve as local party or group leaders and engage in a host of constituency-oriented functions. One really comes to appreciate the human dimension of the representative-constituent linkage as well as its impact on the lives of individual citizens.

Therefore, the case studies presented below focus attention more generally on the title of this book: *Dilemmas of Representation*. Members of Congress make alternative choices about which activities to engage in within their districts. From a normative perspective, the reader is encouraged to think about which kinds of choices are best. Are the legislators profiled here providing "optimal" representation for their individual constituencies? Who is doing the best job overall, and what combination of representative styles would be best for the nation as we head into the twenty-first century?

Overview of the Book

Using public record sources (see below), this book focuses on home styles in a more national environment, the choices legislators make in responding to this environment, and the consequent "dilemmas" these choices pose for constituent representation. To accomplish these goals, this work presents profiles of the home styles of ten legislators chosen from a single, though diverse, state (New York; see chapter 2 for methodology). In accord with the arguments described above, each profile details the "local" and the "national" elements of a legislator's home style along with the factors contributing to such a style.

Each legislator profile is interesting in and of itself, and each contributes to an understanding of the local-national connection. For the purposes of highlighting the other goals of this project—the variation in legislative choices and the larger dilemmas such choices pose for representation more generally—the presentation of the legislator profiles has been organized in chapters so as to emphasize some of the changes that have taken place since the 1970s and to raise the very real dilemmas those changes pose for modern representation. After a more detailed discussion as to the theory and methodology of this work (chapter 2), each of the four case study chapters makes a contribution to an examination of the following concerns:

To begin, can home styles include notable national elements? The profiles of Representatives Maloney and Houghton presented in chapter 3 demonstrate that in addition to the localism highlighted by the legislative literature of the 1970s, national elements indeed have the potential to play an important role in some home styles. The advantages and disadvantages of such representational styles become even more apparent when these two legislators are contrasted with the presentation of self of a more locally oriented representative. John McHugh not only has the electoral freedom to "go national" but also represents a constituency in many respects similar to the area represented by Congressman Houghton. However, McHugh has chosen to focus primarily on concerns that reflect dominant local interests. Thus, the chapter examines the factors contributing to the different responses of these three legislators.

In addition, all members of Congress must deal with the increasingly partisan context of Washington. Chapter 4 adds to our appreciation of the "national" by demonstrating the tradeoffs made by three congresspeople as they develop home styles that attempt to balance increased national partisanship with constituent needs and their own personal concerns. Thus, early on to her advantage but later to her detriment, Republican Sue Kelly jumped on the "responsible party" bandwagon of 1994. Previously loyal Democrat Michael McNulty, similarly confronted with the increasingly conservative tide, was also perceived as jumping on the 1995 Republican bandwagon and therefore as jumping ship not only from his party but also from important segments of his constituency. In contrast, Representative Carolyn McCarthy has developed a home style that has been steadfastly nonpartisan in nature. Thus, confronted with a similar national and partisan environment, these three members of Congress exhibited varying responses to the trend toward increasingly responsible national parties.

Switching gears, chapter 5 highlights a very different national trend, the increasing population diversity across the United States and hence the increasing tendency toward multiethnic or multiracial congressional districts. Because of their extremely diverse constituencies, Representatives Engel and Velazquez face some fairly unique representational challenges; since Rep. Engel highlights constituency service and the commonalities among distinct groups, while Velazquez emphasizes issues of empowerment and difference, their profiles indicate contrasting responses to important changes in American demographics, responses that, as we shall see, also have important implications for the local-national distinction.

Finally, if chapter 3 highlighted ways to "go national," the last two profiles (chapter 6) of Representatives Jack Quinn and Maurice Hinchey return us full circle to Fenno's work, focusing on the continued existence of tensions prevalent at the local level and a congressperson's consequent efforts to balance reelection and primary constituencies. However, as we shall see, even here in two cases where home styles are primarily local, national factors enter in. The national agenda has shaped aspects of the behavior of both these members, and at times, each has been thrust in the national spotlight. In addition, the larger context of a declining economy in both districts has impacted what these members of Congress have chosen for their respective foci of attention, highlighting the importance of extra-district concerns and events.

In sum, as the concluding chapter and the postscript will highlight, in the current political environment, there are more ways than there were in the 1970s for national factors to impact local districts. The changes that have occurred since Fenno's initial work have the potential to pose new challenges for modern-day representatives as they attempt to integrate local and national concerns. By engaging in the conceptualization and profiles to follow, the reader will be better able to think through the implications of connections between local and national politics.

Chapter 2

OVERVIEW OF THEORETICAL AND METHODOLOGICAL CONCERNS

"I'm beginning to be a little concerned about my political future. I can feel
myself getting into what I guess is a natural and inevitable condition—the
gradual erosion of my local orientation. I'm not as enthused about tending
my constituency relations as I used to be and I'm not paying them the
attention I should be." . . . There's a natural tension between being a good
representative and taking an interest in government. "I'm getting into some
heady things in Washington, and I want to make an input into the
government. It's making me a poorer representative than I was."
—Fenno, *Home Style*

"All politics is local," the famous aphorism of Speaker of the House Tip
O'Neill, was the mantra of our generation of congressional scholars.
Everyone recognized that it was overstated, but it was a pretty good way of
summing up the era of incumbency and insulation. Little did we know that
the fit of the aphorism to empirical reality was growing worse even at the
apparent height of the power of incumbency.
—Fiorina, "Keystone Reconsidered"

So, the basic questions have been set out. In the face of a changed political
landscape, what do home styles look like at the end of the 1990s? How do
members of Congress make choices to integrate national-level forces into
their district-oriented presentations of self?

As indicated in chapter 1, a more extensive review of the literature highlighting a changed political landscape will be provided in the individual
case study chapters. It is the purpose of this chapter to focus the reader on
additional aspects of the theoretical framework and to specify the research
design developed to answer the questions set out above.

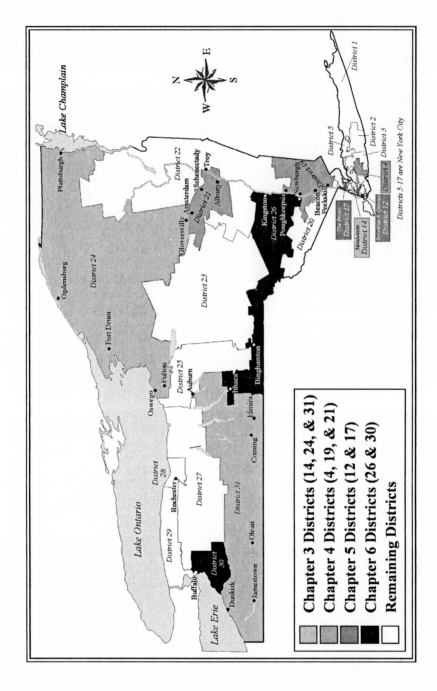

Map 1. New York State Congressional Districts

Chapter 3 Districts (14, 24, & 31)
Chapter 4 Districts (4, 19, & 21)
Chapter 5 Districts (12 & 17)
Chapter 6 Districts (26 & 30)
Remaining Districts

Perspectives on the Local-National Balance

As the discussion of chapter 1 implies, there are now more centralizing forces throughout the layers of national politics including partisanship, recruitment practices, out-of-district groups/PACs (political action committees), and 9/11. Though these forces may impact congresspeople differently, all legislators must take them into account as part of their daily activities. Given a political landslide of one tilt or another, legislators decide whether to jump on the bandwagon and make any alterations or to risk going against national tides and trends.

National factors, then, have the potential to impact local-level politics, and by extension, congressional home styles. So, what might an extremely nationally oriented home style look like, what are the ways members of Congress connect national-level events to what is going on in their local districts, and what then is the connection between the national environment and what takes place in local districts; in other words, the connection between the world in Washington and the world at home?

In the 1970s, one version of a national home style would be to remain in Washington and tout seniority: "I can't come home to present myself in person as much as I once did, because I'm so busy tending to the nation's business; but my seniority, my influence, my effectiveness in Washington is of great benefit to you" (Fenno 1978, 218). When such a representative does come home, one might expect her indeed to engage in a presentational style specifying the ways her time in Washington has in fact benefited the local folks back home.

But, what about legislators who come home often? In addition to their localism, a couple of Fenno's representatives did in fact bring a national perspective to their local presentations of self. Congressman D not only had a primary constituency very concerned over the Vietnam War, but even more, he himself had gotten his political start as an antiwar activist. Congressman F, a product of the civil rights movement, was constantly addressing a combination of local and national issues in his pursuit of racial equality. For these and the other representatives Fenno interviewed, the local predominated, but for several legislators, issue activism and/or identification with social causes reflected extra-district concerns as well.

Thus, wouldn't it be more natural for members today to be more likely to come home and raise nationally oriented concerns in their districts? In addition to senior members touting their accomplishments, a nationally oriented home style could be the presentational strategy defined by a representative who is in his/her district frequently but uses that time to link himself or herself to national issues (e.g., abortion, environmentalism, the Christian Right, etc.), or national figures and parties, for example, President Bush, national Republicans.

So, in this day and age, individual legislators may develop issue expertise, become party leaders or spokespeople, or become involved with concerns inside the Beltway. They vote on roll calls, take positions on issues not always related to their districts, and concentrate on the fortunes of the nation. They act as lawmakers, policymakers, or party leaders. As such, they must find ways to integrate this activity into their home styles.

What are their incentives to incorporate national issues or connections into their local presentations of self? First off, to the extent that politics has become more nationalized, it might simply be harder for legislators to keep the "national" out of their home styles. When, for instance, Speaker of the House Newt Gingrich and the "Republican Revolution" (1994) were at the height of popularity, wouldn't it have been likely that some legislators could benefit from their associations with him while others would be hurt? In any case, wouldn't it have been hard for legislators in their districts to come home and not comment on what Gingrich was doing? Ditto, on the effort to impeach President Clinton (1998), the events surrounding 9/11, and the subsequent war in Iraq.

In addition, constituent factors and legislator backgrounds are major determinants of presentations of self (Fenno 1978). Certain types of constituencies—for example, stereotypically those where constituents are highly educated or attuned to politics—might want their representatives to be more attentive to national concerns. Also, the nature of a representative's primary constituency in particular might impact how issue-oriented or nationally connected a legislator might be. Also, as I began to describe in chapter 1, and as Fenno's Congressmen D and F illustrate, the backgrounds of individual legislators themselves certainly influence their home styles.

But, should we really expect changes in the socioeconomic and political environment to filter down to local districts, and should we really expect members of Congress as a consequence to incorporate national elements into their local presentations of self?

Before proceeding, a brief clarification is in order. The Congress literature described below offers alternative views of the connection between what legislators do in their districts and what they do in Washington. It is helpful to recognize that a representative's Washington activity is certainly a subset of what is happening at the national level, but what is going on "nationally" certainly could be broader than a Washington focus, even sometimes including international events.

That said, an examination of the congressional literature suggests alternative perspectives on the local-national connection. The view from current textbooks infers that there could in fact be very little connection between the Washington environment and what is going on in individual congressional districts. Congress is "a lawmaking institution and . . . assembly of local representatives. The question is how can these disparate elements be reconciled?" (Davidson and Oleszek 2000, 4):

> The answer is that there are really two congresses. One is the congress of textbooks, of "how a bill becomes a law." It is congress acting as a collegial body, performing constitutional duties and debating legislative issues. . . . This congress is more than a collection of its members at any given time. It is a mature institution with a complex network of rules, structures, and traditions. These norms mark the boundaries of the legislative playing field and define the rules by which the game is played. . . . There is also a second congress . . . that is every bit as important as the congress of the textbooks. This is the representative assemblage of 540 individuals. . . . It comprises men and women of diverse ages, backgrounds, and routes to office. The electoral fortunes of its members depend less upon what congress produces as an institution than upon the support and good will of voters hundreds or thousands of miles away. (Davidson and Oleszek 4, 5)

Given this perspective, there could actually be very little relationship between what is going on in Washington and what is going on in a member's district. In Washington, representatives focus on lawmaking. In the districts, they focus on individual constituents and winning electoral support. The focus and activities are different, the worlds don't collide, and a changing political environment might produce little impact on local-level politics.

However, the first quote at the top of this chapter highlights an alternate perspective—Fenno's own view of the local-national connection. As the quote indicates, having been in office for four terms, the congressman is concerned with the potential for the "gradual erosion" of his constituency relationships (Fenno 1978, 216).

Congresspeople actively pursuing national activities perhaps do so at the risk of leaving the local behind. Thus, a seat on a nationally-oriented committee may be stimulating and energizing to a member of Congress in Washington, but such a focus takes energy away from the time (or desire) to deal with the folks at home. A call from the president about an important political matter may be a wonderful ego builder, but it may also lead a member to choose a weekend in Washington over yet an additional trip back to the district. As a congressperson serves more time in office, he or she can become more enmeshed in the Washington scene, more caught up in the duties of a career, and perhaps a bit bored with his/her heretofore successful local routines.

In addition, national-level events and agendas could negatively impact a politician's fortunes within his/her district. For instance, given the preponderance of "conservative" views within the Republican Party of today, a liberal Republican is faced with the difficult job of attempting to please both constituents and fellow partisans. How does such a representative balance loyalty to a more conservative national party and the needs of perhaps a more liberal local constituency?

Obviously, there is a third possibility as to the nature of the local-national connection. Because of the increased nationalization of current politics, present-day members of Congress may be more likely to develop positive connections between the national and the local. They may be able to explain time spent on foreign trips, committee work, or issues as important for public policy, prestigious for the district, or good for the country. As Fenno himself notes, along with their reelection goal, members of Congress may have strong policy or power goals. Rather than a zero-sum relationship between these goals, congresspeople may find positive ways to integrate their interests and needs. They may work on public policies of concern to their districts, may explain to their constituents that national policies are too important to ignore, or they may be partisan loyalists and desire to help their national party succeed in its fortunes. It simply may be easier today to satisfy several goals simultaneously.

In addition, we should expect some degree of consistency between a legislator's presentational style at home and in Washington. For instance, if a congressperson truly enjoys hanging out with the folks back home, wouldn't it make sense that he/she would enjoy hanging out in the Washington scene? If a member is notably issue oriented, is not that member likely to consistently engage in such an orientation?

In this regard, several profiles of Congress members taken from Fenno's own works illustrate the potential for a positive connection between home and Washington. "Still, the question remains intriguing, if only because from time to time House members talk or act as if the behavior we observed at home is repeated in Washington. For example, our issue-oriented

Congressman O, who refuses 'to play the groups' at home, also refuses to play them in Washington" (Fenno 1978, 225). Or, "might not our Congressman B, the well-liked local boy who is so suspicious of 'outsiders,' be handicapped as a coalition-builder in Congress by this exclusive view of politics?" (Fenno 1978, 226).

Similarly, in *Senators on the Campaign Trail*, the two senators who made the most "durable connections" with constituents exhibited home-Washington consistency. For example, "Pell's personal style at home is cut from the same cloth as his personal style in the Senate" (Fenno 1996, 260). "Pryor's elective office ambition at home and his institutional ambition in the Senate have been driven by the sheer love of involvement in politics" (Fenno 1996, 279).

Such home-Washington consistency may be even more likely in today's era. As I argued in the first chapter, there are simply many ways in which the national and the local are interconnected. In addition, several scholars (Fiorina 2005; Jacobson 2001) have highlighted two interrelated trends pointing in the direction of increased local-national connection. Voters today may, in fact, desire representatives to engage in more national activity; as Jacobson puts it, "The minds of voters have become less personal and more explicitly political since the 1970s" (129). When asked what they liked about candidates in the 1990s compared to the 1970s, voters were less likely to mention an aspect of local politics. They were less likely (25% to 15%) to applaud district service/attention, to highlight incumbent performance/experience (19% to 14%) and to mention personal qualities (39% to 37%) (Jacobson 2001, 9). Consequently, Fiorina's examination of aggregate elections demonstrated a similar decline in the importance of the local. Thus, his regressions explaining a member's current vote margin by a combination of that member's past margin (a local component) and the vote for that party's president in the district (a measure of the national component), showed in the face of some diverse conditions (presidential/midterm elections, incumbency/open seats) a general trend toward an increase in the importance of the national.

As Fiorina (2005) concludes, "Indisputably, the elections of the mid- to late-1990s were more nationalized than they had been since the 1960s" (167). Or, as he says in the second quote above this chapter, the "aphorism" that all politics is local may be less apparent in today's modern era.

What factors might have contributed to these changes in voter attitudes? In addition to those already discussed, Fiorina offers some interesting speculations. Activities that distinguished a member of Congress became routinized (Fiorina 2005, 167). Incumbents, while performing the ombudsperson function and cultivating constituencies with the then–most modern campaign techniques, were in short doing everything that Fenno describes as building a career in the district. While once attention-getting, such activities have now become standard behavior. Thus, voters and members of Congress alike may take such behavior for granted. Members simply may not be getting as much political mileage out of their constituency-oriented work.

In addition, with the advent of C-SPAN, other cable channels, 24-hour access to news and the Internet, constituents, especially attentive citizens, certainly have greater access to national-level concerns and might therefore be more likely to hold politicians accountable. Finally, from the perspective of legislators themselves, Fiorina (2005) speculates: "I believe that today's candidates have deeper policy commitments than their counterparts of a generation ago" (171; see also Ehrenhalt 1991).

It simply may be easier in the 1990s to satisfy several goals simultaneously. In turn, it may be easier to develop positive connections between home and Washington. As Davidson and Oleszek (2002) describe it (somewhat in contrast to their earlier view), "National political organizations, issues, and resources shape local campaigns and the way they are waged . . . yet congressional politics is also rooted in local affairs" (4).

The argument of this book, then, highlights the interconnections between the local and the national. While these linkages appear more variable and more extensive than in the 1970s—some politicians today place "national" at the center of their home styles and others stay more local—but, in sum, this book argues that given today's politics, many legislators find creative and positive ways to link the local and the national.

Design

Not surprisingly given Fenno's work, a qualitative design was chosen to answer the above questions. In each of the case studies below, several elements are examined. First off, it is the purpose of each profile to provide an in-depth examination of the home styles of the ten members of Congress chosen for study. A clear advantage of such an in-depth methodology is that it focuses attention on the multidimensional character of the activities underlying a Congress member's connections to his/her district. The case studies of the next few chapters therefore follow in this tradition, in this instance highlighting the variety of local and national elements in each home style.

Obviously, as was discussed earlier, it is another of the advantages of this methodology to put a human face on member activities.

Second, because an understanding of the impact of aggregate environmental factors on home styles implies an understanding of the home-Washington connection for each individual member, each profile includes, in addition to an examination of within-district activity (home style), a discussion of each representative's "lawmaking" activity. In turn, such an analysis allows a full consideration of the relationship (zero, negative, positive) of the local-national connection.

Finally, in order to understand variation, each of the profiles in the next four chapters begins with a description of the two major independent variables in Fenno's analysis: constituency characteristics and a member's background. While an examination of background characteristics may be straightforward, some readers may need a recapitulation of the bulls-eye model Fenno uses to understand the impact of "constituency" on a legislator's behavior. Thus, a full understanding takes us well beyond a description of the most commonly discussed "geographic" constituency (Quinn represents the Buffalo area) and additionally highlights nested sets of subgroups, the reelection and primary constituencies along with a Congress member's intimates. Thus, the "geographic" constituency provides a first cut at how most congresspeople usually describe their districts. In rather apolitical terms, members note such factors as its geography, demographic makeup, and propensity to change over time (Fenno 1978, 1–8).

However, understanding this geographic constituency may only be the beginning of the story. Within its boundaries, the "reelection constituency" is "composed of those people in the district who he (the representative) thinks vote for him" (Fenno 1978, 8). Factors such as partisanship and ideology help delineate this constituency. In turn, the primary constituency consists of even stronger supporters—long-time volunteers, financial contributors, or followers dating back to a member's early career. As Fenno puts it, such a constituency "would provide his last line of electoral defense in a primary contest" (18).

Finally, Fenno (1978) characterizes the intimate sphere as the set of a representative's closest friends, family, and advisors:

> These are the few individuals whose relationship with the member is so personal and so intimate that their relevance cannot be captured by any description of "very strongest supporters." (24)

Why are full constituency descriptions so important? First, as is true for home styles, such descriptions situate a member in his/her district. It isn't enough, for example, to say a member comes from an urban district. Such areas differ one from another, and so describing a member's particular urban area is critical. Even more, the bulls-eye model focuses attention on some important questions about representation. Particularly in the case of a heterogeneous district, a member must make choices about which of his now almost six hundred thousand constituents to pay most attention to. The character of the constituency then poses a strategic problem for each member. For example, two senators representing the same state clearly have identical geographic constituencies but may have a very different character to the remaining circles of the bulls-eye model. In turn, how a member answers these strategic questions has broader implications for which constituents will receive the "best" representation and who will be left out of the representational process.

Thus, the profiles will focus on home styles along with the factors that have the potential to explain them. This said, it is necessary to describe in detail three aspects of the research design: the method, the focus on New York State, and the choice of particular representatives within the state.

Method

As is clear from a long tradition of scholarship on Congress (including Cohen 1995; Fowler and McClure 1989; Malbin 1980; Peters 1990), case studies can yield valuable insights into the attitudes and perceptions of legislators. As Robert Yin (2003) has explained, a case study

> [i]nvestigates a contemporary phenomenon within its real-life context, especially when the boundaries between phenomenon and context are not clearly evident. In other words, you would use the case study method because you deliberately wanted to cover contextual conditions—believing that they might be highly pertinent to your phenomenon of study. (13)

This is an apt description of Fenno's work, which as we know is not only notable for the important theoretical contributions outlined above but is equally famous for its "soaking and poking" methodology. By following representatives and observing them "over the shoulder," Fenno highlighted the importance of member perceptions and the multidimensional character of their district-oriented activities. With such a methodology, he could obtain a sense of what strategies and decisions members were making. He could also, as Yin (2003) noted, describe the interconnections between the context of the constituency and the legislator's behavior.

As will become clear from the profiles presented here, the approach of this work very much follows the spirit of Fenno's "soaking and poking." At the inception of the project, plans were made to collect home style–related information from a variety of sources: observations of legislators at public forums, one-on-one interviews, and analysis of the public record. As evidenced by the sheer number of citations throughout the following chapters, however, it quickly became apparent that an astounding array of publicly available material is at hand and available to individuals interested in understanding the behavior of members of the U.S. Congress. Of course, there are standard reference publications, including *Congressional Quarterly Weekly Reports, The Almanac of American Politics (Almanac),* and *Politics in America (PIA).* There are a surprisingly high number of stories in local, regional, and national press. Finally, and most importantly, the advent of the Internet has not only made this standard information much more easily accessible but it has led to the increasing importance of legislator Web sites as a powerful communication tool to present themselves to constituents.

In order to utilize this amount of publicly available material and to take advantage of the new communication tools, it was decided to take the methodological challenge and to attempt to piece together from the public record good approximations of a representative's home style. Thus, the material for this project is based solely on public record sources. The time period chosen for this analysis mostly focused on the 1990s, with some variation due to the date of a legislator's first election to office. The end point for data collection was September 10, 2001, the day prior to the life-changing events, particularly as they impacted New Yorkers, surrounding the terrorist attacks on America (but see postscript for updates).

So, given that Fenno soaked and poked by crisscrossing the nation and by personally following members, the observations for this project were primarily based on an equally intense research strategy, which unfortunately also included a much more sedentary character.

And what can be gained from a project on home styles that relies so heavily on the public record and so little on "tagging along" with members of Congress? The "outsider" perspective adopted here has the advantage of mirroring the sources available to an interested constituent attempting to glean information as to the activities of his/her legislator. This approach then reflects the perspective of the outsider wishing to obtain information but lacking direct access to his/her representative. Thus, we are depicting home styles as they might become apparent to constituents.

In addition, a reliance on the public record has the advantage of focusing attention on what members of Congress actually do as much as it does on what they say they do. Newspaper reports and Web sites systematically cover bills legislators have sponsored, grants or services they have brought to their districts, or activities members have undertaken in their constituencies. Such coverage not only provides a full picture of member activities but, for the specific purposes of this project, it also provides systematic descriptions of legislator activity at both the local and national political levels.

In order to corroborate these public record sources, several staffers from each member's office were asked to read and comment on the profile of their member. In addition, so much publicly available material was available that sources could be utilized to cross-check the accuracy of the interpretations presented here.

One final note. Though these profiles present considerable descriptive material, they are by no means intended as up-to-date journalistic accounts. What is most important is the descriptions of the home styles, the contrasting styles legislators have adopted, and the factors explaining their individual choices.

As the following profiles make clear, the research strategy employed here appears to have worked well. The profiles both provide solid characterizations of legislator presentations to constituents and also demonstrate considerable differences among the strategies employed by diverse legislators. The bottom line is that there appear to be many fruitful and productive ways to approach the rich concept of home style.

Choosing New York State

Early on, both to narrow the scope of the project and to impose some control on the context in which the representatives operate, it was decided to focus on one state. Such a focus obviously made it possible to simplify choices (from a pool of 435 to 31 representatives). More importantly, by focusing on the state of New York, it was possible to impose some constraints on the context. By isolating interesting similarities, for example, analyzing members from geographically similar districts or from multiracial areas, it is possible to obtain a better understanding of the role of personal factors on home style or get a feel for the range of acceptable behavior within a certain kind of constituency. Similarly, focusing on two ideologically similar members with the potential for different home styles can isolate the impact of constituency factors.

Yet, because New York State is so diverse, it is also possible to obtain substantial variation in the character of its congressional districts. Nationally, with a population of almost nineteen million,[1] New York ranks third, behind California and Texas. On many other dimensions though, it is more "middle" than we might expect, ranking thirtieth in terms of land area and twenty-seventh in terms of median income (http://www.economy.com/dismal). Its population is approximately 70% white (compared to 75% nationally), and its approximately equal (about 15%) concentrations of African Americans and Latinos (mostly in and around New York City) place the state slightly above national averages of just over 12% each (www.dismal.com/regions/states.stm).

More importantly, an incredible variety of cultural and political conditions exist across congressional districts. The constituency descriptions in each of the congressional profiles show that the stereotypes and images of New York as simply a reflection of the urban area in and around New York City are quite misleading.

For example, in addition to its urban areas, New York has some surprisingly rural districts. As Map 1 makes clear, the districts exhibit enormous variation in terms of simple visual factors, including size and shape. Compare, for instance, the sprawling 24th (The North Country) to the 12th, 14th, or 17th, covering parts of New York City, or examine the elongated 26th (with its major cities—Kingston, Binghamton, Ithaca—at opposite ends of the district) in contrast to the 30th, where the city of Buffalo is clearly the hub of its area. Additionally, constituencies vary in terms of their geography (including proximity to waterways and mountains), relationships to county boundaries (not shown on map), and even access to basic transportation including railroads and airports.

Cross-district variation can also be seen by examining demographic data (Table 2.1). Constituencies, for instance, vary from forty-six people per square mile (the 24th) to fifty-eight thousand (the 11th), from 96% minority (the 16th) to more than 95% white. There is also substantial variation in district education, income, and poverty rate.

Politically, too, the state varies. Though New York has leaned Democrat in presidential elections and currently has two Democratic senators (Schumer and Clinton), the state legislature is split in terms of party control (Democrats in the Assembly and Republicans in the Senate). For most of the

TABLE 2.1 Demographic Variation across New York State's Congressional
Districts*

Characteristic	Mean	Standard Deviation	Minimum	Maximum
Land Area (square miles)	1523	2802	10	12393
Population per Square Mile	13731	18174	47	57996
Percent Urban**	90%	16%	46%	100%
Percent Rural	58%	9%	43%	67%
Percent White (Non-Latino)	70%	29%	4%	97%
Percent College Educated	23%	9%	6%	52%
Median Income (in thousands)	34.4	10.56	15.06	56.06
Percent White Collar	63%	9%	47%	85%
Percent Blue Collar	22%	5%	8%	31%

* Most information for Tables 2.1–6.1 comes from *Politics in America (PIA)*, 2000; population per
square mile data come from CQ's *Congressional Districts in the 1990s: A Portrait of America*.

** Note that *PIA* classifies districts as either urban, suburban, or rural, based on the majority area of
the district. Only if there is not a majority area, do they report the percentages of each category, so
percentages do not add up to 100%

last two decades, the delegation to the U.S. Senate consisted of two legendary
members: Republican Alfonse D'Amato and Democrat Daniel Patrick Moynihan, who not only differed in terms of partisanship but also in ideology, priorities, and style. For instance, where Moynihan was an intellectual and former Harvard University professor known for presenting academic-sounding
"tutorials" to the Washington press corps, D'Amato was the practical politician, dubbed "Senator Pot Hole"[2] by his detractors, recognized for constituency service and fundraising capabilities (*PIA* 2000, 906; 1996, 882).

In the House of Representatives, New York is well represented by members of both parties, as the congressional delegation generally runs around
60% Democrat. It will become clear from the profiles that for legislators of
both parties, there is considerable variation in electoral safety. Some members represent solidly one-party areas while others face more closely divided districts.

Despite all this variation, a couple of commonalities about New York
State need to be kept in mind to better appreciate the profiles to follow.
The declining economy ("For three decades New York State has had slug-
gish growth" [*Almanac* 2002, 1031]), which has been so much a factor in
the state's politics, will serve as the backdrop for the home styles of more
than a few of these representatives. As Senator Hillary Clinton poignantly
reminds us:

As I travel across New York, I see firsthand the difficult challenges so many of my constituents face every day. Too often businesses close or downsize. Too many educated young people are forced to leave their hometowns to find jobs. It is time to turn the tide on this trend of low job growth and population loss.[3]

In addition to these economic difficulties, political considerations should be noted. Traditionally, the upstate/downstate distinction is important in New York State politics. Despite the split partisanship of the state as a whole, Democrats have dominated New York City and most surrounding areas, while Republicans have reigned in upstate New York (Schneier 2001). Of the eighteen downstate congressional districts, more than two-thirds have been represented by a Democrat; and of the thirteen upstate districts, the great majority have leaned Republican (Table 2.2).

TABLE 2.2 Characteristics of Project Sample versus Entire New York State Congressional Delegation*

Characteristic	Sample	New York State Delegation
Party	6 Dems, 4 Reps	18 Dems, 13 Reps
Upstate/Downstate	5 to 5	19 to 12
Seniority		
< 5 yrs	2	3
5 to 8	5	10
> 8	3	18
Number of Females	4	7
Latinos	1	2
African-Americans	0	4
Percent Urban		
average	75%	82%
range	65% rural to 100% urban	67% rural to 100% urban
Party Unity		
average	85	84
range	64 to 94	63 to 97
Conservative Coalition		
average	36	48
range	5 to 93	5 to 100

* Information as of 1997; Upstate is defined as districts above Westchester county (districts 19–31)

Moreover, New York State has a tradition of liberal Republicans. Given that such politicians are somewhat more likely to be out of step with the conservatism of their current national party leadership, this ideology has the potential to impact the generalizability of findings (see chapter 7 for more on this).

Choosing the Representatives

As is clear from the chapter previews described earlier, within New York State, ten representatives have served as the focus for the study. At one level, any ten legislators could have been chosen, and much could have been learned from studying them in their districts. From the study of home styles, it has become apparent that any story of a representative in his or her district can yield valuable insight. Yet, to strengthen the work, several specific criteria were employed in making choices. First, the sample was chosen to reflect the diversity of the state. "Here the goal is more typically to study a diverse and usually limited number of observations than to study a representative sample of a larger target population" (Johnson and Joslyn 1995, 185). Furthermore, "intentional selection of observations implies that we know in advance the values of at least some of the relevant variables, and that random selection of observations is ruled out" (King, Keohane, and Verba 1994, 139).

As just noted, the best "intentional" design selects observations to ensure variation in the explanatory variable (and any control variables) without regard to the values of the dependent variables (King, Keohane, and Verba 1994, 140), as the representatives and their relevant constituencies vary on a wide variety of demographic (geography, urban/rural, socioeconomic status, race/ethnicity) and political (party, ideology, seniority) dimensions. Second, within the overall category of representativeness, a special effort was made to include districts that might have been likely to be impacted by 1990s forces and factors. Thus, an attempt was made to include, on the one hand, constituencies that had been affected by demographic and political changes, and on the other hand, districts that have remained more stable. Finally, I consulted lobbyists and legislative scholars in hopes of finding the most "interesting" constituent-representative relationships within the state.

The resulting sample (Table 2.2) included six Democrats and four Republicans, six men and four women, three senior (elected before 1990) and seven junior congresspeople. Four of the congresspeople represent urban areas and the remaining six have more rural or suburban constituencies. The members also reflect a range of ideological views, alternate degrees of "comity," and, as will become apparent, a variety of home styles.

Overall, given the purposely inexact science of qualitative research, it is somewhat gratifying to see how well the sample, at least in terms of basic political characteristics, reflects the character of New York State (Table 2.2). In fact, at the risk of sounding like a Chamber of Commerce advertisement or an "I Love New York" commercial, it appears that the profiles of these ten representatives and their districts will leave the reader appreciating the range of diversity in the congressional districts, along with the consequent variation in representational styles, within the Empire State, adding to our study of congressional politics more generally.

To help orient the reader to the profiles to follow, it is worth stating at the outset that findings indicate that localism is still of prime importance. As illustrated by the headlines from Rep. Quinn's and Rep. Maloney's Web sites quoted above (top of chapter 1), there is no substitute for knowing one's district. Fenno is absolutely right: personal and local connections matter a lot, and the ombudsperson role is very much alive and well, even in a more national environment. In fact, one of the contributions of this book will be to document that an incredible number of examples of the ombudsperson function exist.

But, national factors matter as well. Indeed, these profiles will show some fairly complex interactions between the "local" and the "national." Sometimes there is no relationship between the two, and sometimes they conflict. However, more often than not, national factors figure in some way into the development of even locally oriented home styles and, more often than not, legislators can find surprising and creative ways of combining the local and the national.

Chapter 3

RETHINKING THE LOCAL-NATIONAL DEBATE

> Senator Clinton has been an advocate for children and families for more than thirty years. She brings to the Senate the same commitment and energy that took her to each of New York State's 62 counties during her 16-month campaign.
> —http://clinton.senate.gov/

> You can tell from my accent that I am a lifelong New Yorker. You see, I don't have to fake it. New York isn't just a place I represent; it is my home. . . . I put on my Mets hat when I was 6 years old, and I've been working here ever since. I've stacked mufflers at Linden Auto Parts on Montauk Highway. I played Little League here, I've fished and clammed in our waters . . . prayed in our churches, I've married a wonderful native New Yorker and watched our two little girls come into this world in our local hospitals.
> —Senatorial candidate, Rick Lazio, *New York Times*, 5/21/00

In this first case study chapter, I begin to consider modern home styles in terms of the local, the national, and the interconnections between the two. As might be expected from the preceding discussion, I will argue that in addition to a strong district focus, some home styles today have important national components. Though there is considerable variation both in the level of this national component and correspondingly in the ways each member has found to relate the national to the local, the case studies below, including the profile of a fairly district-oriented representative, will demonstrate considerable interconnections between the local and the national: the world at home and the world in Washington.

In so doing, this chapter poses for the reader the first representational dilemma highlighted throughout this book: Is it more desirable or "better"

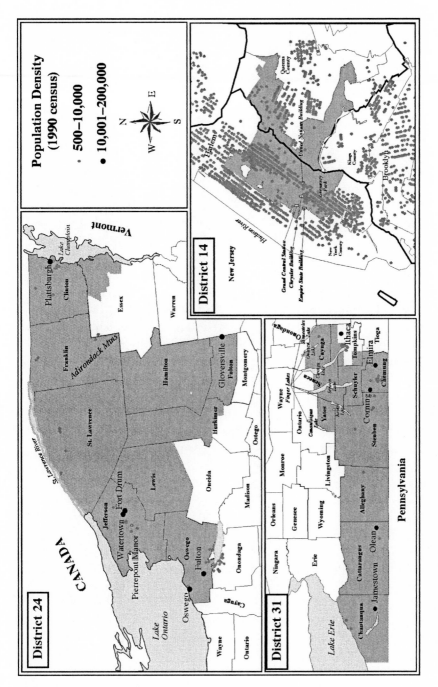

Map 2. Congressional Districts for Reps. Maloney, Houghton, and McHugh.

for a representative to have a local or national focus? What are the advantages and disadvantages of each presentational style, what tradeoffs is a legislator making when he or she chooses one style over another, and which type of representation is "best" for constituents or the nation as a whole?

Nor do we have to look too hard to find illustrations in modern American politics that place these tradeoffs in a very practical context. The historic 2000 Senate race in New York State pitting then-first lady Hillary Rodham Clinton against then-representative Rick Lazio provides a stark contrast, thus helping the reader engage the tradeoffs between a very "national" and a more "local" presentational style. If there was ever a candidate with a national reputation, a former first lady "and the first woman elected statewide in New York"[1] with an activist record and a controversial husband would certainly fit the bill. Viewed objectively, Mrs. Clinton's history of accomplishments at the national level is fairly remarkable, including: Attorney, Children's Defense Fund; Council, U.S. House of Representatives Judiciary Committee; Assistant Professor, University of Arkansas School of Law; Practicing Attorney; and Chair, Presidential Task Force on Health Care Reform (*Almanac* 2002, 1047). As the first quote above this chapter reminds us, Mrs. Clinton has been an advocate for women, families, and children for most of her adult life, has been active in the Democratic Party, and, as first lady, was a key player on many national issues. In these capacities, she clearly has developed, as the first quote above describes it, "energy and commitment" on the national scene.

This perspective offers clear advantages: an individual with such a background can demonstrate considerable accomplishments and can use national connections to enhance the local area. Such a perspective also offers the potential for name recognition and visibility, especially to a challenger. Perhaps more to the point, a candidate/legislator with such a perspective can legitimately claim to be on top of the big picture and know what is going on across the nation. As the founders viewed it long ago:

> Consistently with this view that, as Publius said, the first aim of every constitution should be "to obtain for rulers men who possess most wisdom to discern and most virtue to pursue the common good of the society," the Federalists saw the duty of representatives as extending beyond the particular interests of their constituents to the common good. (Storing 1981, 45)

Indeed, Madison desired a system of government making it most likely that "enlightened statesmen" (Federalist No. 10) would be at the helm. Such "enlightened statesmen" could also legitimately claim that experience at the national level would benefit the local area in terms of political know-how to help local constituents.

As Rep. Lazio could lay a strong claim to being "one of us," his campaign extolled a contrasting view of representation. "A lifelong New Yorker," he typified the constituents of his area, rooting for the local baseball team, working local jobs, and marrying his local sweetheart (second quote above chapter). Thus, Mrs. Clinton was accused even by some Democrats of being a "carpetbagger who had no business running for the Senate in New York" (*PIA* 2002, 671), and "the *Times* said New Yorkers deserved to be skeptical of Clinton when she moved to the state 16 months ago having never lived, worked or voted in the state and having never been elected to a public office."[2] How could she possibly identify with or articulate the needs of the citizens of the state?

Thus, Rep. Lazio was advantaged by his ability to present himself as being well connected to the average New Yorker; Mrs. Clinton, via the "listening tour" that took her to all sixty-two counties of the state, had to catch up, and both candidates had to vie to demonstrate their local credentials:

> Despite the intense national interest in the race, both candidates have tried to present themselves as New Yorkers who are intently focused on local concerns. She wears Yankees caps; he attends Mets games. He has released a tax-cut plan that he says will help the state's small businesses. She touts her economic development plan for Upstate New York. (*USA Today* 9/13/00)

This view of representation to be intimately acquainted with or as "one" of their constituents also dates back to the American founding. The Anti-Federalists of the 1700s visualized a "citizen" legislator who would not only reflect the fundamental values emanating from the constituency but who would also be so steeped in local life, allowing him or her to truly express the same perspective as those being represented. "Effective and thoroughgoing responsibility is to be found only in a likeness between the representative body and the citizens at large" (Storing 1981, 17). And, "Representatives should be a true picture of the people; possess the knowledge of their circumstances and their wants; sympathize in all their distresses and be disposed to seek their true interests" (Melancton Smith qtd. in Storing 1981, 17). Only then could local concerns be adequately appreciated in a large political system.

Thus, although there is potentially a downside to this type of representation (scholars, including David Mayhew, 1974), have expressed concern that contemporary representatives, in their paramount desire for reelection and their emphasis on their local areas, act as a group to generate particularistic and inefficient public policies, there are important advantages to representation in the form of reflecting deeply held local values, including the sense of identification with constituents, the diversity of opinions across congressional districts, and the importance of "local" perspectives. As two of Fenno's congresspeople poignantly expressed it, "I like to come home, and it's fun to campaign" (Congressman C, 86). "It must be terrible to be without roots, without a place to call home. I have a profound sense of identification with these rural people" (Congressman H, 155).

The Clinton-Lazio campaign provides one final lesson, a lesson about the potential for interconnections between the apparently contrasting "local" and "national" representational styles. At least in this particular Senate race, the public appeared to desire legislators who could provide both representational elements. Thus, one commentary observed:

> Contemplating Mrs. Clinton's campaign convinces us that she fits into two important New York traditions. Like Robert F. Kennedy, she taps into the state's ability to embrace new residents and fresh ideas. She is also capable of following the pattern, established by the likes of Mr. Kennedy, Mr. Moynihan and Jacob Javits, that finds New York senators playing a role on the national and world stages even as they defend local interests. (*NYT*, 10/22/00)

Even as she was expected to demonstrate local ties, Mrs. Clinton's national status offered value. In turn, though Rep. Lazio clearly ranked high on the local element, he was not entirely without some national experience, in the form of a record of leadership on housing policy and activity as part of the House Republican leadership team (*Almanac* 2000, 1103–1104).

So, how do lower profile politicians integrate local and national elements as they present themselves to constituents? In the increasingly "nationalized" environment described in earlier chapters, how do legislators integrate the local and the national? The three politicians profiled below are diverse in terms of a wide variety of factors (constituencies, backgrounds, and home styles), and their stories indicate considerable overlap between local and national concerns.

Democrat Carolyn Maloney represents a relatively well-off and diverse congressional district in the heart of New York City. Partly on the coattails of the 1992 Clinton presidential victory and the "Year of the Woman," she translated a New York City Council seat into the defeat of a popular incumbent to get to Congress. By contrast, Amo Houghton represents an upstate rural district. He achieved his congressional seat after an unusually distinguished career as a nationally known business executive. In addition to a strong local presence, both representatives have incorporated important national elements in their home styles, though they do so in notably different ways. Finally, the presentational style of John McHugh, representing the rural "North Country" (Canadian border), is purposefully local, but national factors impact his district as well. (As an added point of interest, though the Houghton/McHugh constituencies are fairly similar, their home styles differ notably, making their comparison thought provoking.) Thus, the juxtaposition of these three profiles begins to suggest differences in what it means to be national, allows us to examine local-national interconnections, and provides a human face on an important representational dilemma.

Consistent with the logic developed in chapter 2, each profile begins with a discussion of the factors thought to impact a home style: constituency/elections and member background. Then, detailed descriptions of the actual home styles are provided.

Carolyn Maloney: Getting Involved at Home and in Washington

As we have seen, Fenno has focused the attention of political scientists on local aspects of politics. Profiling Representative Carolyn Maloney from New York's 14th Congressional District is a good beginning to this book because Maloney's story highlights the interrelationship of local and national factors. Without doubt, local factors and the strengths of Maloney as a candidate and congresswoman matter—it takes political savvy to upset a popular incumbent, to found the Congressional Hellenic Caucus on Greek Affairs and in general to retain office in a politically active constituency. However, in any number of ways, the national context serves as an equally important part of the story. Maloney has, for example, highlighted gender issues, capitalized on national partisanship and associated herself with important national figures, including the Clintons. While one can link many of her national activities back to district constituencies, it is clear that Maloney's use of the "national" goes well beyond what we might expect from Fenno's description of legislative behavior. In fact, the most important observation may be that in Maloney's case, it is hard to separate out what is "local" from what is "national."

Constituency

> New York City, alias the Big Apple, city of promise—and realized potential.
> ... Art mecca for the nation. Engine of America's wealth. The country's
> most populated metropolis. ... Whether shopping Fifth Avenue, sampling
> soul food in Harlem, gallery-hopping in SoHo, touring Central Park in a
> carriage or sipping latte in Greenwich, visitors are embraced in the city's
> contagious pulsation.*
> —*Michelin Green Guide, New York City* online

Put more modestly, Maloney's constituency is part of a historic and important area. Though New York City actually consists of five boroughs—Staten Island, the Bronx, Brooklyn, Queens, and, of course, the main tourist center of Manhattan (see Map 2)—as we shall see, the 14th Congressional District was impacted in a major way by the 1992 redistricting. Once composed solely of a portion of Manhattan, Maloney's district now encompasses the East Side of Manhattan, a sliver of East Harlem, Astoria and Long Island City, Queens, and until 1999, Greenpoint Brooklyn (see Map 2). As the Michelin quote makes clear, it would be an understatement to say that the Manhattan portion of this area is an economic and cultural Mecca for industry, tourism, and the arts, attracting interest and people from all parts of the globe (*PIA* 2002, 697).

Formerly known as the "silk stocking" district "because it takes in some of the wealthiest areas in Manhattan," the 14th is also one of the most urban (100%), with a population density of 43,399 people per square mile (*NYT* 11/4/92) (Table 3.1). The 14th is also the best-educated and wealthiest district in New York State with 52% college educated (highest in the state), 85% white collar (also highest), and a median income of $42,072 (ranks ninth). These rankings place the district among the top third richest in the country, and at least one source describes it as the wealthiest (*Almanac* 1998, 1004).

For a large city with a renowned ethnic heritage, it is interesting to note that the district is surprisingly "white" (about 80%). However, ethnic, religious, and racial diversity impact congressional politics, with the largest concentrations of minorities residing near Harlem (African Americans) and on

*Accessed from: http://www.globecorner.com/t/t7/3792.php

TABLE 3.1 Constituency Characteristics and Election Results for Reps. Maloney, Houghton, and McHugh

	Carolyn Maloney	Amory Houghton	John McHugh
District #	14	31	24
Party	D	R	R
Yr. Elected	1992	1986	1992
District Profile			
Land Area (square miles)	13	6,587	12,393
Population Per Square Mile	43,399	88	47
Percent Urban	100%		
Percent Rural		60%	65%
Percent White	78%	96%	95%
Percent White Collar	85%	50%	49%
Rank (state)*	1	29	30
Rank (nation)**	1	3	3
Percent Blue Collar	8%	30%	30%
Rank (state)*	31	2	2
Rank (nation)**	3	1	1
Percent College Educated	52%	15%	14%
Rank (state)*	1	26	28
Rank (nation)**	1	3	3
Median Income (in thousands)	42.07	25.12	25.69
Rank (state)*	9	27	26
Rank (nation)**	1	3	3
Election Results			
2000	74%	77%	74%
1998	77%	68%	79%
1996	72%	72%	71%
1994	64%	85%	79%
1992	50%	71%	61%
1990		70%	
1988		96%	
1986		60%	
District Vote For President			
2000	D-71%	D-42%	D-47%
	R-23%	R-53%	R-49%
1996	D-71%	D-45%	D-50%
	R-23%	R-42%	R-35%
1992	D-69%	D-34%	D-38%
	R-23%	R-40%	R-38%

*Rank in state: 1 = highest, 31 = lowest.

**Rank Nationally is expressed in thirds: 1 = Top Third; 2 = Middle Third; 3 = Bottom Third.

the Lower East Side (Latinos) (*PIA* 2000, 944). There are also active Greek (Queens), Polish, and Italian (Brooklyn) communities (*PIA* 2002, 697).

Largely because of the 1992 redistricting, the area now runs three-to-one Democrat in voter registration (*Congressional Districts in the 1990s,* 517). In fact, the new "14th is one of those marvels of New York redistricting. It crosses the East River to parts of Astoria in Queens and Greenpoint in Brooklyn, which are three miles apart on either side of the 7th district" (*PIA* 1996, 918) (see Map 2). The additions of these areas had a profound impact on congressional politics. As they contribute fully 20 percent of the district's population, they bring additional demographic and political diversity (*PIA* 1994, 1060). Thus, the Manhattan portion (the old 15th, so familiar to incumbent Bill Green [1978–1992]) is not only better off, but it has been described as a staunchly "urban liberal" (*PIA* 1998) with constituents voting for Democratic presidential candidates throughout the conservative 1980s and showing a tradition of sending liberals (regardless of party) to Congress (*PIA* 2000, 943).

The new areas are different. The education and income levels are significantly lower than the Manhattan portion of the district (*1992 House Races*), ethnic identities (*PIA* 1994, 1060) are strong, residents can be socially conservative (*PIA* 1996, 1061), and perhaps most importantly for purposes of the politics of the 1990s, these areas are substantially more Democratic (*NYT* 11/2/92).

All in all, then, the character of the 14th reflects one of the major cultural and economic centers of the nation, even the world. Constituents are relatively well-off, well educated, and Democratic. All things being equal, a Democratic congressperson newly elected from this area might be expected to develop a home style encompassing national elements and, at least given the Democratic character of the district, to have the freedom to do so.

Background

Born and raised in North Carolina, Carolyn Maloney graduated from Greensboro College (AB degree). Intending to be a lawyer, she spent a year at the University of North Carolina. But a summer trip to New York City changed everything. "I went up to see a friend and never left," she said. "I just fell in love with the place. My father was furious" (*NYT* 12/26/92). She held positions as a public school teacher and administrator for the New York City Board of Education, including teaching an adult education course in East Harlem (*PIA* 2002, 696). In the late 1970s, Maloney decided "that government had a larger impact than any teacher on the education of the city's youth" (*PIA* 2002, 696).

Thus, she switched gears, working as a senior staff person at the New York State Assembly and Senate and rising through the ranks as a professional politician. Then, in 1982, she not only sought elective office for the first time but, partly because "Miss Maloney has shown ability and devotion in difficult state legislative staff jobs" (*NYT* 9/16/82), she also was able to defeat an incumbent for a seat on the New York City Council (Web bio).

It was on the city council that Maloney developed the political base, skills, and issues that would later help her achieve a congressional seat. In addition, she contributed an activist record. Her council district (at least for the years just prior to her congressional bid) was wholly within what would become the 14th Congressional District, so she could network with notable Democratic politicians (Margolies-Mezvinsky 1994). More, as she had as a legislative staffer, Maloney became a vocal council member, on one occasion even suing Mayor Dinkins for what she saw as a failure to engage in a competitive bidding process for certain city contracts (*Newsday* 11/4/91).

She focused on issues that, interestingly, she would continue to espouse throughout her congressional career, including budgets. A strong advocate against waste in government ("Just a one percent improvement in collections would bring in a hell of a lot of money . . . that could buy a lot of cops" [*NYT* 6/24/88]), she founded the council's Committee on City Contracts and wrote a series of laws setting up a computerized system to more efficiently monitor these contracts (Web bio). "She was also the principal author of the landmark New York City Campaign Finance Act" (Web bio). The first woman to give birth while serving as a city council member, Maloney "became a champion of women's, family and children's issues," working, among other things, "to offer a comprehensive package of legislation to make day care more available and affordable" (Web bio).

Rooted in the women's movement, "she gave her first child the middle name Paul, after Alice Paul, [the distant family relative (*USA Today* 2/18/97)] and suffragist who wrote the first equal-rights amendment" (*NYT* 12/26/92). Having personally experienced discrimination, she unhesitatingly spoke out: "When I was young, I never had a job I wasn't propositioned in by an employer. . . . You know if you complained it could hurt your chances for future employment" (*Newsday* 10/13/91).

So, in 1992, the professional politician with an activist record was ready for a try at higher office, and as it turned out, the time was right. Though incumbent Congress member Bill Green was a liberal Republican fitting within the traditions of the district and the ranking minority member of the House Appropriations Committee (*Newsday* 10/28/92), in 1992 he faced several notable challenges: the popularity of Bill Clinton, the Year of the Woman, and the anti-incumbency mood in the nation (*NYT* 11/2/92). Thus, national factors had a considerable impact on local elections. The Democratic National Convention had been in New York City, and presidential candidate Clinton campaigned in the area several times (*NYT* 9/25/92), developing solid support in the 14th, winning 69 percent of the vote in 1992 and 71 percent in 1996 (*Almanac* 2002, 1082).

In addition, the year 1992 saw extraordinary efforts on behalf of female candidates and a subsequent doubling of the number of women entering Congress (Margolies-Mezvinsky 1994). As is quite natural given her background, Maloney grounded her candidacy squarely within this framework: "I announced my campaign on June 28, the day the Supreme Court all but gutted *Roe v. Wade*. When that decision came down, I made my decision and ran" (*Newsday* 11/12/92). "After the Anita Hill hearings, the need for women in public office has never been more obvious" (*Newsday* 11/1/92). Her campaign slogan, "There are more millionaires in the House than women," therefore not only followed up on the women's theme but served as a snipe at Green's economic status (*PIA* 2000, 944).[3]

Maloney's campaign slogan also provided her with another way to link the local and the national. By (fairly or unfairly) emphasizing Green's economic status, she attempted to link the incumbent to the Reagan/Bush political agenda:

> Bill Green has done many fine things, but he did vote for the Reagan/Bush economic package that harmed New York and every other city in the United States. (*Newsday* 11/12/92)

Maloney attempted to associate Green's record in Washington with trends she viewed as harmful to the city. In addition, "even though we had a short period of time to get ready. . . . We were not even able to get a map of the district from the Board of Elections until August" (*Newsday* 11/12/92). Nevertheless, "Ms. Maloney campaigned with puppy dog energy, shaking hands, pushing through crowds to introduce herself, always smiling" (*NYT* 11/10/92). She held "meet and greet" stops where she passed out leaflets ($8 for 100) and increased her name recognition (*NYT* 8/25/92). Maloney also obtained significant endorsements from notable New York politicians and women's groups, including NOW and the National Women's Political Caucus (Margolies-Mezvinsky 1994).

She depended on volunteers and targeted the areas of Brooklyn and Queens newly added to the 14th (*1992 House Races*). As an incumbent, Green had an incredible financial advantage (*Newsday* 11/12/92), outspending Maloney more than three-to-one including five-to-one on mail (*1992 House Races*, 413) and fully ten-to-one on advertising (*Newsday* 11/2/92). A Maloney staff person summed up the effort: "We knew we couldn't compete with Green's mail so we went to the streets and outworked him" (*1992 House Races*, 413).

At one level then, the campaign was a hard-fought contest between two quality candidates with impressive records. With Green narrowly winning the Manhattan part of the district and Maloney carrying the new and more Democratic areas two-to-one (*PIA* 1994, 1060), the final margin of 50 to 48 percent indicates that both Green and Maloney played to their strengths. Both conducted able and hard-fought campaigns.

In addition, the larger context was critical, influencing campaign themes (the "Year of the Woman," the anti-incumbency mood), highlighting party labels (the Clinton effect), and perhaps providing the final boost to the Democrat. Thus, the environment outside the district, in large part, set the stage for the campaign. In short, there would appear to be many linkages between the local and the national in this race.

Home Style

So, what kind of home style might we expect from a candidate who had achieved office on the basis of local and national themes? Given the character of the district, the campaign and the newly elected Congress member, it is not surprising that Maloney's home style would be a mix of local and national factors. To be sure, the local matters.

"As a Member of Congress, providing information and services to my constituents is an important part of my job. . . . You are welcome to visit or call my offices at any time, and my staff will be happy to help or answer questions" (www . . . maloney). This message was not just talk. Maloney attended fully forty district forums during her first year in office (*Newsday* 4/21/93), opened offices in all areas of the district, and kept her family in the district (*NYT* 12/26/92).

In an area known for ethnic celebrations, she participated in the annual St. Patrick's Day and Greek Independence Day (she acted as grand marshal) parades (*Newsday* 3/27/1995). In addition, she uses the *Congressional Record* (upward of five hundred entries per Congress) to commemorate the accomplishments and events of her constituents. Maloney worked to preserve a family-owned East Harlem nursery. "'Now they will be there many more years serving the city with beauty,' said Rep. Carolyn Maloney, who, as a City Council member, helped the business find its current location. 'It really is one of New York's window-boxes'" (*Daily News* 8/26/01). She worked to preserve a crumbling school and "joined a coalition of community groups . . . to announce the formation of . . . [a] community improvement project that seeks to reduce homelessness by providing job-skills training and employment" (PR 11/29/00).

Consistent with Fenno's description of Congress members as officials who never feel safe, Maloney has gone to some unusual lengths to interact with the citizens of her district. Thus, while attempting to secure signatures for a Liberal Party primary in 1994, Maloney described the following event: "There were two women in their eighties, who said that they don't get out much and don't open their door to strangers. They said they would not sign unless the congresswoman herself came to see them. So I did!" (*The Village Voice* 8/8/94). Asked why she was securing signatures for a Liberal primary when she had all but won reelection on the Democratic line, Maloney responded, "You never know. You never know. You never know" (*The Village Voice* 8/8/94).

Interestingly, in contrast to academic views highlighting the generally noncontroversial nature of a politician's work in the constituency (Mayhew 1974; Fiorina 1977), Maloney has also not hesitated to take sides in district controversies. For example, she has advocated to keep legalized gambling off Governor's Island (PR 1/6/98), sided with a neighborhood group to keep a Toys 'R' Us store out of a residential area (*CR* 9/12/95), and sided with a group of longtime but illegal "squatters" threatened by the city with eviction (*Newsday* 10/15/94).

In a very different vein, Maloney even got involved in a fairly unusual squabble: a dispute over the ownership of an escaped bird. Maloney got involved when one of the potential claimants was denied access to the bird and she was present as the "African gray wasn't squawking as it perched in its cage during a sidewalk news conference while humans went cuckoo trying to figure out who he belonged to" (*New York Post* 5/9/01).

Back to reality, Maloney has used the local arena to promote some of her longtime national interests. As she did as a city council member, she has gotten involved in gender-related controversies: "Twenty-two female elected officials will put Police Commissioner Howard Safir on the hot seat next week over reports that cops stood by while more than 50 women were molested in Central Park after the National Puerto Rican Parade" (*DN* 6/30/00). In conjunction with nationally known feminists, including Gloria Steinem, she has worked to ensure the prosecution of a travel company allegedly promoting "sex tours" and child prostitution (*DN* 1/5/00).

Moreover, she has also used constituency forums to put pressure on national leaders, for instance, collecting three thousand postcards to deliver to House Speaker Hastert urging the closing of gun law loopholes (*Newsday* 5/4/01). Even more, she has shown a partisan side, for instance blasting what she perceived as "the anti-woman actions of the new majority" (the Republican-led 104th Congress), characterizing "today's Congress as being 'far more hostile to women's rights than any I remember' and releasing a scorecard detailing that 'women will be hard hit by cuts in Medicare, Medicaid, federal job-training programs for women, family preservation and other programs'" (*Newsday* 4/14/96).

Thus, Maloney can work with a rather partisan style. She prominently displays her party identification on her Web site biography, which begins, "Carolyn B. Maloney, a Democrat." She sometimes performs the functions of party leader, for instance, actively campaigning for city council candidates, and holding forums for Democratic primary candidates from across the state (*Newsday* 4/3/98; *The Village Voice* 11/5/96).

In a decade where many of her party colleagues downplayed their associations with President Clinton, Maloney proclaimed, "I'm proud of the Democratic Party" (*Newsday* 11/4/94). In turn, then-president and Mrs. Clinton and Vice President Gore appeared on several occasions with her (*Newsday* 10/4/94), and she commemorates these associations with photos on her Web site.

Finally, Maloney's constituent work has even acquired an international character, taking her to a Peruvian jail. She visited a constituent (Lori Berenson) sentenced to life in prison by a secret military tribunal for alleged acts of terrorism. Over a multiyear campaign, Maloney has been part of an ongoing effort to secure a fairer trial for Berenson and to generate publicity and attention for the case (AP 6/28/01).[4]

To sum up, Congresswoman Maloney is obviously interacting with local constituents in traditional political ways. As the message Maloney sent to her Greenpoint constituents upon Greenpoint's 1999 re-redistricting out of the 14th indicates, she clearly can demonstrate real warmth toward constituency activity: "I will always have a special place in my heart for the people I worked with side by side and the neighborhood I visited over the years. Congresswoman Velazquez is fortunate to soon be able to call the residents of Greenpoint . . . her constituents" (www.greenpointusa.com).

Issues and a National Focus. However, many aspects of Congresswoman Maloney's home style are national. In fact, it will become clear that a host of factors—the constituency, Maloney's own background, and the environment of her initial election to Congress'—push the congresswoman in a national direction. Indeed, in Maloney's case, it is hard to sort out the local from the national.

Thus, "Maloney likes to speak her mind, whether by taking to the House floor or by writing scores of bills . . . she criticizes the Republican majority for meddling in the census or ignoring the rights of breast-feeding women or failing to protect the elderly from financial fraud" (*PIA* 2002, 696). In the 106th Congress, she ranked tenth in terms of the number of congressional bills she had sponsored, their range covering the jurisdictions of fully thirteen congressional committees (*PIA* 2002, 696). As she sees it, "Instead of standing on the sidelines pointing fingers, I go to work. Instead of style, I've had substance" (*NYT* 10/4/94).

Maloney got involved early, albeit in a somewhat unusual vein. Seeking to gain legislative experience, she looked at the federal budget to find "the stupidest thing there" to address (*Newsday* 4/21/94). What did she come up with but something called the Civilian Marksmanship Program, a program created at the turn of the century "to encourage shooting clubs and marksmanship competitions" (*Washington Post* 11/4/93)? Observing, "I thought it was time to claim victory in the Spanish-American War and get it out of the budget," Maloney introduced legislation that would do just that (*WP* 11/4/93).

What was the outcome? Did Congress jump on the bandwagon? Not exactly. Although the program is still in the budget, Maloney's efforts produced positive results. The Department of Defense responded that it was open to considering options (*Newsday* 4/21/94), and the cause took on more credibility after a Michigan "militia" group allegedly gained access to a military firing range due to the program (*Newsday* 5/6/95). In addition, Maloney was probably right to jump in early; her work earned her some attention from her colleagues along with coverage in some national press (*Newsday* 4/21/94).

The foray into the marksmanship effort indicates that in Congress, Maloney has pursued not only a home style with strong national elements but also a focus on the kinds of concerns marking her precongressional career, in this instance, her perception of waste in government. As such, her committee assignments, including the House Financial Services Committee and the Joint Economic Committee, have focused on the economy. She has used these posts not only to look out for the interests of the 14th (New York pays out $33 billion more to the federal government than it takes back in aid [*PIA* 1994, 1060]) but also "she has worked to modernize financial services laws and regulations while strongly advocating for consumer protections that are up-to-date with the increasingly global economy" (Web bio).

Thus, she has continued her attempts to promote efficiency, sponsoring the Debt Collection Improvement Act in 1995 (*Newsday* 12/7/97) calling for debts (owed by groups including farmers, small business owners, and students) more than 180 days old to be turned over to the Department of Treasury for collection. "We've handed the government departments the tools to clamp down on people who owe them money—yet they continue to let the debt pile up" (PR 9/12/97).[5]

Similarly, to encourage efficiency in the Defense Department, she developed The Best Business Practices for Defense Inventory Act (1997, H.R. 1850), a bill "to require the Secretary of Defense to plan and carry out pilot projects to test various 'best business practices' for defense inventory management" (*CR* 6/10/97). However, it is not surprising that Maloney, representing a liberal constituency, has also been active on the consumer side:

> In addition to numerous amendments in Committee relating to consumer privacy and consumer protection, in the 106th Congress Maloney introduced financial services legislation to: require credit card companies to provide 90-days notice before increasing lending rates; provide banks tools to protect against financial abuse of the elderly; provide loan guarantees for child care facility finance; and require web sites to disclose their affiliations with financial services companies. (Web bio)

Yet, a final point about the congresswoman's work in the financial arena is worth noting. Maloney's efforts on behalf of consumers and constituents takes on an interesting twist when we recall that the 14th district includes important business elements. Referring to her district as "the banking capital of the world," Maloney has been described not only as an advocate for consumers but also as an unlikely (for a liberal Democrat) banking industry ally. Saying, "We have to make sure that what is the most competitive and best banking system in the world remains that way," she has, among other things, helped line up committee support for some key proposals supported by the banking industry and has been tough on the Federal Reserve Board (*American Banker* 11/6/97). Noting that the banking companies in her district "are afraid to criticize their regulator directly," she claimed, "I have to speak for them" (*American Banker* 11/6/97). Thus:

> In the past year, she has helped block a Fed plan to give banks an extra day to clear local checks, accused the agency of interfering with a unionization drive, and sponsored legislation that would stop the central bank from undercutting private companies that compete with its check processing operation. (*American Banker* 11/6/97)

As we would expect from her prior political career, it is also easy to document Congresswoman Maloney's ongoing interest in issues pertaining to women, children, and families. In fact, she began early, telling a group of women activists shortly after her election, "I've got to get us some visibility" (*NYT* 12/26/92). A firm believer in equal rights and opportunities, she has been willing to take a side on some important sociological controversies, arguing, for example, for equality in the military. Separation of the sexes "confines women and makes them unequal. Soldiers must fight as they train. Separation of the sexes during training will only delay difficulties associated with the integration of the field" (PR 12/17/97).

In addition, in her capacity as co-chair of the Congressional Caucus on Women's Issues (106th Congress), perhaps recalling her distant relative, the suffragette from earlier in the century, Maloney has stepped into history: "This year, Rep. Carolyn Maloney, D-N.Y., is picking up where [former representative Patricia] Schroeder left off by sponsoring a version of the equal rights amendment" *(USA Today* 2/18/97). As her efforts also include participation in several important international conferences Maloney is clearly plugged into national and even international networks of women activists (Web bio). She has co-sponsored legislation authorizing a Washington statue in honor of minority women (AP 6/20/00) and has brought her daughter to Washington as part of the Ms. Foundation's "Take Your Daughter to Work" program (*CQ's Washington Alert* 10/18/93).

Reacting to dozens of cases brought to her attention (PR 3/24/98), she has gotten involved in some fairly sensitive territory, successfully sponsoring legislation permitting breastfeeding on federal property.

"It is difficult to believe that in the year 1999, we need to pass a law to allow breastfeeding on federal property," said Rep. Maloney (D-NY). "But, sadly, we do. Women have been kicked out of federal parks, federal museums, federal buildings, and even the U.S. Capitol for doing the most natural thing in the world—breastfeeding a child." (PR 8/4/99)

And, it must have been a fairly unusual event in the eyes of the Washington establishment when, in commemoration of the passage of the breastfeeding legislation: "Today, Congresswoman Carolyn Maloney (D-NY) was joined by bipartisan Members of Congress, moms, babies, and doctors in a 'lactation celebration'" (PR 8/4/99).[6]

Maloney has introduced many other pieces of legislation pertaining to women, children, and families: for example, the Breast Cancer Early Detection Act (1997), the Child Support Enforcement Improvements Act of 1996, and the Child Support Enforcement Act (1996). In addition, she has worked on behalf of international family planning (PR 10/25/00) and she supported quality of life issues for seniors, such as by helping them retain pets in public housing units (*Newsday* 7/23/93).

These activities may go over well among both Maloney's constituents and among a national network of women activists. However, concerns about such issues as sex roles in the military and breastfeeding are genuinely controversial. Maloney actually received the "Bored Legislator of the Year" designation from *Insight* magazine (3/9/98) which apparently didn't think much of her efforts. She also received flack for challenging the "old boy" network on the floor of the House when a fellow (male) representative made what she perceived to be inappropriate comments about the breasts of a female reporter covering congress (CR 6/23/94; *Newsday* 6/24/94).

In a very different but sometimes equally controversial vein, Maloney has pursued her interest in campaign finance reform, advocating for more Federal Election Commission (FEC) funding and serving as a vocal advocate for passage of the Shays-Meehan bill (*Dallas Morning News* 6/8/98; Web bio). There have been other issues as well, many following from the needs of her constituents. For example, Maloney has been part of the effort to bring Nazi war criminals to justice, working over an extended period of time to broaden freedom of information laws (*Jerusalem Post* 8/7/98). To publicize the interests of Greek Americans, she co-founded the Congressional Caucus on Hellenic Issues and has advocated for peace in Cyprus and enhanced U.S.-Greek relations (Web bio).

As should be clear by now—from her style in her district and her work on issues in Washington—there can be a strong partisan side to Maloney's record. Though it was early in her career, she "remained the only Democratic representative from New York State to vote against President Clinton's $246 billion tax hike" (*Newsday* 6/5/93)[7] ("I did not run for Congress to succumb to threats. I was not elected to be a rubber stamp. . . . Everywhere I go in my district, people say the same thing. Cut spending and reduce the deficit. They will respect me more for it in the morning" [*NYT* 5/29/93; AP 5/28/93]). Her party unity scores are generally very high, ranging in the low nineties, and her presidential support scores (Clinton) average around 80 percent.

She more than made up for her controversial vote. Witness her description of life in Washington on a night four months later—the night of the vote on the final version of first-year president Clinton's budget proposals: "It was a hair-raiser . . . I almost had a nervous breakdown on the floor. It was the longest seconds of my life . . . we had the votes but they weren't coming in. The bottom line is—we won" (*Newsday* 8/7/93).

Congresswoman Maloney has demonstrated partisan loyalty in other visible ways, most notably in her role as ranking minority member on the Government Reform and Oversight Subcommittee on the Census. Democratic leaders gave her "primary responsibility for making the case that the GOP was playing politics with the census" (*PIA* 2002, 696). In that capacity, she co-founded the Congressional Caucus on the Census and was vocal in her support for statistical sampling in 2000 (*PIA* 2002, 696). Calling it "the Civil Rights issue of the twenty-first century," she said:

> What's so horrible about counting everyone? In New York, there was an undercount of 244,000 [in 1990], and we can't afford to be undercounted. We have Republicans cutting back our funding dollars, but now they're trying to cook the books so you don't count all the people. (*Newsday* 10/20/97)

A look at the press releases on Maloney's Web site shows that, for instance, in the year 2000, more than twenty of the approximately eighty press releases related to aspects of the Census. Thus, she urged New Yorkers to take part (PR 4/1/99) and blasted Republicans for not providing enough funding ("Republicans created this emergency. . . . They labored in a cynical, partisan way to prevent modern statistical methods from being used to correct the historical racial differential undercount in the 2000 Census—methods endorsed by the National Academy of Sciences and the census professionals [PR 7/22/99]). She went so far as to request that: "Today on Census Day April 1, I call on Gov. Bush to follow the law, open up his census form, fill it out completely, even if it is the long form, and mail it in as the law requires him to do" (PR 4/1/00).

Finally, Maloney continued to emphasize her concerns after the census had been conducted. Claiming that in terms of congressional representation, the three million people estimated to have been missed in the 2000 count equates to five House seats, she arranged to have several Democrats actually leave during a major budget speech by newly elected President Bush (AP 2/27/01).[8]

Discussion

Thus, Maloney's home style reflects a combination of local and national elements. Clearly, as Fenno's work would suggest, there is a strong local component. Maloney, after all, loves the city and has resided there by choice throughout her adult life. She attends parades, interacts with constituents, and works on issues of concern to New Yorkers. In addition, though, this profile has highlighted her emphasis on the national. Events and forces of the 1990s (including increased partisanship, Clinton's coattails, and the women's movement) have not only influenced her Washington activity but all have figured in the development of her home style as well.

Indeed, one is struck by the high degree of consistency between home and Washington. Maloney engages in the same kinds of activities in both arenas, and she does so with the same getting-involved style. Thus, on balance, the local and the national are interrelated, and, at least in Maloney's case, the interconnections between the local and the national are positive; activities in one arena reinforce efforts in the other.

Why is this the case? Obviously, the two independent variables (constituency and legislator background) of this study have a lot to do with the explanation. In fact, if there were ever a constituency with the potential to allow its members of Congress to develop a national focus, New York City (and perhaps other large urban centers) certainly would be considered prime territory. Too, the solidly Democratic character of the district, especially in the aftermath of the 1992 redistricting, would provide leeway for an incoming Democratic representative entering office in part on the coat-tails of a popular presidential candidate of her party. In that sense, at first glance, Maloney's story is a little disappointing as it provides an easy test case for a theory about local-national connections. Is it really so surprising we find major national elements here? At the same time, what is particularly striking and less expected is the extent of the local-national connections and the specifics of the ways in which Maloney incorporates the national into her home style.

One final point remains. Of course, in addition to the impact of Maloney's constituency, her own interests—her history of issue activism, her connection with the women's movement, her desire to make a difference—all point her towards a national home style. Too, for Maloney, the hallmark of this style centers on "getting involved."

There are clearly advantages to this style. Maloney can easily build a campaign record, and more, she can accommodate the concerns of the diverse interests (geographic, ethnic, economic) of the city. There is also a downside to her home style. The flip side of the "getting involved" style Maloney has chosen is the potential for a lack of focus. Hence, early in her career she was labeled a "little spacey . . . a pit bull without a cause" (*Newsday* 11/5/92, 12/26/92).

In what is perhaps an extreme example of how a lack of focus can hurt, Maloney, early in her career, proposed "the Northern Rockies Ecosystems Protection Act" classifying sixteen million acres in five western states as wilderness. Did this act earn her legislative respect? Not exactly. "Western representatives in retaliation offered mock legislation to designate Manhattan . . . as a natural wilderness" (*PIA* 1996, 917). As it turned out, in the congressional debate, she was unable to define some basic terms ("ecosystem") or recall the name of the director of the forest service (*PIA* 1996, 917).

But, overall, Maloney's home style has been successful. She has steadily increased her election margins from her initial squeaker victory to 64 percent in 1994 (her toughest challenge) to upward of 70 percent thereafter, and she has more than made up for her underfinanced campaign of 1992. Given all this, it is perhaps not surprising that she briefly considered a run for the open seat being vacated by Senator Moynihan in the year 2000 (*Newsday* 6/3/99). The fact that she even considered such a Senate run indicates not only her political success but more importantly from the perspective of this work, her ability to balance local and national concerns.

Amo Houghton: Public Service with a Business Slant

To the extent that representatives are first and foremost locally oriented, we might expect them to be relatively like their constituents. We might particularly expect this to be true where the economy of an area is somewhat depressed and where the needs of a district might otherwise go unheard if a member of Congress has a broader agenda. As we shall see, these expectations are, in fact, partially borne out in the case of Amory (Amo) Houghton's representation in the 31st district—he shares many fundamental values with constituents and he consistently expresses a genuine commitment to his home area. However, Houghton's representational style is particularly interesting because of all the ways he is less "like" his constituents and because of the ways he uses national connections to enhance the status of the local area. Thus, it will become abundantly clear that this former CEO of the world-renowned Corning Inc. comes from a background and set of life experiences substantially at odds with not only the average member of Congress but most particularly the average constituent of the somewhat economically depressed 31st district, that the national elements of Houghton's home style form a surprising complement to the local activities we might expect of a representative in such a district, and that Houghton's strong interest in particular national concerns (moderate partisanship, support for some "liberal" social programs, and an interest in foreign policy) go well beyond our image of a member of Congress from rural New York State.

How, then, does an individual so atypical of his constituency nevertheless not only represent them but thrive, with nine terms in office? How does such an individual combine local and national elements to win the trust of his constituents, and how does Houghton translate his business background into the profitable home style we know he has developed?

The following profile seeks to answer these questions by demonstrating the interconnections between the local and the national. Houghton capitalizes on his national status to enhance the economic opportunities in his district. His constituents appear to appreciate a representative with so many national connections. However, in addition to his national interests, Houghton actually would highlight his similarity to his constituents and his identification with their values. Thus, this profile provides another illustration of the ways local and national politics can be connected.

Constituency

Houghton's 31st district, dubbed the Southern Tier, is geographically dispersed, including 6,587 square miles (second largest to McHugh's). It encompasses all of seven counties and portions of three others. Its landscape of farms, towns, and villages is joined by several small manufacturing cities (Jamestown, Auburn, Elmira, and Olean), none of which exceed thirty-five thousand residents.

The district is rural (60%), overwhelmingly white (96%) and 74% with ancestry from Northern Europe (Table 3.1). As its rural character would suggest, constituents are rather dispersed—eighty-eight people per square mile. However, parts of the area defy stereotypes about the homogeneity of such districts. As the *Almanac of American Politics* (1998) describes it, the district consists of "forgotten stretches of territory yet it has an interesting and distinct history" (1047). Thus, the district includes a dozen colleges and universities, the largest grape-growing area outside of California, and the Chautauqua Institute, formerly a Methodist training center and now the site of numerous educational and artistic activities. It contains Native American reservations, the renowned race car track at Watkins Glen, the Finger Lakes, and Mark Twain's burial place in Elmira. The largest employer is Corning Glass, with upward of five thousand employees, but Dresser-Rand, Toshiba, and Cummins Engineering Company are among other businesses with operations in the district (*PIA* 2000, 991). The educational centers and companies such as Corning bring cosmopolitan elements to the area and, as we shall see, suggest the makings for a socially moderate primary constituency.

Like much of the rest of upstate New York, the area has had more than its share of economic difficulties. With a median income of $25,124, a blue-collar percentage of 30 and a college graduation rate of 14 percent, the district ranks among the half-dozen poorest in New York State and in the bottom third of congressional districts nationally (*PIA* 2000, 990; Table 3.1). Thus, any legislator representing the 31st would do well to begin with a focus on economic concerns.

Politically, "the 31st district has been Republican country since the party was founded" (*Almanac* 1998, 1047). Any Republican, even one atypical of his constituents, would start out advantaged in such a district. Houghton indeed won his initial election bid with 60 percent of the vote, and in his subsequent elections he has not received less than 70 percent. Prior to 1998, he had never faced a primary challenge from the more conservative wing of the party (*PIA* 2000, 992). Nevertheless, under certain circumstances, the Republican edge can be cracked, as Clinton carried the district in 1996 by three percentage points over Dole (45 to 42 percent) and Stan Lundine, a Democrat who "defied the political demographics" (*Buffalo News* 10/31/98) to represent the district for ten years, was Houghton's congressional predecessor.

Thus, though Houghton's constituents are rural, Republican, and have undergone economic difficulties, the area is not completely homogeneous. These characteristics set the boundaries and constraints on the home style a representative from the 31st district must adopt.

Background

Amo Houghton's family has been a presence in the district since his great-great-grandfather (also Amory Houghton) opened Corning Inc. in 1851. Now one of the largest companies in the nation, Corning is one of the premier companies in glass manufacturing, producing all sorts of glass-related products. For example, Corning holds "the lion's share of the market in manufacturing electric light bulbs" (*San Diego Union Tribune* 8/7/88) and is a leader in "glass and ceramics technology including fiber optics and photonic components" (Web bio). The company includes Corning Ware products and Steuben Glass and has established a glass museum, which has become a major tourist attraction in western New York (*Almanac* 2000, 1181).

Born in Corning in 1926, Houghton himself (after a stint in the Marines in the 1940s) continued the family tradition by pursuing an education at Harvard University (his family has even endowed a rare book library there [*Almanac* 2000, 1182]). After receiving a degree from the Harvard Business School, he joined the family business in the 1950s. Starting as an accountant in 1951 and rising to CEO at age thirty-eight in 1967, "'He worked very, very hard, harder than anybody,' says Truslow, a long-time associate . . . 'Amo really put us on the map as an international company and a good part of our profits now come from optical fibers, and Amo pushed for that back in 1968 and stuck through it through 17 years of losses. I don't know many business people who would have the courage to do that'" (*BN* 12/10/95).

In the course of his long career, Houghton has served on the boards of directors of some of the nation's premier companies (IBM, Citicorp, and Procter and Gamble), and he was a member of President Reagan's Grace Commission on civil service reform in the 1980s (*BN* 12/10/95). He even ended up in the *Forbes* magazine Business Hall of Fame (*WP* 3/18/93).

At the same time, a strong tradition of public service runs in the Houghton family. Alanson B. Houghton, Houghton's grandfather, served in the House of Representatives in the 1920s and later as ambassador to both Germany and Great Britain (Web bio) while Houghton's father, Amory Houghton Sr., served as ambassador to France. Proud of the tradition, Houghton displays family pictures on the walls of his Washington congressional office (*BN* 6/11/96) and unhesitatingly defends his family background in campaigns (*Elmira Star Gazette* 11/04/90).

Upon his retirement from Corning in 1986, Houghton and his wife were planning to continue the public service tradition in an unusual way: they were intending to pursue missionary work and economic relief programs in Zimbabwe (*PIA* 1992, 1080). But, upon former representative Stan Lundine's nomination to lieutenant governor, a vacant seat attracted Houghton's attention. Concerned that Amo might actually do the unusual and go to Africa, Houghton's brother reportedly phoned then-representative and Houghton friend Ray McGraph of Long Island: "Oh, if you could get him to run for Stan's seat, you would make the family very happy, because he wants to move to Africa and we really don't want him to do it" (*BN* 12/10/95). (Houghton and his wife, however, visit and provide financial assistance to a mission school in Zimbabwe [*PIA* 2004, 739]).

The character of Houghton's initial campaign would set the stage for his ultimate home style. Though he had not been active in Republican electoral politics in the district, the party embraced his nomination (*Albany Times Union* 6/6/86). In turn, Houghton was happy with his choice and articulated campaign themes that would set the stage for his later in-office activity:

> One of the reasons I got into this race was that I felt we needed more businessmen down in Washington. . . . We don't have more people than a lot of these nations. We've just got an extraordinarily efficient and effective industrial arsenal, which is the reason for our power in this world. (*SG* 1/11/87)

In addition, Houghton is consistently referred to as a "nice guy" whose enthusiasm and gregariousness appear to be contagious. A "warm man, quick to smile and slow to criticize" (*The Houston Chronicle* 6/11/96), he is outgoing and enjoys a joke (*BN* 12/10/95). He was (later) even voted number one by House staffers for being "just plain nice" (*TU* 6/26/98).

An illustration of Houghton's genuineness was provided (years later) by Houghton's congressional predecessor: "[Stan] Lundine told the story about how, when he was a Congressman and Houghton was still at

Corning, Lundine attended a luncheon at the plant. 'Afterwards, [Houghton] went into the kitchen and thanked the cook,' he said. 'I remember thinking, "Hey, that's probably something I should be doing"'" (*BN* 10/31/98).

This "people" sense would help Houghton become a shrewd politician. To spice up his 1988 campaign, where he ran unopposed, he thought up the "work days" idea, carrying out stints as a short order cook, disk jockey, and man-on-the-street reporter (*SG* 10/11/88). "I'm in the enviable position of not having to blow my own horn [in order to keep in the public eye]" (*SG* 10/11/88).

In 1986 (and later), the Republican nature of the district gave Houghton, the amateur, a built-in advantage. He ran promising to use his stature, business know-how, and even international connections for the benefit of the area. His 1986 opponent, Cattaraugus County District Attorney Larry Himelein, raised the obvious concerns, charging that Houghton was an "elitist" who would be out of touch with the needs of his not-so-well off constituents and that a background in business did not in fact translate into political know-how (*PIA* 2000, 992).

Thus, the symbol for the campaign became the "Amo Mobile," the recreational vehicle Houghton used to traverse the district. Apparently, the RV, which later would become popular with supporters, was stocked with "liquor and cookies" and was caricatured in the *Wall Street Journal* (10/27/86). The fact that Houghton's other most common means for getting around the district was his private plane only added to the image (*Wall Street Journal* 10/27/86). Thus, it is more than obvious that Houghton is not demographically "like" his average constituent. However, as we shall see, it is in part his uniqueness that has contributed to his political edge.

Home Style

How, then, has Houghton earned and kept the trust of his constituents? How does a former businessman turn successful politician? First, though it might not describe all Congress members in his situation, there is a strong local component to Houghton's home style. His commitment to the area is genuine—he "grew up in this area. He worked here. He knows the people" (*SG* 11/13/98).

Too, Corning Inc. appears to have quite a good reputation and working relationship with the local community and its surrounding areas. Not only was Houghton instrumental in helping the area rebuild after flood devastation in the 1970s, but Corning also financed "a new City Hall and an old town style downtown area that is now a tourist attraction" (*PIA* 1992, 1080). Later, in the early 1980s, when Houghton instituted an across-the-board 5 percent salary cut at Corning in lieu of actual layoffs, the then-mayor commented: "If they feel that pay cuts are necessary to continue in business, I think it is a good thing. They have explained the situation to their employees and have gone about it in a very nice way" (*NYT* 3/23/82).

It follows, then, that as a congressman, "Rep. Houghton is committed to being accessible, and maintains a network of offices in Washington and the Southern Tier and Finger Lakes region. You can visit or call with questions or concerns" (www . . . houghton).

Houghton and his staff put a value on accessibility. He not infrequently makes weekly visits home (*BN* 3/24/95), sends out newsletters, and sometimes ranks high on his use of the congressional franking privilege. "Amo would be disappointed being on the low end of the scale; he'd rather be on the high end" (*BN* 4/5/94).

Nor does Houghton view himself as "above" participating in the normal round of community events. He has thus announced art contest winners at a local high school (PR 5/15/98), celebrated the career of a local sheriff (*BN* 5/20/94), and has problem solved on behalf of constituents— including getting a government investigation into the death of a National Guard member (PR 1/14/99) and helping a child with leukemia attend a Washington Redskins football game (*BN* 1/4/93).

Even more, and this is the strength of his presentation of self, Houghton uses his national stature and position as a member of the business and political establishment to highlight his genuine commitment to public service and his home area. In a way that others without his status cannot, he can use his natural enthusiasm to promote the district: "If I can make people believe in working together we can take on anybody and we can be the best" (*SG* 11/7/90). "I can't build a product, produce a quart of milk, prune a grapevine, or set up a service. That's just not my job. But what I can do is help bring together the best of these activities to promote their value in the outside world and to protect them from the hammerlock of government by bureaucracy and regulation" (*TU* 5/22/88).

Thus, Houghton and his staff have consistently sponsored conferences boosting opportunities for the district: educating business leaders on obtaining government grants (*Houghton Report* 1987), on trade (*BN* 5/17/95), and on tourism (*BN* 5/10/96; 9/9/00). They have also helped companies in the district obtain some significant federal grants: the Schweitzer Aircraft Company received $13.5 million toward the development of a new-style reconnaissance plane used against drug smuggling and terrorism (*BN* 10/22/98), and the race car track at Watkins Glen received $1 million to improve facilities (PR 10/21/99).

In addition, again in a manner that others could not, Houghton has led delegations of district business leaders abroad (to Mexico, Latin America, and Africa) to promote opportunities. "Chile is a really hot country. It's not the biggest country in the world, but it has a big impact on the South American market, and Argentina is coming back from some of the political uncertainties there" (*BN* 11/7/96). "If you're in business, you can't sit around and wait for people to come from Mexico to the Southern Tier" (*BN* 7/8/94).[9]

He has also held town meetings on such matters as educating constituents about New York's inclusion in the New England Dairy Compact (*TU* 2/16/98); has sponsored legislation, along with Representative Sander Levin (D-Michigan), increasing protections for the American steel industry (*Journal of Commerce* 3/25/99); and has promoted rail service and improved transportation throughout his rural constituency (*BN* 6/4/98). Houghton not only advocated for a part of Route 17 to be designated as interstate highway (I-86), but he also enthusiastically participated in the dedication ceremonies as part of an I-86 victory tour (*BN* 12/3/99).

Houghton's activities as a "bridge builder," however, go well beyond the economic. He has used his stature and connections within the community to make things happen in ways others might not have been able to pull off. Early in his congressional career, he inaugurated a unique exchange program between the district's universities and colleges and Nicaraguan students. Originally the idea of Violeta Chamorro, then the president of Nicaragua, the intent was to introduce students to American universities and give them a "free world" alternative to an education in communist countries. The program involved no government funding but effectively took advantage of the district's substantial educational resources: "Here is a way to help a country rather than just posturing. Many times when congressmen go down there, they look at what's happened, they fly down on a military plane, they come back and have a press conference and that's all. Here is a way of saying 'we want to help' in a human way" (*PIA* 1990, 1088).[10]

Similarly, Houghton can use his position to nudge constituents a bit on social issues. Thus, he has spoken out on the role each individual can play in fostering racial tolerance: "The person who runs a store, a schoolteacher, a student or someone like myself [*sic*] in Washington" can do something about racism (*BN* 1/16/98). Indeed, as a member of Congress, Houghton and African American Representative John Lewis (D-GA), in their capacities as co-chairs of the Faith and Politics Institute, have worked to educate other congressional members to the realities of racism by activities including conducting a "pilgrimage" to historic Alabama sites marking the 1960s civil rights struggle (PR 12/6/99; www . . . lewis).

Finally, Houghton even used his wide-ranging connections to accomplish a congressional first: because of his links to Episcopalian groups across the nation, a Massachusetts bishop became the first clergyperson to assume the role (for a month) of a congressional staffer (PR 1/19/00).

In one sense then, Houghton's home style focuses on the local. True to the promises of his first campaign, he uses his stature to boost the district's economy and to expand the range of opportunities available to constituents. At the same time, he certainly brings a national perspective to his local activity. Not every member of Congress could be such an enthusiastic booster for district interests, highlight racism in a rural white constituency, or be willing to work with a bishop from outside his district.

Too, Houghton's work in Washington is very national. The combination of elements that characterize his district style—a national focus, an emphasis on his expertise and interests, and an effort to bring diverse groups together—apply as well to his Washington activity.

As a freshman member of Congress, Houghton received a seat on the prestigious Budget Committee ("'We are delighted to have Mr. Houghton on the committee, particularly because of his stature and background,' commented a committee member" [SG 1/10/87]). In the 103rd Congress, he obtained a seat on the Ways and Means Committee and subsequently has chaired its subcommittee on Oversight. In 1995, Speaker Gingrich appointed Houghton to head a special group responsible for drafting a budget for the District of Columbia (BN 4/22/95).

In these and related capacities, he has brought his expertise to bear on some important national economic issues, issues the average citizen might be more than happy to ignore. For instance, on several occasions, he has weighed in on insurance liability for small businesses, attempting to balance an employee's right to sue with the undue hardship of unlimited liability (PR 10/7/99). He has advocated for simplifying the tax filing process for American companies conducting business overseas (BN 7/13/95), and for Americans more generally, with his sponsorship of the Tax Simplification and Burden Reduction Act (PR 5/12/99).

Similarly, Houghton can bring a unique perspective to other issues ("I probably am one of the only people around here that has ever put in a family leave program" [PIA 1994, 1108]). As he has done in the district,

Houghton has attempted to connect the business community with other groups in society. In 1993, he co-sponsored the School-to-Work Opportunities Act, which encourages schools, businesses, and the government to work together to increase the opportunities for teens without college education. "We are legislating in ways which will affect business for years to come. Over the years, we must build up an understanding of each other" (*BN* 8/13/93).

He also sponsored what some consider to be a pro-business measure, the Targeted Jobs Tax Credit Act, offering tax credits to employers hiring former welfare recipients (*BN* 5/10/95). He is also an active member of a group attempting to increase dialogue between government officials and business leaders, the John Quincy Adams Society (Web bio).

As we might expect given his wide range of interests, it is not surprising that Houghton's Washington activities extend well beyond economic concerns. For instance, he has weighed in on particular foreign policy areas, on controversial debates about "extremist" partisanship in the House, and on social issues.

For most of his tenure in Congress, he has been a member of the International Relations Committee, and has served as vice-chair of the subcommittee on African Affairs. In that capacity, he has traveled with or led congressional delegations to African nations (PR 3/23/98, 12/3/99) and has promoted the economic development of African nations by co-sponsoring (with Charles Rangel and Philip Crane) The African Growth and Opportunities Act (*Almanac* 2000, 1182) and by advocating for increased foreign aid (*PIA* 1998, 1052–53). He has also attended international forums on terrorism (PR 1/13/99), and Speaker Hastert appointed him to the World Trade Organization Ministerial Congressional Advisory Group (PR 10/20/99).

Arising from this interest in Africa, one of Houghton's heroes is Nelson Mandela. Consequently, he led the successful effort that culminated in awarding Mandela the Congressional Gold Medal in 1998 and, quite in character, he served as master of ceremonies for the festivities held in the auspicious Capital Rotunda. Of Mandela, he stated, "He's a big man, he's a hero, he's somebody above the fray. He's somebody who pleads to us to bend to our better natures, and that lesson should not be lost on this country" (*PIA* 2000, 1182). "Forgiveness is what Mandela is all about. I mean this guy Mandela comes out of prison after 27 years, and the first thing he does is forgive his jailers" (*NYT* 9/24/98).

On the national front, Houghton is perhaps best known for his defense of moderate Republicanism. Without doubt, he is a loyal Republican supporter, working for the party in every way he can, mentoring younger Republican members of the Ways and Means Committee (*Almanac* 1996, 982), praising the integrity of fellow partisans he likes ("Jack Quinn is a very forceful, dynamic guy . . . when Jack says something, you can count on it" [*BN* 10/31/94]) and even supporting particular provisions of the Contract with America with which he disagreed for the sake of party unity (*SG* 3/27/95).[11]

At the same time, despite this unquestioned loyalty, balancing party and conscience has been a juggling act for Houghton. In the context of the height of the Republican Revolution, he expressed his dilemma: "If everyone goes his or her own way, then I think you destroy unity we created in the first place. I agonize over party loyalty, what's good for the district, country. There's something different happening here with our contract" (*SG* 3/27/95).

Houghton too has unequivocally decried the increasing partisanship that has occurred during his tenure in office: "Harsher and more belligerent voices do not represent, at least for me, either an appealing or enduring base for growth in coming years" (*Almanac* 1994, 934).

"The Texas contingent [majority party leaders Armey and DeLay] sees things clearly in black and white and imposes the Texas view on the rest of the country. . . . What I bristle at is when I go to a Republican caucus and they're shouting down the voices of reason. It's not the Republican Party I joined and it's not sustainable" (*Houston Chronicle* 6/11/96). "Screaming works, short term, but if you want to get something done, you have to perceive what the other person thinks. If you punish somebody or grab his tie, it doesn't help in the long run. People end up bearing grudges" (*WP* 4/2/96).

Houghton has, in fact, been a leader in strengthening the Republican "center," helping to form groups such as ERR (Extremely Reasonable Republicans) (*Christian Science Monitor* 10/6/92) and the Main Street Coalition, a think tank created for the purpose of restoring "the strength and vitality of the political center in America" (*Almanac* 1998, 1047). True to his character, he even proclaimed (after a surprisingly successful effort in 1996 to increase the minimum wage over Republican leadership objections; see Quinn profile) what would become a rallying cry for moderate Republicans: "The center of the Republican Party is back" (*BN* 5/25/96). However, Houghton added: "The day after I made that rather pompous statement—the one about 'the center is back'—I found myself voting alone. . . . But I still think you don't have to be nasty to wage an effective campaign. This business about being nasty and driving up negatives—NUTS!" (*BN* 6/23/96).

Consequently, it is not surprising that Houghton was one of the organizers of a very unusual event in congressional history: the bipartisan "civility" retreats, which have been held in Hershey, Pennsylvania, during the course of the last few Congresses. Premised on the theory that higher quality personal interactions among members would facilitate better public policy, these unusual get-togethers have been called the "largest gathering of members of Congress outside Congress" (Web bio).

Houghton has also supported moderate Republican causes. Arguing that art programs are "quintessential to the community in which you live" (*PIA* 1998, 1053), he was a leader in the 1995 fight to preserve the National Endowment for the Arts. Similarly, he worked unsuccessfully to protect the Office of Technology Assessment, which conducted scientific research for Congress (*BN* 6/17/95). Quite within his character, it is worth noting that his work on behalf of these agencies included some unusual publicizing efforts: forming a coalition called America for the NEA with New York Democrat Gerald Nadler, bringing nationally known performing artists including Garth Brooks and Kenny G to Washington as lobbyists (*BN* 3/15/95), and holding a press conference with Sally Ride, the first female astronaut (*BN* 3/15/95).[12]

More recently, Houghton strongly defended former president Clinton throughout the impeachment controversy. Not only was he one of only four Republicans to vote against all impeachment articles, but he took the lead in vocalizing opposition within the Republican Party: writing New York *Times* editorials (*NYT* 12/9/98), sponsoring a censure resolution in hopes of forestalling impeachment (*BN* 12/28/98), and even meeting with President Clinton just prior to the actual impeachment vote (*NYT* 12/17/98):

> It can become oddly enjoyable raking over the details, lamenting the moral lapses. It helps sidestep the unadorned thinking required to decide tough issues. . . . Of course there was conduct unbecoming, I deplore it. If a plant manager in the company I used to work for engaged in such conduct, we would have disciplined him immediately. Maybe even dismissed him. But we wouldn't have burned him at the stake. (*NYT* 12/17/98)

In all these ways, it is clear that despite strong allegiances to his party, Houghton doesn't hesitate to speak his mind and declare his independence when he perceives it necessary.

Discussion

What, then, for Houghton is the relationship between his "local" and "national" activity? How did modern politics impact his home style and what, at bottom, does his profile teach us about representation?

Houghton's profile has illustrated a couple of ways in which the "national" and the "local" are interrelated. In Houghton's case, because of who he is and what his experiences have been, it is difficult to sort out one from the other. To be sure, there is a strong "local" component to his home style. He knows the area he represents, and as we have seen, he enjoys person-to-person interactions with constituents. To be sure, too, dating from his initiation into politics, he works hard to develop the local economy and to boost the area. In short, he engages in many of the kinds of activities that are at the heart of Fenno's descriptions of home styles.

Yet, in any number of ways, Houghton puts so much of his own stamp on the job of United States Representative. His initial campaign material pledged to help the local area on the basis of his long experience as a businessman with global connections. Certainly, not every member of Congress would take the initiative to link up with the president of Nicaragua, with southern Democrats interested in civil rights, or with Episcopalian bishops throughout the country; and not every member would work so hard on behalf of his view of where his party should be headed, "and he's not afraid to tell that to the folks back home" (*BN* 6/25/96).

So, on the one hand, because of Houghton's personal stature, there are mostly positive linkages between the "local" and the "national." As one observer described it, "People here see him as a kindly and beneficent lord of the manor" (*WSJ* 6/18/98).

On the other hand, we might expect some conflict between Houghton's local and national activity. Houghton's voting record and moderate stances could have a negative impact on what happens in the 31st. How, as a member of Congress in office at the height of a historic era for your party, do you explain support for moderate Republicanism and some very public deviations from party to your conservative constituents?

Fenno's work provides a partial answer. If your constituents trust you, you can develop the necessary latitude to go your own way under many circumstances. Thus, constituent trust in conjunction with a more moderate primary constituency might go a long way to hold district support. At the same time, while the potential exists for some negative connections between what Houghton does in Washington and his behavior at home, his moderate stances have led some constituents to explore potential candidacies (*BN* 6/23/96; 12/15/98).

For the most part, Houghton has been able to keep these linkages positive. Indeed, if anything, constituents appear proud of his Washington work and national stature. "'I don't think he's a rebel,' said Bob Hardy, eating lunch at the Dill Pickle bar with his wife, Judy. 'He works for what he feels is right. If that makes him a rebel, then so be it'" (*BN* 6/25/96). As Stan Lundine added, "He was the first Republican to say 'enough already' to the talk of impeaching the president. It was one more example of his independence, and that plays well here" (*BN* 10/31/98).

Given the importance of the events of the 1990s, an additional point is worth adding. As has been shown, Houghton certainly was affected by the events of the 1990s. However, Houghton's link to the national began first and foremost with his personality and stature. It doesn't take 1980s or 1990s politics to produce a representative such as Houghton. Indeed, Houghton "may be more what the Founding Fathers had in mind than the politically adept youngsters who win in so many districts" (*Almanac* 2000, 1182).

Thus, there have probably been Congress members like him throughout our nation's history—consider Fenno's discussion of Congressman F, the African American civil rights leader whose celebrity status was so much a part of relationships with his constituents (Fenno 1978), or his later work on Senator Claiborne Pell, the long-time patrician who nevertheless served relatively blue collar Rhode Island for several decades (Fenno 1996).

However, the increasing number of representatives with the potential for a national perspective—the increased numbers of businesspeople (Davidson and Oleszek 2002; Friedman and Witko 2005), women and minorities, and Washington congressional staffers in recent Congresses (see chapter 1)— opens up the potential for a new set of members whose interests and concerns reach beyond the borders of their districts or have the potential to run on a home style that highlights how their national perspectives will translate into local benefits. Houghton may present an extreme case of atypicality, but there are very general implications to his type of presentation of self.

Finally, what more generally does the Houghton profile teach us about representation? This story began with a focus on how a representative so very demographically unrepresentative of his constituents can nevertheless have a long and successful congressional career. In such a case, there will likely always be the potential for charges that this kind of representative is out of touch with the district.

For Houghton, these charges have taken two forms, the first being that his national stature had not in fact produced enough benefit for the district. Houghton's 1998 Democratic opponent, Caleb Rossiter, a former Vietnam antiwar activist and a strong advocate of liberal politics, surprised politicos by making the campaign interesting by catching "people's attention" with a "run for jobs" (BN 10/31/98). More to the point, the Rossiter campaign was important because of its attempts to turn Houghton's arguments about what his national stature had produced for the local area back on themselves. The Rossiter campaign contended that Houghton had not followed through, and despite the rhetoric, had not in actuality done enough to improve the economic status of the district; for example, Rossiter claimed that significant job losses had occurred (BN 10/15/98) and that Houghton's activity on behalf of making Route 17 interstate quality only ratcheted up after an outcry from local officials (BN 8/22/98; 10/30/98).

Second, the demographic mismatch between Houghton and his constituents lurks in the background of all his campaigns. "We need representatives in Congress who understand the problems of ordinary people," claimed a constituent in a letter to the editor (BN 10/16/98). "He can't know what it's like to be worried about paying a mortgage. I'm not saying he's not a good person, but how could he possibly know that?" (1996 Democratic candidate Bruce McBain) (BN 8/30/96).

In an indirect way, Houghton himself demonstrated an appreciation for this view. In the course of the campaign stints he performed with so much enjoyment as a reporter, a cook, and a DJ, he acknowledged: "You never realize the stress a reporter is under. You're trying to get the essence of the story. And when you realize you could make this sound like a good thing or a bad thing" (SG 10/11/88). Simply, you can't appreciate being in someone's shoes until you have done it.

In sum, there is much to learn from Amo Houghton's brand of representing the 31st district. Houghton's story contributes both to our understanding of the local-national distinction at the heart of this chapter as well as to a consideration of the pros and cons of representation by a member so different from his constituents. While it is easy to see the downside of such demographic differences, presenting Houghton's home style from what might be his unique point of view leads to an appreciation of the positive: how a legislator demographically atypical of his constituents can nevertheless be a successful politician. Houghton's results-oriented style, ability to harness resources and bring various sides together, and his unique experiences are indeed valued by the constituents of New York's 31st.

John McHugh: "I Know the Process and I Know the Players"*

By the time John McHugh won a congressional seat in 1992, he had worked in government virtually all of his adult life. He had risen through the Republican ranks as a state legislator, had specialized in district concerns, and, with a degree in public administration, had developed a solid grasp on key issues. It is therefore not surprising that his home style would be one of a professional politician protecting constituent and partisan interests and showing a solid understanding of detail. In terms of the national-local distinction of this chapter, an examination of McHugh's activities illustrates two themes: the importance of the local even in a district where a representative might feel free to choose to "go national" and the ways that national factors nevertheless impact a very local home style. Finally, from a broader and more normative perspective, given that McHugh is a long-time professional politician who knows how to make the process work, an examination of his activities raises questions about the strengths and weaknesses of the style of a politician who, although he doesn't like the term, would be described by most people as a political insider.

Constituency

At first glance, it seems hard to fathom that the label "North Country" could convey any commonality about the 24th district. The first thing that becomes apparent to an outsider is the physical size of the constituency McHugh represents. With a land area of more than twelve thousand square miles (www . . . mchugh), the 24th district literally sprawls across the northern part of New York State (see Map 2). Stretching from the Canadian border, south through the Adirondack Mountains, and down to an area just north of metropolitan Albany, it comprises all, or parts of, ten of New York's sixty-two counties, and in land area it is bigger than eight U.S. states and forty-two nations. Only fifty Congressional districts are larger (www . . . mchugh). An outsider can only begin to appreciate the physical difficulties associated with traversing such a district. As McHugh put it, "You can't get there from here" (*Watertown Daily Times* 6/26/94).

Yet, there is a real sense of identity to this large area and a sense of commonality, which sets very real boundaries for what a representative of this district is expected to do. In many respects, the district shares characteristics with Houghton's 31st (Table 3.1). The district is overwhelmingly rural

*Source: *Watertown Daily Times* 9/13/92.

(65%), with a population density of just under forty-seven people per square mile. There are some small- to medium- (if a population of around twenty-eight thousand can be called medium) sized cities/towns (Watertown, population approximately twenty-eight thousand; Plattsburgh, nineteen thousand; and Oswego nineteen thousand) (www . . . mchugh), but there are also large distances between them. The norm, though, is even smaller towns and landscapes dotted with small farms. The fact that the district contains "the entire American section of the St. Lawrence Seaway and most of the 3.7 million acres of the Adirondack Park" (www . . . mchugh), parts of Lakes Ontario and Champlain, and many other smaller bodies of water enhances the rural character of the district.

Due to a struggling economy (the college graduation rate of 14% ranks twenty-eighth of thirty-one in New York State) and the median income of just over $25,000 (ranks twenty-sixth of 31), economic interests figure importantly in the district's politics (*PIA* 2000, 716) (Table 3.1). Military bases, including Watertown's Fort Drum (12,400 employees) and the Plattsburgh Air Force Base (now closed), figure importantly in district relationships with Washington, as do dairy farming, the St. Lawrence River, recreation, and tourism. As will become clear, though the Republican constituency generally supports cutbacks in government services, because of the role of the military and agriculture, residents also depend on government services.

Not surprisingly given its rural character, the district is overwhelmingly Republican. As the *Watertown Daily Times* observed, "One would never know, from the level of activity, that the Pierrepont Manor congressman [McHugh] comes from a district in which a serious Democratic threat would exceed the spectacle of a volcanic eruption in the middle of the St. Lawrence River" (11/29/97). Thus, despite pockets of Democratic strength due to organized labor principally in St. Lawrence and Franklin counties (*PIA* 1994, 1090) and despite a Clinton victory (50% in 1996), there has not been a Democratic House member in the North Country since 1837 (*WDT* 11/5/94)! So, after his initial 1992 win with 61 percent of the vote, McHugh's subsequent election margins have ranged upward of 70 percent.

In short, McHugh's sprawling district in upstate New York has a particularly interesting character. People (dairy farmers, military personnel) often depend on federal government programs to enhance their economic well-being, and a fairly large range of interests, economic and otherwise, is represented across the constituency. On balance, the district's specific economic interests, coupled with its solidly Republican character, would appear to impose strong constraints on a representative, but also leave room for flexibility on issues of less direct concern to constituents.

Background

John McHugh has spent his entire adult life as a professional politician, rising through the ranks of the dominant district party. Born and raised in Watertown, he was "bit bad [*sic*]" early by the political bug (*WDT* 11/1/92). Inspired by John Kennedy's 1960 presidential campaign, McHugh stated, "I didn't know a Democrat from a Republican at that time. . . . Here was this young guy, there was something different about him. . . . He seemed so disadvantaged politically, being his age, his Irish background, his religious background . . . and I just got caught up into it" (*WDT* 11/1/92). After graduating from Utica College of Syracuse University at age twenty-three, McHugh was expecting to spend a summer taking a roofing job. Instead, he achieved the highest score on a civil service exam and became a confidential assistant to the Watertown city manager, and subsequently a staff aide to State Senator H. Douglas Barclay, focusing on research and relationships with local governments (*PIA* 2002, 716).

Along the way, McHugh earned a master's degree in public administration from the State University of New York at Albany (1977), joined a number of political organizations (including the American Society of Young Political Leaders, the Council of State Governments' Eastern Regional Conference Committee on Fiscal Affairs, and the U.S. Trade Representative's Intergovernmental Policy Advisory Committee on Trade [*WDT* 9/13/92]), and even married the daughter of a local official (*WDT* 11/1/92) (they have since divorced).

It is not surprising, then, that McHugh worked his way up through the party ranks, succeeding Barclay as state senator (1985–1992). "When Doug Barclay took me out to dinner that night and said he wasn't running and would I consider, I felt like I was hit by a planet, I thought I'd found my niche" (*WDT* 11/1/92).

As a state legislator, McHugh chaired several committees and was particularly active on dairy issues: "I think it's amazing that we are not losing more farmers than we are. It's a tribute to their ingenuity and resiliency" (*TU* 4/17/91). He also developed a solid understanding of the dimensions of his constituency:

"My Senate base was critical," he said of Oswego, Jefferson and parts of St. Lawrence counties. "If you include the media market that surrounds it in Lewis and the northern part of St. Lawrence County, you're talking well over 60 percent of the population of the Congressional District. That's an enormous advantage I had." (*WDT* 11/4/92)

When Representative David O'B. Martin (1980–1992) announced his retirement, McHugh was one of several politicians logically placed to succeed him. Though he competed in a primary against Morrison Hosley, who would later run in the general election on the Conservative and Right-to-Life lines, he received significant endorsements, including that of Martin (*WDT* 8/24/92) and all ten Republican chairs of the counties of his district (*WDT* 6/25/92).

Consequently, by outsider standards, McHugh's 1992 campaign was an incredibly easy one. In fact, as the authors of the *Almanac of American Politics* (1998) described it, McHugh was chosen "almost without incident" (1030). Thus, he didn't actually open an official headquarters until August (*1992 House Races*) and raised only $177,000[13] to win his 1992 congressional seat. In 1992 and in subsequent races, Democratic opposition has been weak, as McHugh's opponents have consisted of a retired math teacher (1992), an ex-marine who had worked at Fort Drum (1994), the husband of the retired math teacher (1996), and a parole officer (1998, 2000).

So, benefiting from his party's support and campaigning on experience, McHugh achieved his dream and made it to Congress. Both a cartoon from the 1992 primary (which at the time angered McHugh) amusingly entitled "Natural Selection in the North Country" (*WDT* 10/17/92), and McHugh's response that "his endorsement by the party leadership across the 10-county district 'reflects the effort put forth in the past 20 years on behalf of my party and people in the district that I've had the honor to represent'" (*WDT* 9/13/92) nicely capture McHugh's insider route to political office. It is in light of this background and the context of a rural constituency with clearly defined interests that McHugh would develop a successful home style.

Home Style

Perhaps due to the specificity of district interests and to McHugh's prior experience representing them, his home style is primarily local. More than Maloney or Houghton, McHugh acts as an advocate for the interests, economic and otherwise, of the 24th Congressional District. As a 1994 newspaper endorsement described it, "Rep. McHugh is responsive to the needs of the large geographic area he serves" (*WDT* 11/3/94).

When the editorial added that "[h]e has shown able leadership in helping the North Country focus on explaining to Washington the value of Fort Drum to the nation's defense," (*WDT* 11/3/94), the reference was to one of the new congressman's first efforts, advocacy in the early 1990s centering around the preservation of district military bases.

The Base Closure and Realignment Commission appointed by newly elected President Clinton in 1993 was charged with making obviously controversial decisions about eliminating numerous bases across Congressional districts throughout the nation. Since the bases at Plattsburgh and Fort Drum figured in these discussions, throughout his first year in office McHugh put considerable effort into what turned out to be an unsuccessful attempt to keep the Plattsburgh base open. He took the interesting step of hiring his predecessor, Martin, as a congressional staffer charged with monitoring all activity pertaining to base closings and lobbying for district interests (*TU* 7/7/93). McHugh was active in other ways as well, going out of his way to praise Clinton's commission nominees (*WDT* 1/9/93), proudly presenting Plattsburgh's case to federal officials (*TU* 5/19/93; *WDT* 5/11/93) and requesting access to commission records when Plattsburgh was the only base selected for closing without a Pentagon recommendation (*WDT* 5/24/94). (Later, he interceded on behalf of the role the local Mohawk Tribe might play in the reconversion of the Plattsburgh base [*WDT* 1/4/94]).

At the same time, McHugh was also an important player not only in efforts to preserve Fort Drum from any closure proceedings but also in what turned out to be a successful community effort to expand its scope and facilities; illustrations include but are by no means limited to:

- a training and education center (*WDT* 6/5/97)
- a gunnery range ($17.5 million) (*WDT* 6/5/97)
- a hangar that "would be one of the largest structures in the North Country" (*WDT* 6/16/99).

One sees in all this the importance of having a strong advocate in Congress. By simply keeping the issue on the agenda or speaking out at a meeting, it is possible to make a difference. In protecting the interests of Fort Drum, McHugh has stood up for the importance of army light divisions. "Heavy units need lighter forces to operate between and among them on terrain not suitable for heavy vehicles" (*WDT* 11/7/97). He praised then-governor Cuomo for using a meeting of New York's congressional delegation to raise issues of support for Drum (*WDT* 2/25/94), traveled abroad to visit soldiers of the Tenth Mountain Division (*WDT* 11/15/99), and even had some fun and presented caps to top generals (*WDT* 12/17/94).

Along the lines of representing district interests, McHugh has also been an unwavering backer of dairy farmers (Web bio). In the 1990s, the central issue confronting such constituents was the specter of deregulation of federal price supports. At the height of the push for balanced budgets in the 104th Congress, Speaker Gingrich and the Republican leadership backed plans that would substantially alter the government's role in the dairy industry. In response, "McHugh worked night and day with the more-conservative Rep. Gerald Solomon . . . to ward off a dairy regulation plan that they thought would drive New York farmers out of business" (*BN* 5/25/96). Thus, McHugh reiterated his commitment "to pursue the interest of our dairy farmers and their families" (*WDT* 10/9/95). Even at the height of a period of intense party loyalty, he was one of a handful of Republicans who voted against the major budget reconciliation bill (*WDT* 11/17/95).

Thereafter, in the course of a year-long struggle, details about specific aspects of dairy farming—products covered under regulations, the exact level of price supports, and the particular governmental structures charged with the responsibility of overseeing the programs—were compromised out. While the particulars are beyond the scope of this project, one comes away impressed by the level of detail Representative McHugh and others like him must absorb and discuss.

In the end, an agreement was reached protecting farmers while lowering levels of price supports and leaving room for much future negotiation (*WDT* 3/24/96). This future negotiation, of course, led to revisiting the issues in later Congresses, providing more locally oriented work for McHugh. For example, in 1999, New York representatives wanted an expanded role in the New England Dairy Compact as well as more favorable price supports. "'They pledged to us that the needs of dairy farmers would be addressed to our satisfaction by the end of the session of Congress,' said McHugh. 'We received the leadership's solemn promise'" (*TU* 10/9/99). Later in the session, McHugh got even more specific when he and Representative Tammy Baldwin (D-WI) proposed The Cheese Quality Act of 2000, which would, in part, prevent the Food and Drug Administration from permitting the use of dry ultra-filtered milk in the making of cheese (PR 6/15/00).

What other issues confront the 24th Congressional District? McHugh has expressed disappointment after the Federal Emergency Management Agency (FEMA) failed to allocate money to help the district recover from severe ice storms:

> For three years I have supported requests for funds to assist areas in California struck by fires and earthquakes and aid to areas in the Midwest hit by floods. It seems that every part of the country can reap the benefits of federal aid but the North Country. In our time of need, the [Clinton] administration has turned its back on the people of Northern New York. (*TU* 9/23/95)

Similarly, arguing that "in the North Country's extreme winter weather, the use of generators and the other items (chainsaws, heaters, smoke detectors) were certainly not luxuries they were critical commodities," he has advocated that constituents be reimbursed for "survival items" (PR 1/28/98).

The district's numerous waterways and its proximity to Canada also led McHugh to focus on issues of immigration, recreation, the environment, and water levels. For example, he has served as co-chair of the Congressional Study Group on Canada, has advocated (prior to 9/11) to ease requirements on tourists entering the North Country from Canada (*WDT* 9/8/96), and has also supported legislation suggesting that immigrants who have overstayed their visas pay a one-thousand dollar fee rather than face immediate deportation (*WDT* 11/7/97). He has even publicized concerns regarding low water levels. For example, arranging a tour of the area for appropriate federal officials (*WDT* 5/29/99), obtaining federal funding to study the problem (PR 6/30/2000), and attending a summit of local officials (*WDT* 4/16/99).

In addition, McHugh has advocated for Essential Air Service, a "small but effective" subsidization program guaranteeing transportation to small- and medium-sized communities (*WDT* 8/11/93); for federal technical assistance to ensure quality drinking water (*WDT* 5/7/96); for low postal rates for libraries ("These services are particularly important in rural areas, such as my district, where few alternative delivery mechanisms are available" [*WDT* 9/21/97]); and even for preservation of covered bridges to boost economies and preserve history (*TU* 4/8/98).

Finally, Rep. McHugh, along with other representatives, has recently become an advocate for cormorant control. The uncontrolled breeding of these birds has come to pose a problem first to the fishing industry and consequently to tourism. "Allowing the states impacted by cormorants to address the problem by permitting a hunting season is the only reasonable thing to do" (PR 10/8/97).

Thus, McHugh's main constituency role is as a defender of district interests. He pursues this role, working as a political insider, appearing at hearings, conferring with government officials, and monitoring the latest developments. As the *Watertown Daily Times* has observed, he certainly stays on top of the details (11/3/94).

McHugh interacts with constituents in more personal ways as well. For instance, during his first eighteen months in office, he returned to his district every weekend but one. Due to the physical size of the area, sometimes he and his then-wife would appear at opposite ends of the district:

> I learn more on a Saturday afternoon of questions and answers back home than in a month of Saturdays in Washington. It is a reality check, while in Washington they play to your ego. People won't tell you you are wrong. Back home, I'm not just talking at people, but talking with people. (*WDT* 6/26/94)

There are specific illustrations of contacts Rep. McHugh has had with constituents, for example, interceding with the Army to allow a skating park in Ogdensburg (*WDT* 7/30/97) and educating local officials as to federal grant opportunities (*WDT* 8/26/97). He of course engages in the usual round of personal interactions, honoring a postal worker for her fifty-four years of service with a statement in the *Congressional Record* (*WDT* 6/17/95), helping a veteran with a disability in a year-long attempt to obtain medical benefits (*WDT* 10/28/93), and staying on top of government grant opportunities for constituents, to Alexandria Bay for a new municipal building/fire station (*WDT* 8/6/96), to Watertown for downtown revitalization (*WDT* 9/14/99), and to Saranac (*WDT* 8/9/97) for improvements in housing and an industrial park).[14]

Finally, in 1997, he expressed excitement about his newly constructed congressional Web site, noting particularly the importance of technological communication to a district where traveling to a congressional office might be physically difficult (PR 10/23/97).

On balance, though, McHugh seems to be more his constituents' man in Washington than their man on the street. Constituents can read about him with incredible regularity in the local press, and his staff has participated in "listening posts" sessions with constituents across the district (PR 5/26/00). However, other representatives examined in this book appear to have more frequent contact with individual constituents and are easier to situate regularly at district events. In any case, regardless of whether he is in the district or in Washington, the above pages clearly demonstrate that Rep. McHugh's focus centers on constituency interests and on "representing" local concerns.

Yet, there are also national aspects to his home style. He has not only used his seat on the Armed Services Committee to keep on top of the affairs of Fort Drum and its 10th Mountain Division, but he has broadened his interests to become a policy specialist on certain matters pertaining to military life. For example, he co-chairs the congressional Army Caucus and chaired (until 2001) the Morale, Recreation and Welfare Panel of the House Armed Services Committee. He has used these posts to speak out on additional military matters: advocacy for an "army museum" (*WDT* 6/22/95), concern for fair treatment of military personnel with HIV (*WDT* 4/26/96), and expressed an interest in cigarette pricing at PX posts (*WDT* 6/16/97). Too, since 1995 he has been his committee's representative on the West Point Board of Visitors, a body monitoring education and training programs at the U.S. Military Academy (PR 3/17/99).

In 1997, he added a seat on the International Relations Committee. Very satisfied with this assignment, he explained this would "round out my committee responsibilities." "Where [the] national security [now Armed Services] committee examines global military issues, the international relations committee explores global political interaction, the two form a good complement" (*WDT* 11/26/96). In this capacity, he attended conferences on Russian democracy (Russian leaders are "absolutely committed to the democratic process, and to free and open elections" [*WDT* 4/17/96]) and participated in ceremonies marking the transfer of power in Hong Kong ("From a military point of view to build a wall around China could have consequences that would be disastrous" [*WDT* 6/25/97]) Thus, McHugh can present himself to those interested constituents as a representative who has come to occupy some expertise and clout inside Washington.

Additionally, the Republican takeover of the House provided him with a new opportunity: the chance to head (through the 106th Congress) the subcommittee on the Post Office of the Government Reform and Oversight Committee. In this capacity, Rep. McHugh served as a more active chair than might have been anticipated given the relatively low prestige of the committee (*Almanac* 2000). He emphasized postal reform (the Postal Service should be given "the tools and incentives to adapt itself to the 21st century" [*PIA* 2000, 971]). Given increased competition from both modern technology and other mail delivery services, he focused on ways to increase the viability of the Postal Service. In fact, billed as the most significant piece of postal reform since the 1970s, his proposals have included more flexible pricing policies on stamps: when the post office needs money, prices should be allowed to increase; when things are going well, there should be rewards and price decreases. He also supports fewer limits on first class mail so that the Postal Service can better compete with alternate carriers, and he has advocated for a separate but associated corporation to sell long distance phone cards and knickknacks to increase revenue (*Almanac* 2000, 1165).

Not surprisingly, postal reform has proven to be controversial; McHugh has modified his proposals, for instance accommodating the concerns of competitive mail carriers about equity and of newspapers about bulk mailing provisions (*Journal of Commerce* 12/29/97; *Almanac* 2000, 1165). Though efforts to get a bill out of committee have thus far proved unsuccessful, then-deputy postmaster general Michael S. Coughlin summed up McHugh's effort: "[He] stepped up to the challenge [of postal reform] . . . I think I speak for all of us here when I say that John McHugh has done an exceptional job leading the debate. . . . There's not a voice that wanted to be heard that has not been heard" (*WDT* 5/7/97).

In addition to reform, McHugh (successfully) sponsored legislation creating an independent inspector general for the postal system (*WDT* 10/3/96), and he also sponsored The Prompt Payment Act of 1995 (a consumer would be given credit for a bill payment based on the bill's postmark as opposed to its arrival date [*DN* 9/6/95]). Arguing that a common practice in other nations is to allow commercial mail delivery services (in addition to the government-run post office) to have access to residential mailboxes, he has advocated that the practice be tested here (*WP* 7/11/96), and he has been among those who have lobbied for special postal stamps to be designated to raise funds for medical research (the breast cancer stamp is a successful example) (PR 5/16/00). Finally, McHugh, as we might expect, opposes what he sees as waste in government, even expressing concern when the Post Office bankrolled the cycling team that included Lance Armstrong (PR 8/11/97).

As is clear from the citations to national newspapers in the last few paragraphs (the *Journal of Commerce, The Washington Post, The Chicago Sun Times*), McHugh's postal chairmanship has given him an area of policy specialization. Thus, he can take credit for Washington accomplishments and can present himself to constituents as an experienced legislator. This activity has also generated campaign contributions from all across the nation (fully one-third of his campaign contributions in 1996) (*WDT* 2/1/96).

More generally, as might be expected of someone who "knows the process and the players," McHugh presents himself to constituents as a loyal partisan. Emotionally connected into the establishment of a Republican primary constituency at not only the local but also the state and national level, he clearly feels a bond to his "team."

Thus, he was understandably jubilant at the Republican takeover of the House in 1994, stating, "This is the kind of thing dreams are made of. I have been saying if you don't get excited about this, you better think of another line of work" (*WDT* 1/3/95). He therefore wanted that spirit of unity to spill over into the 1996 party convention to increase the chances of a Republican presidency, and was concerned about presidential candidate Bob Dole's desire to retain an antiabortion plank in the platform (*WDT* 8/9/96).

In addition, McHugh has backed his enthusiasm up with concrete actions, serving as a party whip for the New York Republican delegation and participating in other party-related groups (the Steering and Policy Committee and the Tuesday Group) (*WDT* 1/6/93). He has hosted dinners for Republican candidates (*WDT* 2/10/93), has given excess campaign money to Republican candidates at the local and national levels (*WDT* 2/4/96), and has been included in meetings with then-presidential candidate George W. Bush during swings through the northeast (*TU* 7/25/99). He has even participated in charity baseball games for the Republican side (*WDT* 7/27/93) and played electric guitar in a band of Congressional Republicans, the Amendments (*WDT* 10/12/96).

McHugh's voting record, too, consistently reflects the Republican mainstream, encouraging fiscal restraint, balanced budgets, and increases in defense spending. During his tenure in office, Rep. McHugh has been a champion of fiscal responsibility; lower taxes; protecting Social Security and Medicare; providing stronger, better schools; and protecting America's farmers (Web bio). He supported President Clinton's early budget-cutting efforts (*WDT* 1/22/93) ("We're finally on a path to balance the budget and cut out wasteful spending" [*WDT* 11/3/96]) and later agreed with Speaker Gingrich's similar efforts (*WDT* 3/22/97).

Indeed, The National Taxpayer Union has repeatedly ranked him as a member whose votes have led to more savings than government spending (*WDT* 9/4/94). His conservative coalition scores are consistently above 80, and his party unity scores range from 82 to 94. He has advocated wherever possible for smaller bureaucracy and less red tape, for instance, expressing concern about government purchasing practices ("The current '50s procurement system is unacceptable for the 20th century" [*WDT* 7/28/95]) and supporting welfare reform (*WDT* 7/24/96; 8/2/96).[15]

However, McHugh understands that party loyalty can sometimes conflict with other pressures. As his advocacy for dairy farmers demonstrates, he shows tendencies to deviate from party when the need arises. So, in pressing for the interests of his district, he clearly needs to work across party lines. Thus, his presidential support scores have ranged between 25 and 51. "I voted with Bill Clinton when I felt he was right and against Bill Clinton when he was wrong" (*WDT* 11/31/94).

McHugh voted against term limits (*WDT* 12/24/94), against GATT, and against NAFTA (*PIA* 2000, 971). Though he acknowledged that "there is no question that over the long run, so-called free trade will be the reality of the future. America has to be a player in that process," (*WDT* 10/28/93) after meeting with constituent groups, McHugh's concerns outweighed his support for NAFTA. Similarly, he was one of only forty Republicans to vote for the Family and Medical Leave Act, and one of nine who opposed loan cuts to rural housing (*WDT* 7/21/95). He sided with President Clinton on the issue of comp time (*WDT* 3/28/97), claiming the bill passed by the House on compensatory leave and overtime pay gives employers too much leverage over workers.

In a statement, which is interesting because it acknowledges both the importance of party loyalty and the pull of constituency, Rep. McHugh has summed up the dilemmas he faces when voting: "From my own perspective I would give up the chairmanship [of the House Postal Subcommittee] at any time if voting in the interests of my constituents created a serious conflict with GOP leadership" (*WDT* 10/9/95). Yet, he noted that a "true vote of conscience, one that is important to a member's district, those are things that are understood and are accommodated" (*WDT* 10/9/95).

Discussion

Three themes stand out after reading this profile. First and most importantly, McHugh's home style focuses on the local. He has become knowledgeable and has worked hard on a surprisingly wide variety of concerns that strike at the heart of the interests of his 24th Congressional District. Thus, though his activities begin with a focus on the preservation of military bases and dairy interests, they extend to a wide array of concerns outsiders would perhaps never appreciate (cormorants, covered bridges, etc.). In addition, in McHugh's case, a local focus has not only meant keeping his district's needs on the congressional stage, but it has also meant becoming educated and immersed in the process along with policy detail. Particularly when compared to Representatives Maloney or Houghton, McHugh has stayed "local."

At the same time, even in a district in remote northern New York, the impact of national forces can be felt. By virtue of his Post Office Subcommittee chairmanship, McHugh benefited notably from the Republican takeover of the House. He has followed the "responsible party" model, has generally been a Republican team player and has developed expertise on a few key national issues. Though the local is the most important part of his story, national elements matter as well.

Given his focus on the local, however, one could imagine other ways to represent his very safe one-party district. McHugh has chosen the roles of policy expert and loyal local partisan. Absent from these pages have been instances of Rep. McHugh connecting with individual constituents. While he may in fact play such a role, and to some extent he has to, he doesn't appear to receive coverage for it and doesn't think of himself in those terms. Thus, he may somewhat minimize the role of "accessible" politician. Though he does his share in the district, he perhaps eschews the importance of accessibility and electioneering and he may simply enjoy a focus as his district's man in Washington.

Too, while it goes without saying that McHugh has strong roots in and ties with his district, he is not, strictly speaking, merely a delegate for district interests. After all, he is not a dairy farmer or a member of the military; he has staked out a career as a professional politician and has spent much of his adult life commuting back and forth from Albany and Washington. He certainly knows the district and has innumerable friends and neighbors throughout the 24th constituency. However, it seems inappropriate to describe him as completely "like" his average constituent.

Finally, too, absent from these pages for the most part, is a generalist across a wide variety of policy issues. Given McHugh's safe seat, it is important to note that he defines his role as a specialist. Given the homogeneity of the district, he could probably carve out a broader role if he so chose. As with Reps. Houghton and Maloney, constituency factors matter, but so do the member's own preferences.

Conclusion

As we saw in the introduction to this chapter, dating from debates among the American founders as to the merits of "local" or "national" representation, controversies abound as to the appropriate balance between "local" and "national" elements in legislator home styles. While in recent times, political scientists (Fenno and others) have highlighted the importance of local factors, as we have seen, there are solid reasons to expect national forces to also impact legislative behavior.

The profiles of this chapter provide an initial indication that national factors can in fact prove prominent. In addition to the very clear importance these three legislators place on the local, the Maloney and Houghton profiles clearly demonstrate strong national components. Maloney highlights a broad array of issue interests and the partisan style characterizing legislators of the 1990s. As an essential part of his home style, Houghton uses his wide-ranging national connections to enhance the stature of his local area, decries the intense partisanship characterizing Congress and expresses strongly held opinions on a variety of national issues. Even in the case of Rep. McHugh whose home style is primarily local, national factors matter, pushing him to become involved in military and postal affairs. Thus, these profiles certainly illustrate that there is more than the "local" in the presentation of self of these members of Congress.

Given though the variation in their home styles, what factors impacted the choices of these legislators? Fenno's model suggests that home style arises from a combination of constituency characteristics and legislator backgrounds. To reiterate, the actions of all three representatives are for the most part consistent with the needs of their districts. Maloney's constituents simply have a lot of national concerns. How, after all, can you not take the national stage when you represent a constituency encompassing the hub of Manhattan? And on the other hand, McHugh would be close to committing political suicide if he failed to focus on the needs of the local interests—military bases or dairy farmers—in his rural 24th. Finally, some of the leeway Houghton has to focus on national concerns in part comes because he has done such a good job of meeting local needs.

In addition, as all three of these legislators have put their own stamp on their activities, we see the impact of legislator backgrounds. Indeed, as we have seen, even though Houghton and McHugh represent demographically similar districts—their constituents are rural, relatively poor by objective standards and solidly Republican, their home styles exhibit notable differences. While McHugh, the long-time professional politician working his way up the political ranks tends to highlight the local, Houghton's illustrious business career, family background and strongly held beliefs unquestionably point him in more national directions. He could successfully represent the 31st without addressing the national concerns he champions, and, in fact, advocating for these national interests occasionally proved costly back home. In turn, Maloney's focus on women's issues and partisanship is also consistent with her life-long experiences; though her constituency might require her to "go national," she certainly has leeway as to the particular directions her national emphasis might take.

Thus, for very different reasons, and even given very different home styles, these three representatives appear to be doing a good job. The reader is encouraged to consider which type of representational style might best serve the nation, but the profiles of these three representatives teach us that it is possible to make either the local or a more national style work in light of all the considerations that in fact make up a successful home style.

One final point. In addition to demonstrating the impact of national elements, the material in these profiles highlights strong and mostly positive interconnections between the "local" and the "national." Maloney, for instance, highlights women's issues and loyal partisanship at home and in Washington. Houghton advocates for moderate partisanship and particular social values. It goes without saying that the three legislators advocate in Washington for local concerns and in turn keep their constituents back home informed of their national activities. To the extent that these legislators engage in these types of similar activities regardless of whether they are in the district or in Washington, the profiles suggest that—at least in the current era—the national and the local are more interrelated certainly than Fenno emphasized or political scientists might expect.

Chapter 4

NATIONAL PARTIES, INDIVIDUAL CHOICES
(with Christopher Witko)

> Gingrich is the one responsible for leading the Republican Party out of the
> wilderness of the minority . . . to the promised land of the majority. . . . He is
> singularly responsible for us being where we are now.*
> —Rep. Sherwood Boehlert

> Given the changing nature of the national party, it has become a struggle for
> our leaders to deal with me, and for me to deal with them. . . . In order to
> best represent my state of Vermont, my own conscience, and the principles I
> have stood for my whole life, I will leave the Republican Party and become
> an Independent.
> —Senator James Jeffords, Web press release 5/24/01

If the last chapter depicted the juxtaposition of local and national home
styles in the broadest possible terms, it is the task of this chapter to hone in
on perhaps the most striking and controversial development in current national politics, the rise of increasingly "responsible" and organized national parties. The ascendance of Newt Gingrich, the Republican Revolution, the 1998 impeachment hearings, and the partisanship that has
characterized the work of much of the post-9/11 Congress provide just a
few of the more prominent illustrations of national party agenda setting,
team coordination, and legislator cohesion. As a leading scholar rather dramatically described it, "[O]n two important dimensions, it is as if the immediate postwar era of a relatively strong party-in-the-electorate but weak

*Quoted in Davidson and Oleszek (2000), 163.

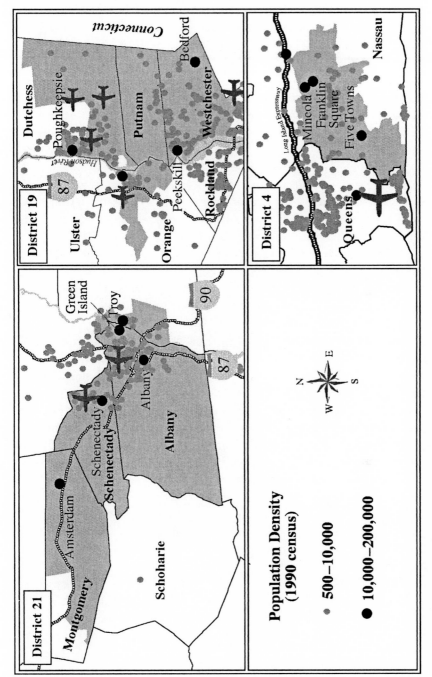

Montgomery

Amsterdam

Schenectady

Schenectady

Green
Island

Troy

90

Albany

Albany

87

Schoharie

Population Density
(1990 census)

500–10,000

10,000–200,000

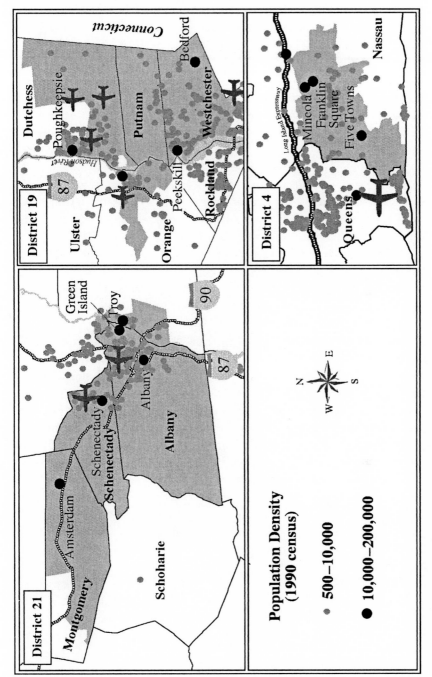

Ulster

87

Dutchess

Poughkeepsie

Hudson River

Peekskill

Orange

Rockland

Putnam

Westchester

Bedford

Connecticut

Long Island Expressway

Mineola
Franklin
Square
Five Towns

Nassau

Queens

N W E S

Map 3. Congressional Districts for Reps. Kelly, McNulty, and McCarthy.

party organizations has been turned on its head" (Bibby 1999, 69), providing the national parties with considerably more potential for leverage over the activities of rank-and-file members.

How have legislators responded in their local districts to this increased leverage of the national (and congressional) parties? We have already seen, as part of their profiles, that all three of the representatives analyzed so far were impacted by national-level partisanship and had to deal with it in their local constituencies. For Maloney and McHugh, representing solidly homogeneous districts of their party, strong party loyalty makes sense. On the other hand, given Rep. Houghton's beliefs about political moderation, the intense partisanship characterizing the modern Congress proved both an asset (he could take advantage of his party's majority status in Congress) and a constraint (he sometimes clashed with party leaders and had to explain those clashes to constituents).

It is the purpose of this chapter to bring modern partisanship front and center. By profiling the contrasting responses of three legislators to the increased role of national parties, this chapter seeks to place a human face on the above question and to highlight the possibilities and dilemmas the current party structure raises for individual legislators.

Some background is necessary. In the first quote above this chapter, Rep. Boehlert hints at the within-party unity and cross-party polarization that have characterized the current national parties, leading to a system close to that described by political scientists as "responsible party" or at least "conditional party" government[1] (Aldrich and Rohde 2001). In such a system, parties "are able to bring forth programs to which they commit themselves and . . . [to] possess sufficient internal cohesion to carry out these programs" (Sinclair 2002, 121). By his positive tone, Rep. Boehlert is clearly pointing to the benefits of such a system, and, when he notes that Speaker Gingrich "is singularly responsible for us being where we are now," he is referring to the series of events culminating with the Contract with America, the 1994 elections, and the Republicans assuming majority party status in the House of Representatives for the first time since 1954, a full half-century earlier!

National parties or party leaders weren't always so important. Throughout the 1960s and 1970s, parties at the national level lacked resources, weren't much involved in congressional campaigns, and party leadership in Congress did not possess many of the formal powers necessary to figure critically in the lives of legislators (Davidson and Oleszek 2004; Kingdon 1989; Rohde 1991; Sinclair 2002). As one of the Congress members interviewed by Fenno (rather colorfully) described the lack of party influence and the resulting candidate-centered politics of the time:

> The party is no damn good . . . they can't organize and they can't raise money. . . . I don't have anything to do with the party organization . . . they have their function. They give you a vehicle to run on. . . . The real function of the party is to have someone to meet the candidate for Congress when he comes into a strange town. You don't know anybody and you don't walk up to the first person you meet on the street. You look for the party members in town to tell you what you ought to know and to introduce you to people. (Fenno 1978, 176)

As is well known, a variety of electoral and congressional circumstances have contributed to the rather remarkable transformation of the role of the national parties from being "no damn good" to becoming both increasingly polarized and powerful. The elections of 1958, 1964, and 1974 brought large freshmen classes of more liberal and activist Democrats to Congress (Rohde 1991) while on the Republican side, the 1964 candidacy of Senator Barry Goldwater initiated the move of the Grand Old Party in a more conservative direction, thus setting the stage for the subsequent Reagan victories and move to conservative politics of the 1980s and beyond (Paulson 2000). Consequently, over the next few decades, the solidly Democratic South dramatically shifted Republican. For instance, in 1953, Democrats held fully 94 percent of congressional seats from the South, compared to 62 percent in 1993 and only 43 percent in 1997 (Abramson, Aldrich, and Rohde, 1994, 261; 1998, 201), leaving the Democratic Party both more liberal and more homogeneous and Republicans with a broader conservative base. In short, at the national level, there has been increased within-party unity and more cross-party polarization.

In addition, campaign finance regulations opened up the possibility for increased national party influence on local candidates. Reforms inside Congress in the 1970s and thereafter granting more formal powers to party leaders (including a greater role in committee assignments and the revitalization of party caucuses) combined with the leadership of some strong speakers (Tip O'Neill and Jim Wright) so that those leaders actually "have been granted powers greater than at any time in the 20th century" (Aldrich and Rohde 2001, 269). And, beginning in the late 1970s, an influx of young Republican conservatives, including Rep. Gingrich (with a desire to be Speaker of the House even dating from his initial term in Congress), used an array of increasingly combative and partisan tactics to make their voices heard, in turn provoking an increased partisanship on the Democratic side (Davidson and Oleszek 2004; Polsby 2004).

These trends culminated, of course, with the 1994 elections. The Contract with America was, first of all, an attempt by the national Republican Party to centralize and develop from the top common themes (a balanced budget, welfare reform, term limits [Bader 1996; Gimpel 1996]) for all candidates. Even more, the importance of the Contract goes well beyond issue positions, as, after the 1994 election: "The House Republican Party acted remarkably like the cohesive, responsible party of party government theory" (Sinclair 1998, 263). In short, "The leaders wanted something more than ideological unity; they wanted a sense of team spirit, a common belief that the party was strong, vibrant and worthy of holding power" (Bader 1996, 353).

For all these reasons, consider that national parties today often impact candidates' initial decisions to run for office (Fowler and McClure 1989) and increasingly participate in the recruitment and training of candidates (Jacobson 2001). National parties also help develop campaign themes and strategies (Hacker and Pierson 2005), including producing "party issue advocacy advertising," which could be aired across many congressional districts (Herrnson and Dwyre 1999, 102). Thus, the party provides "assistance in nearly every phase of the campaign" (Davidson and Oleszek 2000, 62). Also, the national parties have developed close working relationships with interest groups, think tanks, and consultants (Bibby 1999), and members of Congress themselves routinely raise money and contribute to the campaigns of other candidates of their party (Gimpel 1996). Within Congress too, party loyalty provides a route to advancement to leadership positions, and, in turn, leadership places pressure on members to toe the line (Schickler and Pearson 2005). Thus, "party" seems so much a part of every aspect of representatives' lives that "incumbents today do not find it as easy to separate themselves from party leaders, party images and party performance as did incumbents of twenty years ago" (Fiorina 2005, 170–71).

In contrast to the 1970s image of "party" as "being no damn good" at either the national level or inside Congress itself, as Herrnson (1998) has emphasized, the role of the national parties today has become "institutionalized."

What are the advantages and disadvantages of the changes in the party system? Is the movement toward responsible parties good or bad? For some, the current system offers real advantages. Parties behaving more "responsibly" provide a range of benefits: a focus on issues, a clear delineation between the stances of the two parties, and a more national cast to politics (APSA 1950; Beck 1997). "With the same like-minded group of members formulating legislation across a range of issues, policy will display coherence. And, critical for democratic theory, the majority party will be responsible for what the legislature has done and thus can be held accountable by the voters at the next election" (Sinclair 1998, 264).

On the other hand, there is another side to the story, and some see downsides to an increasingly national party system. The dramatic switch of Vermont Senator James Jeffords on May 24, 2001, from Republican to Independent (see second quote above chapter), leading to a crucial change in party control of the Senate, highlights the potential disadvantages to responsible parties; though such politics may produce a unified and efficient government, such a party system might also lead to a less locally grounded politics. Thus, increasing pressures toward party unity clearly make life harder for some members of Congress who have difficulty following the bandwagon, for instance, liberal Republicans such as Sen. Jeffords perceived conflict between the context of a strong party system at the national level and the ability to "best represent my state of Vermont, my own conscience, and the principles I have stood for my whole life."[2]

Other scholars have cited additional costs to responsible parties, including the difficulty of forging cross-partisan compromise and coalitions (Beck 1997), increased pressure on members who must balance the potentially conflicting demands of party and constituency, and the possibility of an overemphasis on issue positions. After all, "party" means so much more to individuals than a focus on issues and a national agenda. For many, "party" has meant an emotional and psychological tie: "Partisan identities meant having a general orientation to others, to citizenship, to history, and to government. Partisan identity matched and expressed other important experiences in people's lives, both linking and distinguishing them from neighbors and strangers" (Miroff, Seidelman, and Swanstrom 1997, 181). Further, there are many levels to "party":

> The activists of the party organization may seek to translate a program or ideology into policy, but they may also seek patronage jobs, other forms of reward or preference, the sensations of victory or the defeat of a hated opposition. The parties' voters may be stimulated by an issue, a program, or an ideology, but they also respond to personalities, to incumbency, to abstract and traditional loyalties, to a candidate or party, or to the urging of friends and family. (Beck 1997, 302)

Thus, a more national, issue-oriented approach to representation detracts from important activities usually performed by political parties: the creation of relationships between heterogeneous groups, the development of social networks, and the desire to foster compromise.

Equally important, these national-level trends also pose representational dilemmas for individual members of Congress as they develop home styles. What impact have these national-level changes had on the average member of Congress in his or her local constituency? How do individual members integrate increasing national partisanship into their home styles?

The three profiles presented below highlight on the one hand the roles the national parties have played in local districts and on the other the variation in member responses to trends of increasing national and congressional partisanship. Partisanship is relevant in all three profiles. At the same time, it will be clear that members of Congress have found very different ways to deal with the current political environment. While Sue Kelly, elected as a freshman member of the 104th Congress, developed a home style in large part in line with the responsible party bandwagon, Carolyn McCarthy, elected two years later, has steadfastly avowed nonpartisanship, and Michael McNulty was a staunch party insider long before the term was in vogue. Taken together, these profiles highlight several themes. Despite trends toward the increased nationalization of parties, legislator responses have been notably variable. The profiles indicate that these differences can be traced to the constituency and background variables described earlier. In addition, these profiles show the multidimensionality of "party." It would be wrong to think of party only in terms of issue orientations. It is true that at times Kelly's career comes close to fitting the responsible party model, but, for McNulty, party arises out of family, a strong social system, and a political career. At the other extreme, Rep. McCarthy had been fairly apolitical before running for office.

In addition, the profiles will demonstrate that the party can both augment and come into conflict with other aspects of a representative's life, including constituency preferences. Finally, following on the ideas of chapter 3, these profiles highlight aspects of the national-local distinction, providing initial examples of (mostly positive) linkages between the two political arenas.

Sue Kelly: Balancing Constituent Interests, Issues, and Party

Sue Kelly, the moderate Republican representing the 19th district, has a home style that incorporates both local and national factors. The biography on her Web site describes her public career as a "model of community and national service" (Web bio). As a member of the freshman class of 1994, she has been closely linked to the national party and has served, particularly early in her career, as a loyal party spokesperson. However, her relationship to "party" is interesting and complex. She has not hesitated to work within the party structure to publicize issues she cares about and to support the needs of her constituents. In addition, the fact of Kelly's gender has placed her in a unique position, helping her stand out among a relatively small number of Republican women, but also bringing her into conflict with the party mainstream on issues such as abortion.

Constituency

The politics of the 19th is particularly interesting because it is a swing district featuring many of the political divisions that have characterized the 1990s. The constituency is largely a suburban and middle/upper-class district, extending north of New York City through the Hudson Valley, to more rural areas near the "largest" small city of Poughkeepsie (population just under twenty-eight thousand). The district encompasses all or part of Westchester, Putnam, Duchess, and Orange counties (including many small cities and towns) (*Almanac* 2000, 1150). Eighty-nine percent of constituents are Caucasian. With a college graduation rate of 32 percent, a median household income of just over $50,000, and a "white collar" population of 69 percent, district residents are reasonably well-off (the district ranks among the top in New York State and in the top third nationally) (*PIA* 2000, 959; see Table 4.1, Map 3). While residents near the southern end of the constituency are likely to be frequent commuters back and forth from New York City, northern parts of the area are surprisingly rural; in those parts of the 19th, agriculture and dairy farming are important, and local economies are poorer.

The characterization of the district on Kelly's Web site is almost quaint: she describes it as "an incredible combination of history and present, hills and valleys, old-time charm and technology of the future" (www . . . kelly). The "old time charm" is represented by the Hudson River, West Point, and historic landmarks including Revolutionary War sites, the

TABLE 4.1 Constituency Characteristics and Election Results for Reps. Kelly, McNulty, and McCarthy

	Sue Kelly	Michael McNulty	Carolyn McCarthy
District #	19	21	4
Party	R	D	D
Yr. Elected	1994	1988	1996
District Profile			
Land Area (square miles)	1,080	1,087	84
Population Per Square Mile	537	534	6,889
Percent Urban	67%	80%	100%
Percent White	89%	91%	74%
Percent White Collar	69%	67%	69%
Rank (state)*	7	9	7
Rank (nation)**	1	1	1
Percent Blue Collar	18%	19%	24%
Rank (state)*	25	22	25
Rank (nation)**	3	3	3
Percent College Educated	32%	24%	26%
Rank (state)*	5	10	9
Rank (nation)**	1	1	1
Median Income (in thousands)	50.33	31.49	50.89
Rank (state)*	3	17	2
Rank (nation)**	1	2	1
Election Results			
2000	61%	74%	61%
1998	62%	74%	53%
1996	46%	66%	57%
1994	52%	67%	
1992		63%	
1990		64%	
1988		62%	
District Vote For President			
2000	D-50%	D-57%	D-59%
	R-45%	R-36%	R-38%
1996	D-49%	D-59%	D-57%
	R-42%	R-31%	R-36%
1992	D-40%	D-48%	D-47%
	R-42%	R-34%	R-41%

*Rank in state: 1 = highest, 31 = lowest.

**Rank Nationally is Expressed in Thirds: 1 = Top Third, 2 = Middle Third, 3 = Bottom Third

Rockefeller family estate, and FDR's Hyde Park home (www . . . kelly). Many hiking areas, along with activities around the Hudson River, mean that outdoor recreation, tourism, and the environment are also important to the area.

Though major layoffs in the mid-1990s placed significant strain on this area, the "technology of the future" is reflected in the dominance of IBM (headquarters in Armonk, a research center in Yorktown Heights, and operations in Wappingers Falls) (*Almanac* 2000, 1150) and other high-tech companies. In addition, the district is home to several renowned companies: Pepsi-Cola, Lloyd Bedford Cox Insurance, and Readers Digest (*PIA* 2000, 959).

Though the district has been described as tilting Republican, current politics are interesting and more complicated (*PIA* 2004, 707). Sociopolitical shifts have altered district politics. Older communities of well-educated, liberal residents have shifted away from their historically Republican roots while communities mostly filled with those moving out of New York City are currently leaving behind their Democratic heritage (*PIA* 2000). It is not surprising, then, that in 1992, President Bush carried the district by only two percent (42 percent to 40 percent); in 1996, Clinton won 49 percent to 42 percent over Dole; and in 2000 Gore won 50 percent to 45 percent over G. W. Bush (*Almanac* 2002, 1099).

Too, as one might expect of residents in a relatively well-off district, political interest is high. Consequently, factions within each party exist and, as we shall see, matter politically.

When, in 1994, Republican representative Hamilton Fish Jr. announced his retirement, it meant more to the district than simply the end of a political career. A thirteen-term incumbent, Fish's family has literally been politically active since Revolutionary War days. One ancestor had been secretary of state to President Ulysses Grant, and another had been the member of Congress most disliked by Franklin Roosevelt (*PIA* 1992, 1048). Fish himself had been the epitome of moderate Republicanism. A member of the House Judiciary Committee during the 1974 impeachment hearings, he had been a champion of civil rights and a voice of moderation as the Republican Party grew more conservative in the 1980s (*PIA* 1992, 1048). It would be an indicator of the complex politics to come that, upon Fish's retirement, one of the contenders seeking to succeed him would be his son, Hamilton Fish III, running however as a Democrat.

In sum, though constituents in the district are doing relatively well, and though traditions of moderate Republicanism predominate, a changing economy and the presence of an active and interested constituency mean that a Congress member's actions will be noted and that Republican victories are not assured. Thus, district heterogeneity affords centrist candidates opportunities in terms of room to maneuver, but also sets constraints in terms of the potential for challenges from both the Democratic "Left" and the Republican "Right."

Background

Like many of the freshman class of the 104th Congress, Sue Kelly was an amateur without prior elective office. Perhaps ahead of her time for a woman of her generation, she has brought a unique set of experiences to bear on her congressional career. She graduated from Denison University in Ohio with a BA in botany and bacteriology, earned a master's degree in Health Advocacy from Sarah Lawrence College, and worked as a Harvard University researcher (Web bio). She has operated several small businesses, including a building renovating company and a florist shop. In fact, part of her 1994 campaign was financed with $150,000 she was saving in order to begin yet another small business (*Almanac* 2002, 1095). She has also worked as a patient advocate, a rape crisis counselor, and a junior high school teacher (*Almanac* 2002, 1095).

However, unlike many of her congressional cohort, Kelly has long been active in civic and party affairs, and this seems to have naturally led her to politics. She served as president of the local PTA (she has raised four children and is now a proud grandmother) and was a co-founder of the Bedford League of Women Voters (Web bio).

Nor is she a stranger to partisan politics. In the 1970s, she served as a campaign manager for State Assemblyman Jon Fossell (*Almanac* 2000, 1151). Therefore, in the course of a long behind-the-scenes career, she honed her political skills. She worked on "local, state and national campaigns" (*PIA* 2000, 959), made connections with nationally known Republicans, including Jack Kemp, and participated in activities including the New York State Republican Party Family Committee.

Interestingly, Kelly had actually worked as a local coordinator for Hamilton Fish Jr. (*PJ* 8/14/94). Nevertheless, she later found herself on an unusual collision course with Fish. Fish's campaign manager had allegedly commented to a *Poughkeepsie Journal* editorial board in 1992 that he would oppose abortions "for some lady who doesn't want to get fat" (*PIA* 2000, 960). Angered by these comments because she thought they trivialized abortion by linking it to cosmetic purposes, Kelly gave the names of pro–abortion rights Republicans to Fish's Democratic opponent and, dressed in a black cloak, she demonstrated outside of Fish's office holding a sign that read: "Fish = Women in the Dark Ages" (*PIA* 2000, 960).

As they reflect the influence of both local and national factors, and as they demonstrate an interesting balance of party loyalty combined with independence from party, Kelly's 1994 primary and general election campaigns nicely set the stage for her subsequent home style. To achieve initial election, the former businesswoman first faced a tough seven-way primary. "I'm running because what I have to say needs to be heard and nobody else is saying it. I'm looking forward to this race because people of this district have a number of choices" (*PJ* 6/14/94).

Kelly was right. Her campaigns in 1994 did give voters a choice. Though as might be expected, all seven candidates in the Republican primary supported the Contract with America and favored government cutbacks, Kelly was the only woman in the race and the only candidate to take a pro-choice stand (*PIA* 1996). In contrast, her chief opposition came from former representative Joseph DioGuardi (1985–1989) (*PIA* 2000, 959–60), who would later run on the Right-to-Life line. DioGuardi, who must have eagerly wanted political office, had previously served in the Westchester district south of the 19th and had been defeated twice (1988 and 1992) by Nita Lowey (*Almanac* 2000, 1151). He accused Kelly of being a "Democrat in disguise" due to her pro-choice stand (*PIA* 1996, 931) and cited the importance of his prior congressional service as a boon to the district.

Kelly's response was interesting. Not only did she attack DioGuardi for his carpetbagger status ("Sue didn't need an atlas to find her way around," claimed Kelly's spokeswoman, Ashley Heyer [*PJ* 9/2/94]), but she also found ways to highlight the value of her own life experiences: "Business and health care are the two things that will hit most people's pocketbooks hard for the next five years, and that's what Congress is going to be talking about for the next five years. I'm somebody who has the experience of both" (*PJ* 8/14/94). In addition, she suggested that her gender would actually offset her lack of elective experience. "I'm not worried about not having enough power to do something. The Republican House women do the best they can to nurture each other's careers because we know we're up against a lot just being women" (*PJ* 8/14/94).

Though in the primary she failed to capture the support of the local Republican party (she was, of course, endorsed for the general election), she was able to attract the support of organizations such as the National

Women's Political Caucus-Westchester (*Yonkers Herald Statesman* 11/3/94) and the backing of New York City mayor Giuliani and his then-wife, who was advocating for women's issues (*NYT* 2/24/00).

Mostly, Kelly achieved a reputation as being a strong campaigner able to highlight her ties to the constituency. As the campaign progressed, she spent eighteen-hour days crisscrossing the district in a camper and increasing her name recognition (*PJ* 10/23/94). In that capacity, she has been described as "phenomenal in one-on-one politics" (*PJ* 9/19/94). For instance, according to former Westchester State Assemblyman Jon Fossel, "She's one of those rare people who gets along with everybody from the guy who runs the gas station to the chief executive. But she's also sharp in terms of political knowledge and strategic thinking" (*PJ* 8/14/94). "People who meet Sue Kelly like her. No one is going to win this race on radio and TV," claimed political consultant Jay Townsend (*PJ* 9/19/94).

Ultimately, Kelly beat DioGuardi. Though, consistent with district heterogeneity, the margin of victory, twenty-three to twenty, shows that both candidates had strong support.

The general election was also a hard-fought contest between DioGuardi (Conservative and Right-to-Life parties), Fish III, and Kelly. As a newspaper editorial described it, "all are credible candidates, and each has brought a different political spin to the often interesting campaign exchanges" (*PJ* 11/2/94).

Democrat Hamilton Fish III, a human rights activist and magazine publisher with *The Nation,* was described favorably, even by a newspaper that ultimately chose to endorse Kelly: "The younger Fish, 43, is bright, committed and quick with intelligent answers to complicated questions. He is a worthy heir to the great Fish tradition of public service" (*PJ* 11/2/94). He attracted the support of traditional Democratic groups such as the New York State AFL-CIO (*PJ* 10/2/94) and considered himself organizationally strong in every part of the district (*PJ* 9/14/94). He also had the support of his father, which obviously counted for a lot in the area.

As she again traversed the district in her van, Kelly's campaign highlighted the themes she had developed in the primary. She again pointed to her varied experiences as a Republican and as a woman. "I know what it's like to have that terrible stretching that sometimes occurs when you have to be a woman and a business owner" (*PJ* 9/14/94).

Importantly, Kelly also capitalized on national trends. She continued her enthusiastic support for the Contract with America and obtained the endorsements of Bill Paxon, chair of the Republican Congressional Campaign

Committee, and district resident/gubernatorial-upset-winner George Pataki. In an astoundingly Republican year, Kelly received 52 percent of the vote to Fish's 37 percent and DioGuardi's 10 percent. Thus, not only was her election a part of the historic Republican takeover of the House, but it increased the ranks of the minority of Republican women in general and pro-choice women in particular (*NYT* 12/17/94).

Thus, in Kelly's election, we see the imprint of local politics, state-level forces, and national factors. The Republican bandwagon, which contributed to her win, combined with Kelly's own campaign skills and her interesting prepolitical experiences, counted as well. These elements would contribute to the development of her home style.

Home Style

Of all the representatives we have studied, particularly early in her career, Kelly comes closest to fitting the "responsible" party model. Consistent with the national tides, which helped her achieve office, and with the message of her own campaign, she presents herself to constituents as a party loyalist. Thus, she enthusiastically supported the themes and symbols of the 104th Congress. "It's amazing the number of people in my freshman class who seem to have the same sense I do that it's essential that the government start thinking about how it spends its money. . . . This is the first time in more than 100 years that Congress will work on Inauguration day" (*PJ* 1/1/95). "I want to continue to make government smaller and smarter" (*PJ* 10/22/98).

Indeed, she supported votes on the Contract with America 90 percent of the time (*PJ* 10/11/96), served as an assistant majority whip since her initial election to Congress, and even occasionally acted as a media spokesperson: representing the Freshman GOP class (CNN 12/14/95), supporting Speaker Gingrich's work on budget negotiations (CNN 4/24/96), and defending Bob Dole's choice of her friend Jack Kemp as vice presidential nominee (CNN 8/12/96).

In articulating her issue positions, Kelly uses language consistent with Republican themes, speaking on behalf of tax cuts, state flexibility for education spending, and a general streamlining of the bureaucracy. "That's us. That's the middle class" (*PJ* 8/17/97). For instance, she has successfully sponsored legislation seeking to eliminate capital gains taxes for people earning $70,000 or less upon the sale of a principal residence (*PJ* 4/29/95). She has also lobbied against the marriage penalty tax:

Working couples shouldn't be penalized simply because they are married. . . . This is a flaw in our tax system that needs to be fixed. This is an unfair tax and working couples in my district need relief. (www . . . kelly)

Kelly has also chaired the Small Business Committee's subcommittee on Regulatory Reform and Paperwork Reduction, where she has acted to streamline red tape in government, to increase mileage reductions when driving for charitable use, and to promote women-owned businesses (www . . . kelly). Similarly, Kelly has argued that teachers and local administrators should make educational decisions: "What if a school district doesn't need hundreds of new teachers, but needs a new roof? I really believe local school officials, not Washington, ought to be in control of the [federal] money because they know best what schools need" (TU 1/18/00).

There are even times when Kelly's enthusiasm for party has gone beyond the call of district or duty. Occasionally, she might in fact have been electorally smarter to distance herself from the "Republican Revolution."

A case in point involves her record on the environment, particularly in the 104th Congress. In his capacity as an environmental lawyer, Democrat Robert F. Kennedy Jr. later expressed the opinion, "In the 19th Congressional District, which has a long and illustrious history of giving green leadership to the nation, Sue Kelly is a disappointment" (NYT 4/26/98).

Thus, in 1995, Kelly supported a conservative-backed proposal to amend the Clean Water Act of 1972 ("There are certain laws, that become sacred cows, and it's very important that we sometimes address sacred cows.") and voted for the use of more cost/benefit analysis on environmental regulations (PIA 2000, 959).

More recently, her support for a congressional office of Regulatory Analysis to examine the impact of government regulations on business has come under fire and has been interpreted as promoting business interests over health and safety concerns (NYT 4/26/98). (It is important to note that Kelly defended her early actions: "I signed the Contract with America, and I'm an environmentalist. As far as I can see, I haven't done anything off that message" [NYT 4/26/98]).

Indeed, some of her later actions are more environmentally friendly, as she has sponsored the Hudson River Habitat Restoration Act, advocated for land acquisition for Sterling Forest, and lobbied against delays in the PCB cleanup of the Hudson River. She is a member of the House Trails Caucus and has aspirations to write a book about walking tours in her district (NYT 2/24/00).

Similarly, despite a divided and concerned constituency (staffers reported receiving as many as one thousand phone calls a day for a three-day period and eight thousand e-mails [*PJ* 12/17/98]), Kelly followed the party lead on the Clinton impeachment controversy: "A CEO in my district would be fired for this. An attorney in my district would face disbarment, a member of my staff dismissed. All would face prosecution" (*PJ* 3/16/99).

Finally, in 2000, Kelly engaged in very partisan attacks against one of her newest and perhaps most famous constituents: then-Senate candidate Hillary Rodham Clinton. Tapped by the national Republican Party to be a point person, Kelly accused the Clintons of interfering with the privacy of their neighbors due to their own security needs (*NYT* 2/24/00). She attacked Mrs. Clinton for using public money to fund campaign trips (*NYT* 2/24/00). Most telling, however, is her claim that candidate Clinton simply doesn't understand the needs of New Yorkers: "We need to stop a certain carpetbagger from Arkansas from being the next senator from New York" (*TU* 4/12/99). "She does not know New York. You need to live here. You need to have the background and understanding. . . . There isn't a neo-socialist cause she won't shove down our throats" (*NYT* 2/24/00).

Issues. Thus, Kelly's Republican loyalty has been important. Particularly during the 104th Congress but also throughout her career, party connections are a crucial aspect of her home style, and she has defended them in the context of her subsequent reelection runs (see below). At the same time, to portray Kelly as only a party loyalist would be misleading. For example, her party unity scores between 1995 and 1998, ranging from 84 (1995) to 66 (1998), are lower than one might expect given her outspoken partisan attachment. More consistent with her somewhat unique prepolitical experience, she presents herself to constituents as someone desiring to put her own stamp on the issues she cares about. Thus, party loyalty may serve as the backdrop for her activity, but working within the party structure, she has advocated for particular issues. Her comment after introducing herself to Speaker Gingrich is interesting and indicative of her ability to balance concerns about party with her issue focus: "Being female has been an advantage for me. I have had direct access to Newt on issues that are of concern to me like nutrition for children and meals on wheels for the homebound. I have found Newt to be very responsive" (*PJ* 2/27/95).

Thus, consistent with her campaign themes, she attempts to translate the experiences from her varied background into legislation. For example, she has focused on health concerns, sponsoring legislation to expand health insurance coverage for mastectomies and subsequent reconstructive surgery (H.R.3224, introduced 11/4/99). She has advocated for the rights of doctors and patients to make decisions without undue interference from HMOs. As a person with lyme disease (*TU* 6/24/98), she (in the 106th Congress) chaired a Congressional Advisory Committee on that concern and has served on several other health-related caucuses and task forces including those on cancer, home health care, and international AIDS.

Kelly has also advocated on behalf of veterans, working to change federal formulas by which hospitals are ranked for federal assistance, attempting to expand nursing care for veterans with disabilities and advocating for assistance in ensuring that veterans have full knowledge about available benefits (www . . . kelly). The issue of federal funding formulas for VA facilities is particularly controversial in Kelly's district as current allocation methods appear to involve shifting money from the Northeast to other regions of the nation (*PJ* 7/16/97) and because such formulas raised the potential for hospital closings in Kelly's district (*PJ* 8/6/97). As Kelly perhaps overemphasized, "Over my dead body are they going to close Castle Point or Montrose" (*PJ* 6/22/97).

In addition, Kelly and other New York legislators have worked— through letters to government departments, meetings with constituents, and even a Gingrich trip—to publicize quality of care issues in general and to rectify a fairly unusual controversy (in 1998, claiming the fiscal year had ended and spending time had run out, a regional VA director returned $20 million to Washington [*PJ* 7/19/98]). Among her efforts to turn the balance of VA money around, Kelly invited Speaker Gingrich (in the context of a campaign appearance on her behalf) to visit: "I wanted him to see what we have. I hope that's one more step toward getting our money back" Kelly exclaimed (*PJ* 7/10/98).

Arising from discussions with domestic violence workers in her district and from her own experiences as a rape crisis counselor, Kelly introduced an anti-stalking bill in 1999 (www . . . kelly). "The prevalence of this crime may be news to many who think stalking is a plague only of the rich and famous," said Kelly, "but it's an all too familiar occurrence to people who work in the area of domestic violence who encounter people affected by stalkers every day" (www . . . kelly). As her Web site explains, "Recent research has shown that more than 1 million women and more than 370,000 men are stalked every year. It has been revealed that there is a strong link between stalking and domestic violence" (www . . . kelly). In the 106th Congress, this legislation was expanded to include "cyber stalking" (PR 8/7/99).

Kelly's work on stalking, marriage taxes, and breast cancer makes clear that she takes a consistent interest in women's concerns, either giving them primary focus or adding a women's slant on her other areas of interest (health and taxes). As she herself has noted, the simple fact of her gender places her in a unique and sometimes controversial position within the Republican Party. As is well known, most congresswomen are Democrats. In fact, at the start of the 106th Congress, the fifty-eight women split forty-one to seventeen in their party affiliation (Davidson and Oleszek 2000, 175).

Even more, Kelly has chosen to be involved. For example, unlike many other Republican women, she has been an active member of the Congressional Caucus on Women's Issues and its co-chair in the 106th Congress. Notably, she has incorporated this Washington activity back to district concerns. For example, she consistently speaks to women's groups, for instance, by participating in ceremonies honoring the 150th anniversary of the Seneca Falls Convention for Women's Rights (*PJ* 9/28/98), addressing students at Marist College, and presenting the keynote speech to a group of New York State Republican women (*TU* 11/7/99). At the Seneca Falls celebration, her remarks echoed traditional themes of the 1848 gathering: "Women need to be able to make a choice to stay home with their kids and work in anything they want to, because they can" (*PJ* 9/20/98). "You learn you can do just about anything you have to when you have a bunch of kids running around" (*PJ* 12/5/97). Kelly also received an award from the Enterprising Women's Leadership Institute (*TU* 4/30/98).

Kelly's opinions are all the more interesting because they can be controversial. Critics on the Right and Left have not always been pleased with her views. Her vocal pro-choice stand has generated opposition within the national Republican Party. In 1996, with the support of pro-life members of her congressional party (including Christopher Smith, NJ, and Robert Dornan, CA), Kelly's 1994 primary opponent, pro-life former Rep. Joseph DioGuardi, attempted yet another primary challenge. Kelly, however, obtained the support of party leaders, as Speaker Gingrich attempted to dissuade DioGuardi from running (*PIA* 2000, 957) and penalized Rep. Dornan for his endorsement (*Los Angeles Times* 8/1/96) by removing him from a panel on defense appropriations and prohibiting his overseas travel for the rest of the term (*Los Angeles Times* 8/1/96).

However, Kelly's pro-choice views have been controversial to the Left as well. Although initially an opponent of any sort of ban on partial birth abortion, she reversed her position when the executive director of the National Coalition of Abortion Providers admitted to lying by underestimating the incidence of such procedures. Kelly explained, "When you get into doing it on a healthy woman, with a healthy fetus, very late term, what are we talking about here? Because I can't get a clear reading from either side of the fence, I changed my vote" (*Almanac* 2000, 1151).

As she did in the case of the environment, Kelly has defended her pro-choice stand. In fact, despite controversy around her, she sees no particular problem with it: "I'm a Republican. Republicans believe in letting local people make their own laws. I believe strongly in personal freedom. Every time I've checked, the district is pro-choice" (*NYT* 7/21/96).

Even though Kelly supports women's rights and appears at conferences honoring women leaders, her general views on women's issues sometimes appear a bit more traditional than the average Democrat might espouse. "Because we are caregivers and educators your perspective changes unalterably in many ways . . . women lend a compassion to Congress that, quite frankly, I don't think would be there without us" (*PJ* 12/5/97).

Similarly, Kelly commented ironically on Hillary Clinton's activity on behalf of her husband: "They have a child. While she can do as much as she wants to support and amplify him (Clinton), she also has the role of a mother. She is a working mother" (*PJ* 10/1/95). Democratic women in general and Mrs. Clinton in particular would surely agree. The roles of wife, mother, and caregiver are, of course, important. At the same time, as the profile of Representative Maloney and the well-publicized activities of Hillary Clinton indicate, some women take an even stronger stand than Kelly with regard to breaking down stereotypes and traditional gender roles, emphasizing the need for equality.

It is therefore not surprising that some of Kelly's attentive constituents feel their congresswoman could be more active at the local level. For instance, a spokesperson for at least one group in her district, the Westchester Women's Agenda, expressed unhappiness with Kelly, contending that, "[she] has not been a presence, certainly not in Westchester County—not at child care meetings and not at domestic violence meetings" (*PJ* 2/21/99).

Constituency Activity. Rep. Hamilton Fish Jr. was once described as "renowned for his constituency service" (*PJ* 1/1/95). As her interactive campaign style makes clear, Kelly also enjoys connecting with constituents and continuing Fish's tradition, even taking it to the next level of computerizing service records (*PJ* 1/1/95).

Some examples bear out these contentions. Kelly holds regular town meetings and forums involving groups ranging in number from six to eighty (*PJ* 8/17/97). She has introduced groups of seniors to the Internet, showing them how to access her Web site: "I really think that any type of community outreach is really imperative to seniors" (*PJ* 5/8/99), and she also has promoted reading programs by showing young children she can recite Dr. Seuss's *Green Eggs and Ham* by heart (*PJ* 3/16/99). She presented a new flag to a local church (*PJ* 3/5/99), toured the Great Swamp to promote environmental concerns and programs (*PJ* 3/5/99), and worked on Academy Day, a program promoting recruitment opportunities at West Point (www . . . kelly*)*.

The constituents Kelly has worked with also include some very well-known individuals. For instance, she worked to assist marathon runner Khalid Khannouchi with a citizenship request so he would be eligible to compete in the 2000 Olympics (an injury, however, prevented such competition [*TU* 11/7/99]). Similarly, she petitioned that actor Christopher Reeve (who, incidentally, declined an opportunity to run against her in 1998) receive an achievement medal from the National Endowment for the Arts (*TU* 3/22/98).

In an unusual example of a constituency concern, Kelly has even asked the secretary of the army to deal with the problem of "unexploded shells" as a safety hazard in and around the West Point area (www . . . kelly).

Even more than personal interactions, Kelly is proud of the federal largess (by her count almost $100 million) that she has helped bring to the district. This, she said, offers "real solutions for working families, and I have accomplished a great deal" (*PJ* 10/26/98). For example, "last Congress, Sue spearheaded the effort to bring home $27 million for a new veterans nursing home in Montrose, NY and successfully secured $35 million in important transportation infrastructure projects in the Hudson Valley" (www . . . kelly). She has worked with the city of Poughkeepsie to obtain a $3.7 million grant for a major parking garage, has announced grants for $5.7 million for housing at the Bill Koehler Senior Complex in Mahopac (PR 11/19/99), and has worked with local realtors to obtain a Fannie Mae grant pilot project helping low to middle income homebuyers (*PJ* 3/22/97). She has gotten grants promoting early literacy ("They didn't go to every school district in the nation. They came here because these people have vision" [*PJ* 6/16/98]), and has traveled to China on behalf of local business (*PJ* 1/3/97).

Finally, consistent with expectations suggesting that an educated constituency would desire their representative to be on the forefront of modern
technology, Kelly's Web site is well developed, going far beyond the basics.
For instance, not only does the site provide descriptions of her constituency
and her accomplishments, but it also includes a fairly extensive history of
the district dating back to Revolutionary War days and links to "Recess,"
which contains information on the "lighter moments" of Congress, "Congressional Recipes" ("The Official New York State Muffin"), "Interesting
Questions about the 50 U.S. States," and "Numerically Speaking" (the
"30–27 Vote of the New York Delegates when ratifying the Constitution at
Poughkeepsie on July 26, 1788") (www . . . kelly).

All this attention to constituents might be seen by some as an attempt to
balance out controversial associations with the 104th Congress by highlighting less controversial activities. Kelly would interpret her actions differently. She said the millions of dollars she got for new buses and other
transit projects in "Westchester, Putnam and Dutchess counties were 'anything but pork.' They offer help to 'thousands of commuters' as well as seniors who don't own a car" (*TU* 3/7/99).

Discussion

More than most of the other representatives in this study, Congresswoman
Kelly has followed a "responsible party" model, and her home style has
certainly held advantages for her. She capitalized on the 1994 Republican
bandwagon and used the party agenda in her campaign themes. As a member of the majority party, she has been able to advance more of the issues
she cares about, and, as her willingness to be partisan in the early stages of
the Hillary Clinton senate campaign shows, party loyalty has also helped
Kelly generate publicity and attention for her own accomplishments.

Yet, Kelly's subsequent reelection campaigns demonstrate the risks of
adopting such a party-oriented strategy and highlight the need to balance
this type of strategy with consistent constituency service. As was true in
1994, the 1996 general election in part offered a choice based on a responsible party model. DioGuardi again ran on the Right-to-Life and Conservative lines. On the Democratic side, Dr. Richard Klein was so upset with the
tenets of the Republican Revolution that he gave up his medical practice in
order to make a congressional run. "I honestly believe that the Gingrich
revolution has caused more harm to the health and safety of the people in

the Hudson River Valley than any major medical catastrophe," Klein said (*PJ* 10/11/96). "Sue Kelly ran as a moderate and she's a definite radical. This is a moderate district. Who is she representing with that kind of vote?" (*PJ* 4/17/96). Klein thus framed the electoral choice in terms of what was going on in the national arena and attempted to link Kelly to broader partisan trends.

Kelly's response was interesting. In a moderate district, she could have backed off and attempted to disassociate herself from national trends. In part, she did. Kelly acknowledged that the Republicans might have made some mistakes: "I think they were [scared] by a lot of harsh rhetoric and a sense that there were many people in my freshman class who were unyielding on a number of issues and were perhaps jeopardizing any kind of conclusion on the budget issues because of their hard stance" (*PJ* 4/17/96). "It took me a while to settle in. There was so much legislation coming so fast in those first 100 days, and I didn't have the historical perspective on it," Kelly said (*NYT* 4/26/98). However, on balance, she expressed pride in Republican accomplishments and was happy Speaker Gingrich made campaign swings through the district in both 1996 and 1998: "I'm not going to back down on what I started. If he wants to associate me with Newt Gingrich, I voted for 100 percent of the Contract with America. That's good public policy" (*PJ* 5/23/96); "We can cut taxes and still preserve the safety net" (*PJ* 10/17/96).

In 1998, Kelly again faced a political amateur, Dick Collins, a teacher at local prisons (*PJ* 11/1/98). Attempting to associate Kelly with the national scene, he charged that she didn't adequately understand the needs of her average constituent. For instance, he argued that Kelly and Gingrich were "close from the beginning" and that "Kelly looks so nice but is really quite conservative: she's been helping him send all our federal money down to Georgia. The least he could do is come up here and raise some money for her" (*PJ* 6/9/98).

These two elections show the advantages and disadvantages of following a responsible party model. Kelly's 46 percent win in 1996 (in a multi-candidate race) is an indication that her activity was satisfying enough constituents. Yet, the closeness of the margin cycles us back to appreciating the political divisions inherent in an affluent and attentive swing constituency. In 1998 and 2000, perhaps with some of the partisan warfare more under control, and perhaps because Kelly increased her focus on district service, she was able to increase her victory margins to the 60 percent range.

In sum, jumping on the responsible party bandwagon can be a plus, yet, as Kelly's profile indicates, attentiveness to constituents, identification with district needs, and the continuing charges of "carpetbagger" that were relevant in the Kelly campaigns also highlight the limits of a responsible party system.

Michael McNulty: Interactions among Party, Constituency, and a Changing Political Context

> Congressman Michael McNulty represents the residents of the Capital
> Region in the distinguished tradition of his predecessors, Sam Stratton and
> Leo O'Brien. . . . We upstate Democrats are somewhat more conservative
> than our political brethren elsewhere, and our Congressmen have reflected
> that in their votes in Congress.
> —Letter from constituent (*TU* 7/17/96)

The above letter, striking at the heart of Michael McNulty's home style, also highlights the forces and controversies that have shaped that style. Primarily through a variety of constituency activities but also through his issue positions, McNulty very much sees himself sometimes as a political independent but mostly as "representing" his constituency. To invoke, as the letter writer did, the word "tradition" for the description adds a particularly appropriate dimension to this representational style. Not only is McNulty himself an experienced politician sometimes faulted for being too much of a political insider, but the history of his family has been inextricably intertwined with, and even a contributor to, the long-standing and unique Albany Democratic political "machine." Thus, as we shall see, the larger district context—an important political and party legacy—contributes a unique perspective to modern political events.

However, the letter writer's description, "We upstate Democrats are somewhat more conservative than our political brethren," begins to articulate present-day interactions among party, constituency, and a changing political agenda. As the letter hints, after the Republican takeover of the House in 1995, McNulty's attempts to satisfy "centrist" elements at home meant that he sometimes cast votes at odds with national Democratic Party positions. In addition, local political struggles factor in, and the "we" of "we in upstate New York" is often not as single-minded as the letter writer implies. Not only have there been important splits and disagreements within the local Democratic Party, but also current trends toward suburbanization and a service-based economy have led to changes in McNulty's constituency since the heyday of the political machine.

Thus, the description below of McNulty's representation of the 21st Congressional District is, on the one hand, a story of an exceptionally strong fit between a legislator and the dominant segment of his constituency. However, it is also the story of a sometimes independent-minded representative at times operating in a changing political context.

What are the implications of all this for the "responsible party" system of the 1990s? First off, to focus on "responsible parties" is to focus on "party" at the national level of government. Although the "machine" politics are a bit unique, McNulty's story serves as an important reminder of the crucial role local parties can play in shaping events. To overfocus on what is going on at the national level misses the two-way interconnection between local and national political parties.

Moreover, as was the case for Sue Kelly, to focus on responsible parties is to highlight the importance of issue positions. As will become clear below, family ties, social interactions, and serving constituents are equally notable aspects of meaningful party activities. Finally, in the broader terms of the local-national distinction, which is the focus of this book, profiling McNulty's representational style demonstrates some ways national factors can have a surprising impact on an otherwise local presentation of self.

Constituency

Any understanding of McNulty begins with an understanding of the geographic constituency. As implied above, the 21st is interesting both because of its unique economic and political history and because of the profound changes that have occurred over the past few decades. Geographically, the district is relatively heterogeneous (despite a lack of really large cities) and rather dispersed (a land area of 1,087 square miles). Primarily an urban area (80%) (*PIA* 2000, 965), this portion of central New York includes the medium-sized cities of Albany (population just under one hundred thousand), Schenectady (sixty-three thousand), and Troy (fifty-two thousand). In addition, numerous suburbs have sprung up, particularly around the state capital of Albany, and they have become politically important. Over time, the city of Albany has lost voters to the suburbs, dropping its share of the county vote from 65% in 1941 to 41% in 1968. In 1995 it was 27%, the same as the "suburb" of Colonie (*TU* 12/8/96). Finally, the fact that the 21st includes portions of Montgomery and Saratoga counties contributes a surprising rural element to the district.

Economically, too, the constituency is rather heterogeneous. The area has long had a strong manufacturing base. In fact, as lumbering (Albany), textiles (Troy, "The Collar City"), and steel (Cohoes) were once important to the district's economy (*Almanac* 2000, 1156), the area has actually been described as the "birthplace of the American Industrial Revolution" (www.renscochamber.com/ourcommu.html). In addition, in the twentieth century, the presence of General Electric (Schenectady) and the Watervliet Arsenal made defense-oriented industries relevant to the district's economy.

Concomitant to this manufacturing heritage, it is important to note that immigrant populations, including Irish, Italians, and (pre-Revolutionary War) Dutch (the 21st is 91% white), have impacted the district in such ways as participating in the subsequent Democratic political machine and taking somewhat conservative stands on social issues such as abortion (see below) (*PIA* 1996, 937). In addition, there has long been an active Jewish community (Kennedy 1985).

Today, however, as in other areas of New York State, sectors of the industrial economy have been in decline. Many of the industries that contributed to the area's prosperity in an earlier time no longer exist or are smaller in scale. For example, companies such as GE have "cut its work force deeply over the last decade" (*PIA* 1996, 937), and cities including Schenectady and Amsterdam (Montgomery County) have undergone economic difficulties.

Consequently, the area's economy has diversified. In addition to manufacturing, "nearly half of all employment in Albany is in the public sector" (*PIA* 1996, 937), and the economy has a more service-oriented base. A variety of health care, educational (*PIA* 1996, 937), and even high-tech industries (the area is now billing itself as Tech-Valley [www . . . mcnulty]) provide a significant presence in the 21st. All in all, a median income of $31,000 and a 24 percent college education rate indicate that, despite economic downturns, district residents are doing fairly well compared to state and national averages (Table 4.1).

Politically, too, the story of the 21st reflects both strong traditions and increasing diversity:

> Albany continues to have one of the nation's most famed Democratic political machines, dating back to 1921, when Daniel O'Connell and his brothers and local aristocrat Edwin Corning took control of City Hall. They never

really relinquished it: O'Connell died in 1977, still boss after 56 years, and his early partner's son, Erastus Corning II, was mayor from 1942 until his death in 1983. (*Almanac* 2000, 1156)

Thus, "sustained by legions of city and county employees, [and] by a certain creativity when it came to counting votes" (*Almanac* 2000, 1156), Democratic Party domination not only flourished but also ensured that an "old boy" network of politicians almost completely controlled the political landscape.

Given this dominance, it is no surprise—in fact, an understatement—to note that McNulty's reelection constituency is solidly Democratic. His predecessor, Sam Stratton, held office for thirty years, demonstrating the strong partisanship of the area. In turn, McNulty has won all his general elections with upward of 62 percent of the vote (*Almanac* 2000, 964). Yet, as the area changes, local Democratic Party strength is not quite what it once was (*TU* 12/8/96). Given reforms of the past couple of decades, the "machine" has less control over patronage in city jobs. Further, recent challenges to the political status quo have resulted in "insurgents" achieving election to local legislative posts (*TU* 11/5/89).

In sum, the 21st has a unique and interesting sociopolitical history of immigrant populations, industrialization, and Democratic Party dominance. As we move into more modern times, the legacy of the past combines with economic shifts, a move to the suburbs, and increasing political independence to set the stage for the story of a congressional career that reflects the traditions of the area but also represents the potential for change.

Background

McNulty's family tradition combined with his own ambition propelled him into the Albany County political scene. In a fairly amazing political story, three generations of McNultys have dominated the politics of the Village of Green Island in Rensselaer County (population 2,490) (www.census.gov/cgi-bin/gazetteer), subsequently using that as a base to achieve greater electoral success.

McNulty's political heritage may be traced back to 1914, when his grandfather, John Sr., was elected tax collector of Green Island and, twenty years later, became Albany County Sheriff (*PIA* 2002 711). Similarly, John McNulty Jr., father of the current representative, has himself engaged in more than a half-century of local political activity, including serving as mayor of Green Island while almost an octogenarian. Even more, other family members have held public positions: McNulty's uncle, William, served as an Albany County legislator; his sister, Ellen, worked on the town board of Green Island and was also mayor; and his brother, Jack, was vice president of the Green Island Board of Education (*TU* 12/30/88).

Despite their domination of Green Island, it is important to note that relationships between the McNulty clan and the Albany Democratic machine have been somewhat in conflict. In the 1930s, McNulty's grandfather was sheriff. As McNulty explained the relationship between county "bosses" Ed and Dan O'Connell and his family, "He was close to Ed; Ed gave him the nod. But during the [first] term Ed died and Dan took over. Many people who were in good graces with Ed were not in good graces with Dan, and my grandfather was one." According to the *Times Union,* "Dan O'Connell refused to endorse the elder McNulty for a second term as sheriff, creating a political rift that lasted for decades" (*TU* 3/4/90). In 1973, McNulty's father avenged the rebuff. Opposing the machine, he ran successfully for his father's old position of Albany County Sheriff, mounting the first successful challenge to the O'Connell/Corning network (Kennedy 1985). (To complete the story, several years later, Mike's father was ousted by the machine in a controversy over the sheriff's overtime budgets and resigned, only to be appointed by then-governor Cuomo to the state Commission of Correction [*PIA* 2000, 964]).

For Michael McNulty, a political career was never in question. Indeed, it was a fulfillment of his grandfather's dream (*TU* 7/19/88). He obliged, early on expressing interest in politics. For example, he recalled a strong desire as a twenty-one-year old to attend the 1968 Democratic presidential convention. After several unsuccessful attempts to obtain credentials from then-Albany Mayor Erastus Corning II (how many twenty-one-year-olds would have been likely to have such contacts?), he got in touch with a friend in Chicago. According to McNulty, his friend's father, "seeing me crushed, said, 'Kid, you really want to go to that convention, don't you? Would you mind doing a little work?'" (*TU* 8/28/96). Thus, McNulty served as a security guard, at one point actually shocking Mayor Corning by checking the mayor's credentials (*TU* 8/28/96).

After graduating from Holy Cross in 1969 with (what else?) a major in political science, McNulty was elected to the Green Island Town Board, becoming "the youngest Town Supervisor in New York State at the age of 22. Subsequently, he served as Green Island's Mayor and entered the State Legislature in 1982" (Web bio).

His election to represent the 21st district (formerly the 23rd) demonstrates the power of the still-influential Democratic organization. Sam Stratton, the incumbent of thirty years, unexpectedly announced his retirement on the last day candidates could legally be taken off the ballot (*Almanac* 2000, 1156). Under New York law, such circumstances allow party leaders the opportunity to select candidates. Within a few days after the Stratton announcement, Albany County Democratic leader J. Leo O'Brien, along with other officials, selected McNulty as the choice (*Almanac* 2000, 1156), a choice ratified in a less than one-hour meeting at the Albany County Airport. "'I'm going right back on that plane,' emphasized O'Brien who flew in, and then out, from the Democratic presidential convention" (*TU* 7/21/88).

For obvious reasons, critics denounced the selection procedure (*TU* 9/12/88). However, in this solidly Democratic area, the voters apparently did not object too much, because McNulty won the 1988 election with 62 percent of the vote, and except for a very close primary in 1996 (see below), he has won subsequent elections quite handily.

Home Style

Local Roots. McNulty's roots and his family's tradition of involvement in the political/partisan life of the district are the hallmarks of his home style. He highlights the fact that in many ways, he is just like any other person in the district while at the same time acknowledging and using his status as a powerful political insider. McNulty's firm belief in service to the district dates from a young age. While his contemporaries might have been out playing baseball or working a paper route, McNulty's memories are of politics. McNulty said his grandfather warned him to "never take anything for granted and get out and see the people" (*TU* 10/14/86). He explained, recalling his childhood, "The phone would ring during dinner and my father would be off to help someone—no problem was ever too small" (*TU* 10/14/86).

Thus, McNulty presents himself to constituents as a regular guy looking out for their interests. He has five district offices located throughout the 21st (www . . . mcnulty). His family has continuously resided in the district, and he makes weekly trips home.

So, McNulty's allocation of resources and presentation of self are primarily district-oriented. A local paper describes it well: "Now McNulty is a mainstay at Democratic functions, from picnics to funerals, and is on the campaign trail even in years he is not running" (*TU* 8/25/96). For example, he regularly frequents district events such as swearing-in ceremonies for new citizens, participates in sleep-a-thons to publicize the Homeless Action Committee (*TU* 3/10/99), and attends awards ceremonies for groups working to advocate for people with disabilities (*TU* 6/20/01). He has attended retirement parties for local officials (*TU* 11/28/95) and has eulogized deceased firefighters as longtime friends (*TU* 10/9/99). Along with these types of activities, he regularly visits temples (*TU* 6/28/99) and churches, and he speaks at local venues including educational institutions (*TU* 5/24/93; 5/23/96). Along with other elected officials, he has recently participated in an antiracism dialogue (*TU* 4/30/01).

It is therefore clear that over the course of his career, McNulty has developed extensive contacts and connections throughout the Capital District. Nevertheless, he sometimes pays particular attention to specific groups within his primary constituency. He has stayed involved in his home base, the area in and around Green Island, even involving himself in local controversies (*TU* 4/12/94). Too, McNulty remains a loyal party man, speaking frequently to Democratic groups, sometimes taking sides in intraparty disputes (*TU* 3/27/97), and employing staff who themselves have strong party ties (*TU* 5/22/97). Finally, he has developed important links to elements of the Capital District Jewish community, working for a $400 million loan package to help Soviet Jews (*TU* 3/31/90), sponsoring a sense-of-Congress resolution to bring Nazi war criminal Alois Brunner to trial (*TU* 10/24/91), and receiving the Cup of Life Award from Congregation Ohav Shalom for "his support of efforts to secure the freedom of Ethiopian Jews" (*TU* 6/28/91).

McNulty (having himself lost a brother in Vietnam [*TU* 7/6/98]) also demonstrates a consistent interest in the concerns of veterans (*TU* 10/21/98; 6/11/96). Most notably, in conjunction with several colleagues, he engaged in a decade-long campaign leading to the construction of a veteran's cemetery in the Capital District (*CR* 7/12/99). "There is a considerable amount of veterans in this area and [the cemetery] has received strong support, they have been sending me letters to advocate it and I've been doing that," he said (*TU* 6/16/90).

Thus, McNulty spends considerable time in and around the 21st cultivating constituents. In addition, as we might expect given his background in "machine" politics, he is known for a strong desire to expand the district's economy and preserve jobs. As was true of Stratton before him, he has worked tirelessly to protect jobs at the famed Watervliet Arsenal and other defense-oriented industries. Following Stratton, he initially sought a seat on the House Armed Services Committee and advocated for district interests. He worked with New York senator D'Amato to restore $30 million to the defense budget to produce weapons at the arsenal (*TU* 11/15/89), and gained a $7.52 million arms contract for the facility (*TU* 2/16/98). In 1997, he and former Republican Congressman Gerald Solomon (22nd district) convinced General Johnnie Wilson, head of the Army Material Command, to delay a decision about cutting jobs until after touring the Watervliet facilities (*TU* 10/10/97). He has supported arsenal growth through the development of private sector contracts as well (*TU* 12/2/93) and helped to secure a contract to build 162 cannons, with the possibility of building more than four hundred total (*TU* 11/23/00).[3] As a grateful employee summed it up, "If not for the tremendous effort of our congressional delegation, led by Rep. Michael McNulty, the Watervliet Arsenal would have lost more than 50% of our future workload" (*TU* 7/31/00).

Expanding on this role of bringing federal largess to the 21st, it is not surprising that McNulty has helped secure a steady stream of grants for the district:

- Grant to build a visitors' center in the economically struggling city of Cohoes—$1.2 Million (*TU* 5/31/90)
- U.S. Department of Justice grant to invigorate drug courts in the city of Troy and for Rensselaer County that provide drug treatment and services to misdemeanor drug offenders—$241,000 (*TU* 7/14/98)
- Aided the Whitney M. Young Jr. Health Center, providing service to low-income citizens—$500,000 (*TU* 12/9/99)

Finally, McNulty has promoted district interests in other and more unusual ways. He nominated a local band to represent New York State in a series of performances at the Kennedy Center (*TU* 11/25/00). With his help, several landmarks—including the Kate Mullaney (leader of the first women's labor union) Historical Site (*TU* 2/9/99), the Mull House and Cemetery (in Coeymans, serving nineteenth-century Hudson River communities)—have been designated as historic buildings. And, on August 8, 1999, a plaque was unveiled commemorating the Harmony Mills complex as a "textile titan that clothed the nation in calicoes and muslins while weaving together the city's economy" (*TU* 8/21/99). Most recently, he inserted in the *Congressional Record* a tribute to the Glenville Air National Guard, the unit responsible for the difficult and much-publicized evacuation of cancer patient Dr. Gerry Nielson from the South Pole and "the only guard unit trained to fly such a dangerous mission" (*CR* 10/20/99).

In short, McNulty devotes considerable time and energy to promoting the interests of the 21st. He not only looks out for the district's economic interests, but he stays connected with many constituents and advocates for a wide variety of district concerns. Perhaps he does so because, as a labor leader put it in supporting his first congressional campaign, "He's one of us" (*TU* 9/6/88).

Party Roles: Insider and Independent. In addition to his work on behalf of constituents, McNulty is a loyal party man among Washington Democrats. Like Sue Kelly, he has been a key part of both his party's official leadership team and the wider network of social connections among Washington Democrats. Nevertheless, also like Kelly, McNulty's issue positions sometimes deviate from those of his national party's mainstream. If for Kelly these conflicts arise primarily due to strongly held beliefs, McNulty would explain his differences with national Democrats in terms of a fundamental desire to represent the positions of his constituents.

To begin, as has been true in the district, McNulty has been a part of the Democratic Party leadership ever since his initial election. In 1989, he was appointed the only freshman member of the executive committee of the Democratic Study Group ("I'm honored by it, and I am delighted about the recognition it gives my district" [*TU* 2/14/89]). Subsequently, he was selected as Freshman Majority Whip for the Northern Region of the country (Web bio), Majority Whip-at-Large, and Minority Whip-at-Large after 1994 (Web bio).

His pleasure in these appointments was captured in an interview during his first term in office: "In the corridor, McNulty is handed a letter. . . . Reading it, McNulty shows no expression, then lets out a 'Yo.' The letter—which he didn't expect for at least another week—was from [former Congress member and party leader] Gray, notifying him of his Whip-at-Large Appointment" (*TU* 3/4/90).

Similarly, the congressman has achieved committee assignments to his liking and has advanced relatively quickly up the rungs of the committee hierarchy. His initial assignments included Armed Services, his first choice:

He's talking again about his favorite subject—how he got on the Armed Services Committee. He's so serious. He knew the Democratic Caucus Steering
and Policy Committee recommends appointments. "Knowing that . . ."
McNulty continued.

"How did you know?" he is asked.

"I made it my business to know it." (*TU* 3/4/90)

A short four years later, "as a reward for toiling away quietly as a vote-
counter for the party" and his work in the Democratic whip system (*PIA*
1994, 1080), he was offered the possibility of an even more prestigious assignment. In considering his set of options, his first choice for a new committee was Appropriations. However, upon learning that two other New
York Democrats wanted the seat, he demonstrated collegiality and bowed
out of the running (*PIA* 1994, 1080). What he settled for, however, was a
pretty good alternative: the prestigious Ways and Means Committee (*PIA*
1994, 1080). (There he has remained, except for a brief time in 1995 when
the juggling of committee positions temporarily cost him his seat.)

Given his success inside Congress, it is not surprising that he is also
plugged into more informal party networks. To appreciate this, it is only
necessary to refer to the 1990 article quoted extensively above. Its full title
is, "A Day in the Life of Michael McNulty" (*TU* 4/30/90). As such, it is
probably a good indication of McNulty's role as a party insider to note that
two other events he attended on that presumably typical day included a re-
ception hosted by high-ranking Democrat Charles Rangel (NY) and a dinner engagement at the National Democratic Club (*TU* 3/4/90). Similarly,
on a much sadder note, he went out of his way to eulogize former commerce secretary and Democrat Ron Brown (*TU* 4/4/96). In addition, he has
used these national connections to his electoral benefit, drawing prominent
Democrats, such as then–vice president Al Gore and first lady Hillary Clinton, to the 21st for political events and fundraisers (*TU* 7/20/98; 6/20/99).

Nevertheless, when it comes to issues, the story is different. In accumu-
lating a voting record that is a "centrist philosophy that reflects the views
of the people of the 21st District," and that "represents independence" (*TU*
10/3/94), McNulty deviates from his party more than might be expected
based on his role in the party hierarchy.

In light of this "centrist philosophy," there are times, of course,
where McNulty is very supportive of his party's positions. For example,
he was in favor of important Democratic legislation early in the Clinton

administration including AmeriCorps, Family and Medical Leave, and the economic stimulus package (*PIA* 1996, 964). He has also been solidly behind traditional Democratic initiatives involving government intervention on behalf of those in economic need and providing jobs. Thus, he voted to raise the minimum wage, voted against allowing employers to offer their workers compensatory time off instead of overtime pay (*PIA* 2000, 964), and opposed welfare reform. (In response, McNulty "is sponsoring a bill called the Hunger Has a Cure Act," to ensure that underserved groups retained benefits [*TU* 11/25/97]).[4] Similarly, again following the Democratic line, he has stated that education, Medicare, and social security should have higher funding priority than defense or tax cuts in the event of a budget surplus (www.vote-smart.org).

At the same time, it is very easy to find illustrations demonstrating his independence from party. In 1995, he was one of only a few Democrats to support a $10 billion bill for local block grants for fighting crime. "'I voted for it because it gives more decision-making powers on how the money is spent to leaders of local government,' said McNulty, echoing the GOP line. 'In particular, this bill gives a bit more money to the localities than the President's bill which was a very good bill because the local match goes from 25 percent to 10 percent'" (*TU* 2/23/95). Though he liked the bill supported by his own party's president—and said so—he nevertheless was happier with the Republican alternative.

In addition, the Irish Catholic McNulty has been more conservative than many Democrats on social questions and has, in particular, amassed a consistent record opposing abortion under most circumstances. At the beginning of his career, the abortion rights organization NARAL had him pegged as firmly antichoice (*TU* 9/8/96). Though he supports the idea of family planning, he only favors abortion in cases of incest or rape and when the life of the mother is in danger (www.vote-smart.org). In contrast to many other Democrats, he has supported parental notification when minors seek abortions and against a measure designed to promote safe access to abortion clinics (*PIA* 2000, 965). In 2001, he was one of only fifty-three Democrats to favor granting rights to an unborn fetus (*TU* 4/27/01).

All in all, as an indication of his deviation from party, he supported thirteen of fifteen items (except for tax cuts and welfare reform) in the 1995 Contract with America (*Almanac* 2000, 1157). It may not be surprising then that McNulty is "one of a handful of New York Democrats (regularly) endorsed by the conservative, not the liberal party" (*Almanac* 2000, 1157):

I not only would not reject the Conservative Party nomination, I'm going to actively seek it. I've run with the support of the local Conservative Party three times in a row, and I hope this time will be the fourth. . . . Of course your main allegiance is to your own party. If you run on an additional line, it doesn't mean you adopt somebody else's beliefs or any platform that they might adopt. (*TU* 3/4/96)

In addition to these differences of beliefs, McNulty differs from many Democrats because he also "thrives on foreign policy issues, and there [is] none of that at the state level" (*TU* 3/4/90). In fact, his enthusiasm has taken somewhat unusual forms. As a contrast to public stereotypes of many legislators who, in their roles as politicians, simply engage in talk, he has actually traveled to and visited a rather astounding number (approximately fifty) of nations, including countries on all six continents as well as the North and South Poles (Web bio). He is clearly proud of these trips, as artifacts and souvenirs (including a small clay statue of a rabbi McNulty acquired during a trip to Ethiopia, an olive wood carving of the Virgin Mary brought back from Bethlehem, and a photo of McNulty and two American bishops taken while he was studying in Rome in 1967) line both his current Albany office and even more, the relatively unfurnished apartment that he occupied in Washington early in his career (*TU* 3/4/90).

McNulty has other foreign policy interests as well. He served on a congressional delegation accompanying President Clinton on the historic first-ever trip to Northern Ireland by a United States president (*TU* 11/30/95). He has consistently followed the Balkan peace process, joining a fact-finding delegation to Sarajevo and Zagreb, Croatia, in 1995: "As our government asks more than 20,000 American soldiers to risk their lives on foreign soil, the least our elected officials can do is take a first-hand look at the conditions they will face'" (*TU* 12/9/95). He has visited Mexico to investigate drug control and environmental standards (*TU* 2/13/99), Cuba to examine the healthcare and food shortage situation (*TU* 2/16/00), and Armenia to observe the violations of civil rights ("That all ended in 1991, and I was there to see it. I was one of the four international observers from the United States Congress to monitor that independence referendum. I went to the communities in the northern part of Armenia, and I watched in awe as 95% of all of the people over the age of 18 went out and voted in that referendum" [*CR* 4/21/99]). As he has in his district, McNulty has consistently expressed concern about global humanitarian issues. He was a longstanding member of the Select Committee on Hunger (Web bio), traveling to African nations including the countries of Sudan and Ethiopia (*TU 5/17/90; 5/21/89*).⁵ And, most recently, to signal the importance of the nation to a new administration, he was part of a congressional delegation visiting Greece (*TU 1/26/01*).

In terms of roll call votes, he has built up a record that is "more supportive of defense department priorities than many Democratic colleagues" (*PIA 1992, 1052*). For example, "he voted in 1989 against capping production of the B-2 'Stealth' bomber and in 1990 against a deep slash in funding for the strategic defense initiative" (*PIA 1992, 1052*). He has supported a proposed amendment to the Constitution to ban desecration of the flag (*TU 6/13/97*).

Finally, he has been described as a vocal supporter of the policy of the first President Bush toward Saddam Hussein (*PIA 1992, 1052*). However, when it came to a vote on deploying troops to fight, his record displayed his characteristic brand of independence. First, he remained loyal and voted for the Democratic leadership's proposal for economic sanctions and, when it didn't work, he voted to send troops, "one of only three democrats who voted for both" (*PIA 1992, 1052*).

In sum, McNulty balances his insider status with a fairly independent voting record, particularly in the areas of social concerns and foreign policy, but also in some key domestic arenas. Although it would be a stretch to call him an issue-oriented congressman (he doesn't sponsor many bills and doesn't include many statements of issue positions on his Web site), he has nevertheless developed his own viewpoints and ideas and is unafraid to side with the opposition party. However, to an outsider, the degree to which his issue positions reflect independence is particularly striking because of the social connections and status he so enjoys within the Democratic Party and because of his links with the legacy of a powerful political machine. It would be easy for him to simply follow the party line.

Discussion

This profile began by highlighting the important political traditions and relative conservatism of the historically Democratic 21st district. Because of his fit into these traditions, Rep. McNulty's home, locally oriented, and partisan-insider style probably developed naturally as a reflection of his perceptions of constituency desires and his own set of life experiences.

In turn, there have always been critics of this locally oriented home style. Charges that the congressman has been too much of a "political insider" are natural and perhaps appropriate given the circumstances of his initial election to Congress (*TU* 10/17/90). In addition, segments of the changing constituency, particularly liberal elements, can argue that McNulty's focus on local interests detracts from his attention to national issues; and, that when he does assume an issue focus, that focus takes on a conservative bent, even pointing to similarities between Rep. McNulty's voting record with that of staunch Republican former representative Gerald Solomon (*TU* 1/14/90) on abortion, flag burning, and school prayer (*TU* 10/29/94).

However, in the wake of the particularly polarized politics of the 104th Congress, criticism of McNulty, at least temporarily, ratcheted up. In the course of his first few years in office, his party unity scores averaged in the high eighties. Between 1994 and 2000, this average slipped a bit, to approximately eighty, hitting its low of sixty-five in 1995. Thus, during the 104th Congress, his failure to stand with the national Democrats increased the alienation of some constituents (*TU* 3/20/95); a newspaper headline from 1996 actually asked, "Is Rep. McNulty a Real Democrat?" (*TU* 9/8/96).

Thus, in 1996 a combination of circumstances—a publicized change in the political agenda as the Republicans gained control of the House, a more heterogeneous constituency, and a good candidate—coalesced. Despite a lack of elective experience, challenger and environmental advocate Lee Wasserman proved himself an energetic campaigner with very credible credentials. More, he attempted to link McNulty to House Speaker Newt Gingrich: "And when the Albany environmentalist talks about the four-term congressman, the name of Gingrich is certain to follow" (*TU* 8/25/96), "more than any other Northern Democrat, according to *The Almanac of American Politics*" (*TU* 1/7/96). "Mike has repeatedly voted for Newt Gingrich, he has repeatedly voted against choice, he has the highest ranking of any Democrat north of the state of Mississippi by Pat Robertson's Christian Coalition'" (*TU* 8/22/96).

The campaign proved to be only a temporary challenge to McNulty's record, though; the details of this controversial primary are beyond the scope of this profile. But abstracting from the charges and countercharges, which lasted for months, are underlying philosophical views about representation, which place McNulty's home style in a broader perspective. Wasserman was clearly advocating for the "responsible party" model with its focus on issue activism and receptiveness to the agenda of a national party. He was clearly implying that, in the face of the 1994 Republican takeover of the House, McNulty had a choice to make: to stand loyally with his national party or to "jump ship" and go with the winning side. According to Wasserman, McNulty had chosen to jump ship.

Yet, if the Wasserman campaign can be viewed as taking the national perspective, McNulty offered a more practical view. He reiterated that he was a good politician who had been following the wishes of his centrist constituents but who had the courage to deviate from party when appropriate. "McNulty said his contract votes were common-sense measures and that the majority of his 800-plus votes in the past two years illustrates he is a Democrat in good standing" (*TU* 9/8/96). While he doesn't always support the Democratic platform, McNulty explained, "[t]hat doesn't mean I don't support them on most occasions. The point that Lee completely misses is that people like politicians who have the courage of their convictions, who listen to their own constituents" (*TU* 3/4/96).

In addition, McNulty reminded voters that a campaign is not just about issues. In keeping with his home style, he highlighted the tangible benefits he had helped bring to the district by taking partial credit for:

> [t]he construction of Exit 8 on Interstate 90, which should help the Rensselaer Technology Park; the Exit 26 bridge project off the New York State Thruway, which will be fully federally funded when ground is broken this spring; and the consolidation of the National Science Foundation's Antarctic research team at Stratton Air Force Base. (*TU* 3/10/96)

"I'm talking about jobs . . . that's what people are interested in" (*TU* 7/22/96).

Finally, the circumstances of 1996 refocus attention on the role of the local party, which is at the heart of this story. Despite primary opposition (ultimately Wasserman garnered an astounding 43 percent of the vote), the "machine" was still strong enough to provide notable advantages to its chosen candidate.

In short, the lessons from the Wasserman campaign and the McNulty profile more generally highlight the interactions between party, constituency, and a national agenda, or, more simply, between the national and the local. Many national elements worked themselves into this profile—the 1996 primary with its emphasis on the merits of "responsible parties," the changing national issue agenda and even the trips to foreign lands, which McNulty so enjoys.

At bottom, however, McNulty's profile is a local story, highlighting the importance of party in the district, constituency needs, and a locally oriented home style. For the most part, as is made clear from the many wonderful anecdotes relating to Democratic party history within the 21st that have turned up in the research for this profile, McNulty's fit with the dominant traditions of the district is exceptionally strong, and it is consequently not surprising that the congressman has chosen to focus on constituency service, personal connections, and party activity. Thus, it is also not surprising that the 1996 campaign was as much about a changing local constituency as it was about national party politics.

This story then is about the interactions among local and national factors. There appears to be a cycle: even in a district where local traditions are so much a part of the story of the life of the current congressman, national factors enter in and have the potential to impact local politics. Yet, at the same time, an adequate understanding of those national factors requires that they be interpreted through the context of the local district. Thus, a complex interaction between a changing constituency, several layers of a political party, and the larger national agenda have come together to shape the events of this story and have contributed to an appreciation of particularly interesting political dynamics.

Carolyn McCarthy: Politics Made Personal on Long Island's 4th

With party discipline at the modern-day high described earlier in this chapter, one would expect that incoming freshman in the latter part of the 1990s would have strong partisan loyalty. In the aftermath of the Contract with America and the very partisan 104th Congress, we might expect that candidates seeking a congressional seat in 1996 might have to pass a party litmus test. This might be particularly true for would-be congressional candidates who were given considerable support from all levels of the party hierarchy. However, not only has Democrat Carolyn McCarthy (New York's 4th Congressional District, Long Island) not toed the Democratic party line, but she has actually maintained her lifelong Republican party registration (until 2003) (*Newsday* 10/28/98) while sitting in Congress and has steadfastly espoused a brand of "commonsense," "nonpartisan" politics, which she argues is essential for finding forward-looking solutions to difficult political issues. "Carolyn was elected to Congress because of her common sense approach to the problems facing Long Island's working families and her legislative agenda reflects this" (www . . . mccarthy).

Thus, understanding the factors underlying McCarthy's political choices is instructive not only in helping us to appreciate one congresswoman's story but also because it provides us a better appreciation of the limits of the "responsible party" system in the United States.

Constituency

As is true of Long Island generally, the 4th is described as "a heavily sub-urban area with most of the residents commuting daily into New York City. . . . A major commercial center, the Fourth District is also home to thousands of businesses" (www . . . mccarthy). Located around "the southwest corner of Long Island's Nassau county and . . . eastern Queens" (*PIA* 2000, 921) (see Map 3), the district is not only over-whelmingly suburban, but in fact, "the area of Garden City is one of the nation's first suburbs" (*Almanac* 2002, 1055). As McCarthy herself has noted, the proximity to New York City means there is much commuting back and forth either via the Long Island Railroad or several fairly con-gested highways, making transportation an ongoing district concern (*Newsday* 3/6/97).

The 4th is largely white and middle or upper middle class (69% white collar, seventh of thirty-one in the state, top third nationally; median in-come $50,887, second of thirty-one in the state, top third nationally [*PIA* 2000, 921; see Table 4.1]). Residents are well educated (26% college edu-cated, ninth of thirty-one in the state (*PIA* 2000, 921)), and the district is home to numerous universities and colleges.

Yet, the economy of the area has had its ups and downs. Thus, after the "decline of the defense industry on which Long Island was heavily depen-dent . . . the district continues to rebuild and diversify, focusing on technol-ogy and small business" (*PIA* 2000, 921). Perhaps as a consequence, the economic mix of residents is actually more diverse than the overall num-bers quoted above suggest. For instance, there is a sizeable "working and lower middle class" element in the 4th (*Congressional Districts in the 1990s,* 503) seeking local employment (at "John F. Kennedy International Airport [across the district line in Queens' 6th district], Belmont Park race track, and large shopping centers such as Roosevelt Field and Green Acres" [*PIA* 2002, 677]).

In addition, the 4th has the largest minority population (26%) of any dis-trict on Long Island, a population concentrated around the east end of the district (Hempstead, Uniondale, New Castle, and Roosevelt) (*PIA* 2000, 921) (see Map 3). While still predominantly middle-class, these towns have higher poverty rates than the rest of the district or Long Island (*CDs in the 1990s,* 503). There is also a sizeable Jewish population heavily concentrated in the "five towns" of Inwood, Lawrence, Cedarhurst, Woodmere, and

Hewlett. Also, because just fewer than 50 percent of district residents are of Irish or Italian ancestry, and because Rockville Centre houses Long Island's Roman Catholic Archdiocese, the Catholic Church is a force in district affairs (*CDs in the 1990s,* 503). As we shall see, this Catholic presence can give the constituency a conservative cast on social issues, including abortion.

Also, as is true of Long Island generally, the 4th has historically been viewed as Republican territory. Though McCarthy believes that party affiliation is not uppermost in most voters' minds ("the majority of people in my district and on Long Island are not politically active" [*Newsday* 5/25/97]), Nassau County's GOP organization has long been one of the strongest party machines and most "well oiled" around the country (*Newsday* 11/22/98), spawning such legendary politicians as former Republican senator from New York Alfonse D'Amato. Thus, "the district which includes the Nassau County Seat of Mineola, is a stronghold for the County's GOP organization" (*PIA* 1996). Similarly, the nearly all-white communities of Valley Stream, New Hyde Park, Garden City, and Franklin Square are consistently Republican bastions (*CDs in the 1990s,* 504).

So, the 4th has traditionally voted Republican for president, and since 1962, it had been represented in Congress by Republicans (*PIA* 1990, 1005) including Ray McGrath (1980–1992), David Levy (1992–1994), and Daniel Frisa (1994–1996).

But as this recent turnover in congressional representation indicates, there can be some volatility in voting, especially in the 1990s. In turn, this volatility is one of several factors holding out the potential for Democratic inroads in the district. The sizeable working and lower-middle-class population, the growing number of African American and Latino residents, and the Jewish population lend support to Democratic candidates (*PIA* 2002, 677). Indeed, currently, party registration only runs three-to-two Republican, with a sizable proportion of independent voters sometimes holding the balance in close contests (*DN* 11/5/96).[6] Bill Clinton carried the district with 47 percent and 57 percent of the vote in 1992 and 1996 respectively, Al Gore received 59 percent in 2000 (*PIA* 2002, 677), and the Democratic Party has fielded high-quality congressional challengers. In addition, constituents have been described as "socially moderate" (*PIA* 2000, 921).

Thus, McCarthy's geographic constituency is suburban and reasonably well-off. Though it leans Republican, both its demographic makeup and political character highlight the potential for close and competitive elections.

Background

The story of Carolyn McCarthy's entry into politics is by now more than familiar. In the early 1990s, running for Congress or even giving much thought to politics at all would have been far from the mind of the "life long resident of Mineola" (Web bio). McCarthy had spent her life as a housewife, mother, and nurse, content to let her husband, Dennis, be the center of attention at any public gatherings (Web bio). The closest she came to political activity, in her words, had been "as a volunteer who helped clean up the beaches each spring" (*Newsday* 5/30/96); even in the course of the 1996 congressional campaign, she had to be reminded of some basic political facts: Geraldine Ferarro had not in fact been "kicked off" the Democratic ticket in 1984 and Richard Gephardt (who called urging her to run for Congress) was actually the minority leader of the House (*Newsday* 5/21/96).

In the aftermath of the tragic and much-publicized shooting on the Long Island Railroad (December 1993), which left her husband dead and her son Kevin seriously injured ("I don't want it to be my whole identity, but obviously that's how people know me. So it's a double-edged sword" [*Newsday* 10/29/96]), this heretofore nonpolitical housewife first took an active role in her son's rehabilitation (*London Sunday Times* 8/8/99). She also became a nationally known gun control advocate:

> Q: Not everyone turns an event like that into activism. Why did you?
> A: It was a simple question from the press: What did I think about guns? I think my answer was, "I don't understand why guns are so easy to get." At that time Gov. Mario Cuomo was trying to pass an assault weapons bill, and reached out to me. (*Newsday* 10/29/96)

When the congressional incumbent of New York's 4th Congressional District, Dan Frisa, voted to repeal a federal ban on certain semiautomatic weapons in 1996 (a ban she had worked to get passed), McCarthy understandably became angry not only at Frisa's vote but even more at what she saw as his subsequent refusal to take time to speak with her:

> For McCarthy, the events that made her run started happening in March, when Frisa voted to repeal the assault-weapons ban that President Clinton had signed into law. McCarthy was disturbed, but not enough to run. Then, at a May fund-raising event for Bob Dole, she saw Frisa and asked him to explain his vote. She didn't like the answer, which she described as gobbledygook, and her campaign was born. (*New Orleans Times Picayune* 7/21/96)

After another disappointment—the Republican Party refused to allow her to challenge Frisa in a primary—McCarthy made the decision to run as a Democrat.

So, especially early on, this profile reflects the unusual story of a housewife-turned-celebrity who, thanks to considerable help and a reputation as a "quick study," learned to become a successful politician. Not only was the candidate's name recognition unusually high for a challenger, but she was even described in words such as "icon" and "heroine" (*Newsday* 8/29/01; 7/31/96). An "array of cameras and satellite dishes" (*Newsday* 7/31/96) from all over the globe followed her as she went about the business of campaigning. She was covered in the "Los Angeles *Times,* Washington *Post* and is even about to get the Good Housekeeping Seal of approval" (*Newsday* 7/31/96).

In addition, from the perspective of partisanship, in a year when the Democratic Party had hopes of regaining control of the House of Representatives, it is not surprising that the competitive nature of the district and the name recognition of the candidates ensured that this would be "one of the highest profile races in the country" (*Los Angeles Times* 7/5/96). The National Democratic Party put considerable effort into the race, with the Democratic Congressional Campaign Committee making it "a top priority" (*Newsday* 9/29/96). McCarthy received a prime time speaking spot (after Hillary Clinton) at the Democratic National Convention (*PIA* 2000, 921), and nationally known Democrats (Hillary Clinton, Al Gore, and Jesse Jackson) made 4th district appearances on McCarthy's behalf (*Newsday* 10/3/96; 10/28/96). Then-congressman Charles Schumer actually "lent her his best campaign strategist, staff members, [and] moral support" (*Newsday* 11/1/98); Rep. Floyd Flake held fundraising breakfasts (*Newsday* 10/31/96); and Rep. Gary Ackerman attended campaign events. McCarthy also received aid from women's groups such as EMILY's List (*Newsday* 11/12/96) and labor (*Newsday* 10/20/96).

How did McCarthy translate this celebrity status and national attention into the defeat of an incumbent of the district's majority party? What kind of developing political style enabled this former "ordinary citizen" to obtain a seat in Congress? Despite all the help she got from national Democrats, the first clues can be provided by the "ordinary citizen/regular person" phrase that McCarthy has often used to describe herself: "I want to go to Washington and put a face on government. I have no political experience and I am proud of it. . . . I don't care if you're a Republican or Democrat; I'm one of you" (*Newsday* 9/29/96). "'Carolyn is a once in a life time candidate; she is the people' added Gerry Moan, chairman of the Nassau Independence Party, on the announcement that she would be running on that party's line" (*Newsday* 7/15/96).

Partly due to her celebrity status (people were constantly asking her "how's Kevin" and telling her she had "guts for running"), McCarthy developed "human connections" with citizens. As one constituent described it, "There's a certain pride here for us when we see her on the cover of the magazines" (*Newsday* 5/25/97).

As a lifelong New Yorker and a long-standing resident of Mineola, McCarthy could also emphasize her roots in the district. She could tell union workers that her father and brother were boilermakers and that her mother was a buyer for Woolworth: "'I come from a union family,' McCarthy reminded the 50 union representatives, all men" (*Newsday* 9/29/96). She could tell blue-collar workers that she had been from a relatively poor family (*Newsday* 10/29/96). Thus, when she said, "I am one of you," she meant that instead of bringing political experience to the job of legislator, she would bring to office the practical experiences of wife, mother, and nurse.

Thus, she described the difficulties of her campaign in very nonpolitical terms: "It's like having a baby; you'd never do it if you thought about it" (*Newsday* 10/29/96).

In addition, McCarthy stressed a "commonsense" cross-partisanship that would later be one of the hallmarks of her home style. "I'm going to be running as a Republican on the Democratic line. . . . As far as I'm concerned, labels mean nothing" (*Newsday* 5/21/96). Thus:

> McCarthy is a registered Republican woman from the suburbs who opposes assault weapons, who supports a woman's right to abortion, who doesn't talk scary about cutting entitlements and who bears a certain resemblance to all the best next-door neighbors you ever had. (*Newsday* 7/16/96)

"In addition to gun violence, she emphasized issues impacting children, the elderly and the environment. Their minds are made up; they're voting for Carolyn," acknowledged the chairman of the Nassau County Republican Party (*Newsday* 10/30/96).

Another way McCarthy was able to make a cross-partisan appeal was simply by doing her homework. "No one realizes how I worked," she said. "We went local first, then state, then federal. That's the way you go" (*Newsday* 8/29/96). And her diligence was duly noted by others. "'I thought she was a one-issue candidate, but she surprised me,' said Jack

Kennedy, president of the Building and Construction Trades Council of Nassau and Suffolk counties" (*Newsday* 9/29/96).

Not surprisingly, McCarthy's grassroots campaign generated considerable enthusiasm. She was well funded for a challenger, accruing $967,221 in 1996. And she amassed many engaged supporters. "In a county with virtually no Democratic organization, McCarthy has more campaign workers than she can use" (*Newsday* 9/29/96). One woman even came from Israel to volunteer (*Newsday* 11/6/96).

Of course, "normal" politics played a role in even this unusual campaign. Whatever people thought of McCarthy personally and however much they identified with her story, political strategy still mattered. McCarthy had to campaign in a difficult district against an incumbent with political strengths of his own, including common people appeal: "Dan Frisa lives around the corner and down the street from his parents' original Levitt house on Pilgrim Lane in Westbury." He was experienced in the political arena, having served as a state assemblyman (*NYT* 11/3/96), having pulled off an upset victory in 1994, and having been described as "unerringly loyal to the Republican leadership's congressional agenda" (*Newsday* 10/24/96).

To his advantage, he could accuse McCarthy of being a single-issue candidate and of being too strident on gun control in a district where many people valued the right to own guns.[7] As an extension, he would "paint his opponent as a liberal who advocates abortion rights and opposes the death penalty and is allied with Rep. Charles Schumer (D-Brooklyn) and former New York Gov. Mario Cuomo" (*Newsday* 9/29/96). He would claim that his views were more in keeping with those of constituents. "I work and represent you in Washington as I know you would me . . . because I am you and you are me" (*Newsday* 9/29/96). Regardless, McCarthy herself pulled off the upset with a victory margin of 57 percent (*PIA* 2002, 676).

Home Style

A description of McCarthy's home style could begin with a discussion of any number of traditional political categories. She and her office emphasize services to constituents. According to one local official, "[I]t's an attention to the district . . . that he hasn't seen since Ray McGrath. . . . She seems to be taking a leaf out of [former congressman Ray McGrath's] book and dealing directly with the people" (*Newsday* 5/25/97).

So, McCarthy has returned to her district every weekend (*Newsday* 5/17/97), speaking about commerce and industry on Long Island (*Newsday* 4/13/97), about women's history at the opening night of a film festival (*Newsday* 3/7/97), and about law enforcement at the dedication of a memorial in honor of fallen officials (*Newsday* 6/22/97). She has been the featured speaker at college graduations, for instance, personally identifying with Adelphi University students by acknowledging that she had taken courses there as an unregistered student because she lacked the money to matriculate (*Newsday* 5/19/97). She has held town meetings publicizing the need for increased health coverage for children (*Newsday* 7/2/97), has participated with middle school students at their first legislative forum (*Newsday* 1/4/98), and was involved in the ribbon-cutting ceremony for a halfway house for rehabilitation (*Newsday* 12/5/98). She has worked to obtain funds to improve the water treatment system in Hempstead (*Newsday* 6/28/98) and has been involved in veterans' issues to help ensure that Long Island hospitals could receive their fair share of reimbursement (*Newsday* 7/24/98). Along with then–Republican representative Michael Forbes, she "packed food cartons" to publicize issues of hunger (*Newsday* 7/9/97). She has been a part of the New York delegation's efforts to make permanent a temporary office of the Immigration and Naturalization Service (*Newsday* 11/4/97); and, she has worked with Senator Schumer "to drop the charges against a Long Island man" navigating a plane that flew into a wire, killing civilians at an Italian ski resort (*Newsday* 3/6/99).

Throughout, she has sought citizen input on vote decisions. "When running for office last fall, McCarthy promised to bring the opinions of her neighbors to Congress. So, with the House of Representatives set to consider two bills that directly affect women with breast cancer, she decided to get local input before casting her vote" (*Newsday* 2/4/97).

As indicated by her participation at forums with students and college graduation ceremonies, McCarthy emphasizes her work with young people. In fact, for a variety of reasons (she believes that education is at the root of gun violence, her committee assignments included Education and Workforce, and education is important to her suburban constituents), one of the distinguishing characteristics of McCarthy's home style is that she spends considerable time in local schools:

> Mr. Speaker, I have spent the last week traveling throughout my district in Mineola, Garden City, Uniondale on Long Island, and meeting with hundreds of children. I have visited their classrooms, met their teachers, and

watched them work on computers, listened to their lessons and heard them read their books. . . . These are visits that have made more clear to me that our children are one of our Nation's most precious resources. (*CR* 2/11/97)

When speaking to students her message is clear and supportive. "I know a lot of times you don't get a lot of pats on the back for what you've done. . . . Now you're an example for the whole country. But don't let it go just for this year. Keep up the good work" (*Newsday* 5/28/97). She regularly salutes a "school of the month" on her Web site and encourages politically active students (*Newsday* 3/19/99). McCarthy is particularly interested in what young people have to say about gun violence. "When these students came to Congress and saw some of the discord going on with the gun debate, they asked, 'Why doesn't Congress have conflict resolution counselors like we do at school?' What a great idea! That's exactly what I'm trying to do here" (PR 10/22/99).

McCarthy has also worked the more conventional political circuit, for instance, organizing meetings between Washington and district officials:

Many village leaders of all political persuasions turned up at the meeting Monday, hoping for a chance to get the congresswoman's ear on a certain matter of local importance. "Our water system is over 100 years old," said the mayor of Rockville Centre, Eugene Murray, "and we need some help with funding to replace the four-inch pipes." Glen Spiritis, the Community Development commissioner of Hempstead Village, came looking for some help with the clean up of a pollution plume that has seeped into the village's aquifer from nearby Roosevelt Field, once the site of a government air strip.[8] He waited in a long line behind Guido Cirenza, a trustee in the Village of Valley Stream, who was wondering how the federal government might help with the dismantling of the old village incinerator on Arlington Avenue. (*Newsday* 2/5/98)

McCarthy and her staff have followed through on these requests, working on a variety of issues crucial in the 4th district. For instance:

Finding a way to move people around Nassau's frequently gridlocked commercial core without using cars is probably the county's single most important economic imperative. . . . Reps. Peter King . . . and Carolyn McCarthy . . . are seeking federal money to design a transit system that would get people out of their cars and offer a reliable way to move around the hub—perhaps on elevated trains. (*Newsday* 3/6/97)

McCarthy, too, has highlighted the somewhat surprising educational needs even in her affluent suburban district. She has acknowledged, for example, the problem of lower than expected literacy rates (PR 8/2/01). She has publicized poor conditions—overcrowding and serious repair needs—in suburban schools ("There's been a great deal of talk about the state of urban and rural schools. . . . This survey shows that many of the schools in suburban Long Island are in serious need of repair" [*Newsday* 2/10/98]. "Everyone thinks this is an extremely rich area, but the reality is that much of the Island is middle class. . . . I wanted (Secretary of Education) [Riley] to realize that a lot of our schools are old, they need construction—they could use some help" [*Newsday* 3/31/99]).

Similarly, in 1997, she was pleased to receive an assignment to the Small Business Committee because "small businesses—of which there are 83,000 in Nassau and Suffolk Counties—were such an important part of Long Island's economy" (*Newsday* 2/7/97), and she expressed particular support for women-owned businesses:

> I am proud to inform you that New York ranks third out of the 50 states in the number of women-owned firms as of 1996, second in employment, and second in sales. (*CR* 3/10/99)

Taking a very different tack, one could also begin a discussion of McCarthy's home style by examining her issue positions. Of course, she has continued her activities on behalf of ending what she calls "gun violence" (*Newsday* 5/25/97). "Whenever our nation faces a tragedy such as the one in Arkansas or the one last year at the Empire State Building, I get media calls from all over asking the question: 'What can we do?'" (*Newsday* 3/30/98). McCarthy is a significant proponent of gun control legislation, a person who expects her staff to work around the clock every time others are killed by gunfire in America (*London Sunday Times* 8/8/99). Starting at home, she attends reunions of the families impacted by the shooting that took her husband's life. "It has been three years. We have new children. . . . We have people who are happy. All of us have gone forward" (*Newsday* 12/8/96). "But for me and, many other victims, each new incident moves us to work harder for the day when the violence will end" (*Newsday* 3/28/98). "On the Internet tonight, we will be called gun grabbers and we will be called fanatics. But we're just trying . . . to save another family from going through what we've been through. Is that so terrible?"

(*DN* 2/24/98). She supports other victims ("I told him you're going to have a bad day now and again but get over it" [*Newsday* 2/24/98]), speaks at rallies in her district in support of "child access prevention legislation" (*Newsday* 5/3/97), and praised Governor Pataki's efforts when he "signed a wide ranging package of state controls" (*Almanac* 2002, 1056).

Even more, she participates in Washington rallies, holds press conferences, such as with (former) Representative Constance Morella (R-MD) to publicize the Million Mom March scheduled for Mother's Day 2000 (*NYT* 10/31/99), and speaks around the country on the lesser known aspects of gun violence ("The hidden cost of gun violence to the nation's health-care system is something no one is talking about in the emotional debate between gun-control and gun-rights advocates." [*Seattle Times* 5/24/00]).

An unusual incident illustrates McCarthy's "'dual role' as victim and congresswoman" (*Newsday* 5/25/97). In the aftermath of a shooting incident at New York's Empire State Building in which the gunman was not from the United States, McCarthy "got so mad she put in a call to the White House. President Bill Clinton called back, and asked her what he could do to help" (*Newsday* 5/25/97). A few days later, she was invited to the Oval Office ceremony where Clinton signed an executive order implementing new regulations that would require gun-buying foreigners to show a government-issued photo ID for at least ninety days from the state in which they were trying to buy a gun (*Newsday* 5/25/97). Later, at a survivor gathering, "clearly proud to be able to tell fellow survivors about her success, she recounted the story of her telephone call with Clinton" (*Newsday* 5/25/97). And not surprisingly, every time the House considers gun control, McCarthy weighs in on the debate.

So, "when a Republican-offered juvenile crime bill came to the floor in May 1997, McCarthy and her allies including Rep. Schumer (*Newsday* 5/9/97) on the gun question sought to add language to the legislation requiring child-proof trigger locks on all guns" (*PIA* 2000, 920). Her logic was straightforward: "It is a simple safety lock. We have bills that make it impossible for children to get into an aspirin bottle. Do my colleagues not think we should do the same thing with a gun?" (*NYT* 6/22/97). Interestingly, though the specific amendment didn't pass, the publicity generated from the controversy enabled the Clinton administration "to accomplish a non-legislative solution" when major gun manufacturers agreed to include trigger locks (*PIA* 2000, 921).

Later, in 1997, Representative John Murtha offered an amendment to a Treasury and Postal Appropriations bill loosening restrictions on the importation of certain types of assault weapons. While Murtha and others argued that these guns were simply "relics and curios" of historic interest, McCarthy claimed this old material could be converted into usable weapons (*PIA* 2000, 920). She surprised everyone who thought she was too much of a novice to understand parliamentary procedure by pointing out that Murtha's amendment was nongermane. In turn, Murtha surprised her "when he motioned her to the back of the House Chamber. . . . 'Been watching you. You're one tough broad.' . . . So he says, 'You can sit in this corner anytime.' So I took him up on it" (*Newsday* 10/21/98) and got some help learning the legislative ropes.

Finally, in the aftermath of the shootings in Littleton, Colorado, Congress became embroiled in controversy about the regulation of gun shows. Naturally, McCarthy had a strong opinion about the issue:

> "I am not willing to wait another year, I am not willing to wait any longer until there's another shooting," McCarthy said. "I happen to believe Congress has a moral obligation to stop this. I happen to think that we can do something about this. I'm tired of people saying, 'What can you do? We can't do anything.' I don't believe that." (*Boston Globe* 4/23/99)

Though Republicans have generally opposed regulation by the federal government, public pressure led to calls for some members of Congress and the gun industry to make changes. "We are looking for something that is responsive to public sentiment but that will not eliminate, or unreasonably restrict, the possibility of weapons sales among law-abiding citizens at gun shows," said the chief lobbyist for the NRA (Baker) (*WP* 6/9/99).

So, in the context of the controversial gun show debate in Congress after Littleton, McCarthy offered an amendment to a Judiciary Committee bill requiring a three-day waiting period if a computer background check indicated a problem (*Newsday* 7/11/99). She and other Democratic legislators lobbied hard for their proposals but "she knew, in a way that she did not know just three years ago, that it was hopeless by the time she made her speech" (*Newsday* 6/22/99).

Even when McCarthy knew her amendment would be beaten (the Republican leadership had scheduled a vote on a less restrictive proposal offered by veteran Democrat John Dingell), she nevertheless made an emotional late-night last stand on the floor of the house: "'Let me go home,' she said. 'Let me go home. I love working with all of you people. I think all of you are great. But somehow we sometimes lose sight of why we are all here. And I'm trying to remind you of that'"[9] (*NYT* 6/18/99).

McCarthy, however, is not a one-issue congressperson. "One of the reasons she got elected was one big issue, but some people are no-issue candidates," said Rep. Peter King (*NYT* 6/22/97). In fact, "Mrs. McCarthy has steadily expanded her areas of expertise, adding care for the elderly and education issues to her repertoire" (*NYT* 10/27/00). For example, she has used her seat on the Education and Work Force Committee (until the 107th Congress) to pursue her view of better schools. Consistent with her work at home on behalf of education, she has been concerned about teacher training. In 1998:

> Flanked by local school administrators, McCarthy yesterday announced legislation to overhaul the way teachers are trained across the country. The proposed "Teacher Preparation Improvement Act" calls for more federal funds and support for teacher recruitment, training college education majors in cutting-edge technology and placing prospective teachers in classrooms for more clinical experience. . . ." We should reach out for the best so we can have the best in our schools." (*NYT* 10/27/00)

On a lighter note, she supported education by celebrating: "Techies Day allows us to recognize and applaud today's technology professionals. In addition, it brings current techies and schoolchildren together in hopes of encouraging more of them to pursue careers in science or technology" (*CR* 10/5/99).

Also, "McCarthy has become an important player on health-related bills. Consistent with her work on breast cancer cited above and with the high incidence of the disease on Long Island, she has advocated for more federal funds for research" (*PIA* 2002, 677) and "released a study showing that Long Island women with breast cancer pay excessive prices for their medication" (*Almanac* 2002, 1056). "She supports efforts to give managed care patients the right to sue their health care plans, pointing out that members of Congress and fellow employees already have that right. 'If it's good enough for us, why isn't it good enough for everybody else?'" (*Almanac* 2002, 1056). "She worked on HMO reform with John Dingell who had opposed her on some gun issues. She helped to reverse Medicare cutbacks for New York hospitals" (*Almanac* 2002, 1056), commissioned a study that "tracked the prices, in both independent and chain stores within her . . .

district . . . of five brand-name prescription drugs most commonly used by the elderly" (*NYT* 8/15/99), and advocated for money for children with learning disabilities (*PIA* 2000, 921).

Most recently, "Congresswoman Carolyn McCarthy (D-NY), joined by U.S. Senators Max Baucus (D-MT) and Chuck Grassley (R-IA) and Representative Connie Morella (R-MD) today introduced bipartisan legislation to monitor America's health care safety net" as it effects "uninsured and vulnerable populations . . . often the last resort for patients who are unable to afford health care" (PR 9/12/00).

Finally, McCarthy has pursued other interests. She has worked on issues of concern to veterans:

> I was proud to vote for a budget last year that provided the largest funding increase in the history of the Veterans Administration. After several years of neglecting veterans, that was only the first step. Next, we have to take care of veterans' health care needs. (PR 7/30/01)

She also supports the work of the Congressional Caucus on Women's Issues: "'We'll address child care next year," McCarthy said. 'We got four of seven [bills]. That isn't bad'" (*Newsday* 10/4/98). So, she related to the concerns of a delegation of women parliamentarians from Northern Ireland who "shadowed" her and Rep. Peter King for a day to get a sense of the workings of the United States legislature: "They're in the minority like we're in the minority . . . I mean, there's 48 of us and 435 members, so we've had to build up our own strategies, also. That's why we have the women's caucus" (*Newsday* 9/28/00).

At the same time, in addition to the importance of her constituency work and her issue positions, perhaps the overriding aspects of McCarthy's home style are based on two interrelated themes: the human connections and sense of identification she conveys to constituents and her consequent emphasis on nonpartisanship or bipartisanship. In *Senators on the Campaign Trail,* Fenno (1996) has written persuasively about the necessity for congresspeople to be consistent in their activities. The more they stay true to a focus, and the more they stay true to who they really are, the easier it will be for constituents to trust them.

Of course, some of McCarthy's image as being above politics comes from her status as a celebrity. "Honorary degree in hand, McCarthy waded through a receiving line of professors, students and parents. . . . 'Can I just shake your hand?' Angela Cona, 22, made her way to McCarthy as well, and sheepishly held out her graduation program for an autograph" (*Newsday* 6/2/97). Even younger students have been influenced by her. "Going to college and becoming a cardiologist will enable me to help others. I know I can make a difference in many lives just like my role model Carolyn McCarthy did," wrote an eighth grade winner of a "Follow a Leader" contest (*Newsday* 11/30/97). In a different vein, stopping at restaurants, McCarthy has found special salads made in her honor (*NYT* 6/22/97).

But, celebrity aside, as she did in her 1996 campaign, McCarthy presents herself as an "ordinary citizen" using her life experiences to inform her political efforts. Of course, she participates in the "gun violence" movement as not just an advocate and politician but as a survivor still dealing with personal experiences. "You think you've moved on with your life—you look at how much has changed over the years, but there's really no such thing as closure" (*Newsday* 12/8/97).

She brings her experiences as a career nurse to bear on her health care stands. Drawing on more than thirty years experience as a nurse, she has supported flexibility in hospital stays for mastectomy patients ("The treatment has gotten better but not to the point of being released in 24 hours." [*Newsday* 1/30/97]), urged members of Congress to participate in blood drives ("One day, I was going up to Speaker [Dennis] Hastert and [Majority Leader] Dick Armey and asking them to donate. . . . All the members were saying 'What's she doing?' but I know what a difference it can make" [*Newsday* 9/9/01]), and expressed anger at cigarette companies for withholding information about the hazards of smoking ("The only thing wrong with the $368 billion, Marlboro man-killing tobacco deal . . . is it doesn't hit the industry harder. I would have liked more" [*DN* 8/31/97]. "'I'm a nurse; I should know better than this (smoking cigarettes)' she sighed. 'I've tried to kick the habit. I've made it 72 hours. I've made it three weeks once'" [*Newsday* 9/2/97]).

Finally, even her advocacy for increased federal aid to support children with learning disabilities (*PIA* 2000, 921) stems not only from her view of a fair system of education but also from her own experiences. "As one who has struggled with learning disabilities as a child" (*PIA* 2000, 921), she has had to adapt to dyslexia in her life as a politician. On receiving an award from the Lab School of Washington as the learning disabled person of the year, she spoke of the accommodations she had to make: since she is unable to read her speeches quickly, she must study them in advance, and she has taught herself to give the kind of off-the-cuff speeches that characterized her 1996 campaign (*Newsday* 11/9/97).

In short, McCarthy presents herself as an ordinary citizen who happens to be in Congress. In fact, she believes that "being down there just four months now, I am more than confident any citizen can go down to Congress and learn the job" (*Newsday* 5/5/97). In this regard, her opposition to term limits takes on particular significance:

> Mr. Speaker, today the House of Representatives will vote on term limit legislation. I have always believed in citizen legislators who work hard for the people, who accomplish things to make their communities a better place to live and then step aside after a few terms to let others into office to achieve new goals. It is what I have believed in and the kind of representative I am. At the same time, I also believe in devoted public servants, citizens who dedicate their lives to learning the laws and doing good things for others. I believe Congress needs people like Senator Bob Dole and Patrick Moynihan, people who spend their lives working to improve our lives. Term limits will deprive people of their choice between citizen legislators and public servants, and we do not need that. (*CR* 2/12/97)

It is not surprising then that "nonpartisanship" and "bipartisanship" are hallmarks of McCarthy's home style. For example, she was excited to be coming to Congress in 1997 "because freshmen from both parties seem fairly moderate. Everything that leadership has said from Gingrich to Gephardt is that we will work together and that's what the American people want" (*Boston Globe* 12/13/96). "I don't get up in the morning thinking I am a Republican or a Democrat. I am just a person who went into office" (*Almanac* 2000, 1110). "The days we don't play politics here, we get a lot done" (*Newsday* 6/18/98).

Thus, she meets regularly with Republican freshmen and insists on reading the position papers of both parties.

> But recently she and her staff members, career Democrats all, worked together on a speech. "They basically wrote down what I said," she says. "But what they put in, which I didn't say, was, 'And the Republicans and the Republicans and the Republicans.' I took the stuff out, and I told Beneva"—Schulte, her chief of staff—"I don't want any bashing in any of my speeches. That's not who I am." (*NYT* 6/22/97)

"In other words, call her a politician, a representative, a Democrat or Republican, but what you get is someone who's refusing to be defined by or confined to any of the boxes, partisan or otherwise, that politicians often fit neatly into" (*Newsday* 5/25/97).

So, McCarthy has gone out of her way to make friends with members of the Capitol Hill community and to do her homework. "The sergeant came over and told me I was the first congressman from New York to say hello to him" (*Newsday* 11/16/96). She purposely had dinner with fellow freshmen representatives from all sides of the political spectrum, some of whom she said, "Probably thought I was some sort of a gun nut" (*Newsday* 5/25/97). Other Congress members like her. "Her demeanor is such that we know she is not brash or a show boater. She's just very matter-of-fact" (*Newsday* 11/26/96). "She's like a kid from the neighborhood who ended up in Congress. She doesn't have that attitude that she's the only honest person who can come in and save the country," said Rep. Peter King (*Newsday* 5/25/97). "'She's there when the committee meetings begin, and she speaks out when she has something to say,' said Rep. Dale Kildee (D-MI). 'She speaks not to be heard but to be listened to, and she doesn't hog the mike'" (*Newsday* 5/25/97).

Even more, she has in fact struck up quite a friendship with King, who has advised her "not to take politics so personally" (*Newsday* 6/22/99) and who, when she first came to Congress, "guided her through the intricacies of the White House Correspondents Dinner" (*Newsday* 5/17/97). Her camaraderie is more about principle and less about party. When her picture turned up in the newspapers with then-Republican Senator Alfonse D'Amato's arm around her shoulder the day Chuck Schumer announced his Senate campaign, she couldn't understand why people were upset (*Newsday* 5/25/97).[10] Later, at the height of Schumer's 1998 Senate campaign, she steadfastly refused to endorse not only her friend Schumer, but also other Democratic candidates. "My staff gets exasperated with me; I don't give endorsements" (*Newsday* 11/1/98).[11]

In legislating, McCarthy likes to say she's above partisan politics. She has a rule: No bill goes out of her office without a Republican co-sponsor. McCarthy views the rule as her way of breaking through the political rhetoric that's marred her enjoyment of being a lawmaker. That bipartisan spirit was recognized when Gov. George Pataki signed an anti–gun violence bill in her district two months ago—despite being Republican (*Newsday* 10/31/00).

Nonpartisan or not, McCarthy has also had to cast some extremely difficult votes. So, as we might expect, given the nature of her district, votes on partial birth abortion techniques are controversial for her. In 1997, for example, she decided to vote not to prohibit such procedures despite the urging of advisors to take an easier way out with her constituents (*PIA* 2000, 921). McCarthy however agonized over the vote because, as is true of her attitude toward abortions more generally, she does not condone the procedure but was upset when the House leadership would not allow a vote on a measure that would have provided an exception in the ban to protect the health and future fertility of the mother (*Newsday* 5/25/97). "I don't support partial-birth abortion, but they pushed me into a corner" (*Newsday* 5/25/97). She explained:

> I started to think about all the things I've been trying to do. . . . I started to think about gun violence—all this stuff came into play. If we don't back the mothers, what are we doing? The mothers who are having children. And having women have children who don't want to have children—that's the cycle of violence, which contributes to child abuse, and all the other things that go with it. (*NYT* 6/22/97)

In response, "within a week, Nassau County District Attorney Denis Dillon criticized a local child abuse prevention group for asking her to speak at its annual meeting" (*Newsday* 5/25/97), and she has been confronted by constituents participating in the annual March for Life in Washington, D.C. (*NYT* 1/22/97).

Voting on the impeachment of President Clinton also proved a difficult decision for McCarthy. Though she would come to support the President on all four final votes, she was one of only thirty-one Democrats to vote for an initial inquiry against him late in 1998. "'This may be the toughest vote I ever cast,' she said after consulting academics, constituents and colleagues" (*Newsday* 10/10/98). After attending a women's caucus meeting to hear Mrs. Clinton, she stated, "'I think we have a constitutional obligation to investigate.' The House Judiciary Committee has outlined 15 potentially impeachable offenses in seeking authority to continue with its investigation. 'The only way we are going to bring this to a close is for the process to go forward. . . . I am convinced unless there is something else, these charges are not impeachable offenses'" (*Newsday* 9/16/98).

As a side note, it is interesting that the day after the vote, in the context of a gun control rally on the White House lawn, Mr. Clinton nevertheless offered campaign help to McCarthy (*Newsday* 10/10/98), and during the subsequent 1998 campaign, taped telephone messages from the president were played to all registered Democrats in the 4th district (*NYT* 11/5/98).

Discussion

The story of Congresswoman Carolyn McCarthy illustrates the way one amateur made a successful congressional career. It shows the interplay between local and national factors in any number of ways. McCarthy clearly advocates for ending gun violence at any level of government. The work she has done on behalf of education, veterans, or health care have local and national ramifications. As we have seen, though her opponents have charged that she focuses too much on the national at the expense of the local (*Newsday* 10/31/00), she has thus far successfully linked and integrated aspects of the local and the national.

Perhaps the most interesting aspect of McCarthy's home style, however, is her steadfast insistence on nonpartisanship and bipartisanship. It should be clear from the above profile that she is a sharp politician. Therefore, we should view her nonpartisanship in part as a political strategy and assess its benefits and costs. We have already examined its benefits: nonpartisanship helps McCarthy connect with citizens of the predominantly Republican 4th district and accords her a certain amount of legitimacy arising from being "above politics." (In fact, some charged that her 1998–2000 opponent, New York State Assemblyman Gregory Becker has "consistently taken easy, party-line votes and would contribute to Congress hyperpartisanship" [*Newsday* 10/29/98]). Consequently, as a member of the minority party, cooperation with the majority has enabled her to impact legislation. "I came to the realization this is going to take a while," she said of her gun control goals. "Once I accepted that, I started looking at networking: I'm going to make a lot of friends on both sides of the aisle and look at smaller issues, step by step" (*Newsday* 10/31/00).

So, earlier this term, she introduced a bill to fund stronger enforcement of existing gun laws. When the legislation languished, however, she put bits of the proposal in other bills and succeeded in getting funds for five hundred new federal agents to tackle gun problems (*Newsday* 10/31/00).

Similarly, each year, with the help of Republicans, she has inserted amendments in education bills, changing the way schools report violent incidents and building mentoring programs for teachers (*Newsday* 10/31/00). In addition, "the Children's Health Act passed Congress with her proposal to improve day care, the first step to funding criminal background checks of day care providers, renovating facilities to meet health standards and a host of other projects" (*Newsday* 10/31/00).

However, nonpartisanship has had its downside, a downside that serves as a reminder that McCarthy, as successful as she might be and as hard as she might work, simply represents a district of the opposite party. As Frisa had in 1996, Becker could charge that she was too liberal for the district ("including a vote against a ban on late-term abortions that had infuriated opponents of abortion rights in her district, which includes the headquarters of the Roman Catholic Diocese in Rockville Centre" [NYT 11/5/98]) and that she was a single-issue candidate (NYT 11/5/98):

> "I think the people of the district are asking, 'Where are the achievements?'" said Becker, 46, a deputy Hempstead planning commissioner from Lynbrook. "They realize gun control is a very important issue, but they realize that nothing has gotten done. The other issues that the people care about in the Fourth Congressional District are left by the wayside." (Newsday 10/31/00)

McCarthy has also been criticized for her nonpartisanship by Democrats who say that if she wants a longer career in Congress, she needs to clarify her party loyalty.

Most importantly, the downside of nonpartisanship is that one runs the risk of needing to activate core supporters, especially in an era when responsible parties are a key to success. In that sense, McCarthy's 1998 victory margin of 53 percent (four points less than two years before) "was a reality check. . . . I think everybody thought it was a walk in the park because I won by 16 points in the first election. Everybody liked me. It was like, 'Who would vote against me?' I had a hard time raising money. People thought I didn't need it and I didn't have a race'" (Newsday 10/31/00).

Similarly, a nonpartisan style could make it harder for an incumbent to defend behavior while in office. Some could, for instance, find McCarthy's overall voting record confusing. Her unwavering activity on behalf of gun violence clearly allies her with important Democrats from President Clinton on down, and her support for issues including partial birth abortion and an enlarged federal effort on behalf of education also place her firmly in the Democratic camp. In fact, "In her two terms, McCarthy has sided with the Democratic president about 70 percent of the time and with the Democratic Party about 82 percent of the time" (Newsday 10/31/00). However, McCarthy's presidential support for Clinton and party unity scores were, in fact, "[t]wo of the lowest percentages among New York Democrats. . . . McCarthy has bucked the Democrats several times this term, especially on tax issues" (*Newsday* 10/31/00). So, to protect herself from future misunderstanding as to the nature of her activities, McCarthy began sending out more mailings targeted at seniors, veterans, and other groups to tout her achievements (*Newsday* 10/31/00).

In sum, Congresswoman McCarthy's profile shows that even in an era of strong political parties, nonpartisanship still matters.

Conclusion

In this chapter, we have examined the home styles of three New York State representatives in an era of an increasingly responsible party system. While much has been written about the Washington side of the party equation, less is known about how national trends impact the average member of Congress. How do members integrate national partisan concerns into their home styles and how do their home styles, developed locally, impact the national context?

Our look at three representatives suggests a number of conclusions. To begin, even at a time when scholars and politicians alike focus attention on the notion of responsible parties, our case studies show the limits of a responsible party system. Of these three members, Sue Kelly, as the party loyalist and even party spokesperson, particularly in the 104th Congress, most closely fits the model. However, her pro-choice stand on abortion along with other positions demonstrates that even Kelly cannot be portrayed as simply a knee-jerk partisan blindly following leadership. Michael McNulty is the party insider who, not infrequently, votes more conservatively than the majority of his Democratic Party. Meanwhile, Carolyn McCarthy eschews partisan politics as much as possible.

These case studies also highlight the multidimensionality and complexity of "party." Allegiance to party involves more than agreement on issue stands. These representatives have taken on very different roles with respect to party, and for each congressperson, the relationship with party can be multifaceted. For instance, for McNulty, party not only connotes long-standing district roots but involves his relationship to the local Democratic organization, his national activity as a party whip, and his sometimes party-deviating set of issue positions. McCarthy may advocate nonpartisanship, even to the extent of refusing to endorse candidates of her own party, but she maintains her registration as a Republican while sitting in Congress on the Democratic side. Her nonpartisanship can be viewed as a political choice, which has the advantage of fitting with her district's needs, but has the downside of alienating potential partisan allies. Like McNulty, Kelly is involved in her party's whip system; unlike him, she has taken on the additional role of media spokesperson, thus attaining more national visibility.

The selection of a home style is, of course, a personal choice and these members have carved out varied roles with respect to party. Fenno (1978) has suggested that a combination of constituency factors and a member's background are determinants of home styles and we see these factors at work in the cases of these three representatives. Sue Kelly's strategy of jumping on the national bandwagon makes sense in light of her relatively well-off suburban constituency. Though not a solidly Republican district, hers is a district with a shifting population and a population concerned with issues highlighted by the Contract with America: smaller government, tax cuts, and balanced budgets. For Congresswoman Kelly, a strategy integrating local and national forces appears quite reasonable.

In turn, the solidly Democratic nature of McNulty's constituency, along with its strong party tradition, suggests that McNulty's activity on behalf of his party also makes sense. The character of his district gives him leeway to take positions that sometimes deviate from those of the national party, and his own preferences come into play as they impact the strength of his issue convictions and his preference for an insider strategy. For McCarthy, nonpartisanship may be a personal choice natural to an amateur politician, but it also makes political sense as a way for a Democrat in a Republican district to present herself to constituents.

Finally, these findings focus attention on the importance of context. McNulty, first elected to Congress in 1988, had his highest defection rate from party in the 104th Congress at the height of the Republican revolution. Sue Kelly, initially elected in the wake of the 1994 upheaval, took on the role of national party spokesperson. Partly as a reaction to her predecessor's zeal for the Contract with America, McCarthy, first elected in 1996, chose to downplay any form of partisanship. Even in the course of an eight-year span, members enter Congress under very different conditions and electoral tides and, in turn, these tides shape behavior.

Chapter 5

THE LOCAL-NATIONAL CONNECTION AND THE REPRESENTATION OF MINORITIES

(with Michael Rogers)

"We fought publicly with Jimmy Carter almost every day of his administration," William Clay (D-MO) recently said. "It's no different, Democrat or Republican. We will challenge anybody who seeks to undermine the basic interests of our people [African Americans]."
—Canon, *Race, Redistricting, and Representation*

"I see myself as participating in an effort to enhance the quality of life for all Americans," says Representative John Lewis (D-GA). "The point of the [civil rights] movement was to create in America a truly interracial democracy, so what affects one segment of the population affects all of us. So it's not a civil rights concern, it's a people issue."
—Canon, *Race, Redistricting, and Representation*

While New York's political presence in the House has been declining steadily over the past decades (forty-five House seats in 1960; twenty-nine after 2002), it has also witnessed the influx of a vibrant and vocal new political force in the country's largest metropolitan area, New York City. As New York has been forced to relinquish more and more House seats, it has also felt the modern push for increased minority representation. Nor, as we know, are these increases in minority populations unique to New York State. What is happening here may be particularly dramatic, but parallel trends are occurring across the nation. Clearly, our nation's population is becoming more diverse, and some estimates show that as early as fifty years

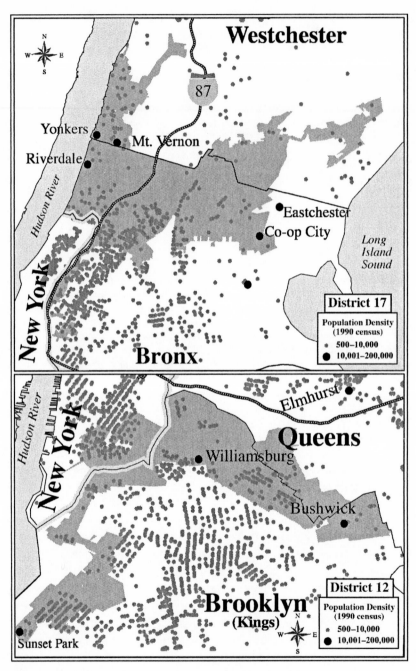

Map 4. Congressional Districts for Reps. Engel and Velazquez.

from now, Caucasians will no longer comprise the majority (*Population Bulletin* 6/00). Consequently, there is a growing push in many areas of American life—schools, the workplace, and, of course, politics—toward understanding and accommodating multiracial and multicultural perspectives.

In addition, changing sociopolitical roles hold out the potential for multiracial or multiethnic congressional districts unlikely just a few short decades ago. In the aftermath of the civil rights movement (forty "years ago the United States was a country in flames" [Farley and Allen 1987, 1]), the American political system has opened up to face the concerns not only of African Americans but also of women, Latinos, and other formerly underrepresented groups. This being the case, society faces difficult choices about sometimes competing values. Where "white" (male) Americans might have once been the only political force acknowledged by most members of Congress, today "white politicians cannot write off the black vote any longer. They cannot do it. The black vote in South Carolina may not elect by itself a United States senator, but that vote will decide who that United States senator will be," said Rep. Robin Tallon (SC) (qtd. in Swain 1993, 146–47). Turnout among African Americans, Latinos, and other underrepresented groups has been increasing (Miroff, Seidelman, and Swanstrom 1998, 109; 130), the support of minority constituents has been increasingly courted by "white" candidates ("Latinos, wooed energetically by both sides, are seeing and hearing Spanish-language ads and literature promising—as the Bush signs say—*un nuevo dia.*" [*Milwaukee Journal Sentinel,* 11/2/2000]) and the minority vote has been credited with impacting election outcomes, including helping President Clinton weather the impeachment storm in 1998 (Davidson and Oleszek 2002, 108).

Consequently, Congress today is a more diverse body than it was in the 1970s. The number of women and minorities has been steadily increasing so that the 107th House includes sixty-one women, thirty-six African Americans, nineteen Latinos, three Asian and Pacific Islanders, and one Native American (Davidson and Oleszek 2000, 127–28).

These new members have the potential to bring different perspectives to Congress, to shape the political agenda and to serve as role models (Carroll 2002; Fenno 2003; Gilligan 1982; Lublin 1997; Swain 1993; Thomas 1997). How, then, does a member of Congress, minority or white, represent a multiethnic or multiracial district? How does a legislator decide whether to fashion a home style around the needs of a select group of constituents (at the risk of alienating others) or to develop more broadly based appeals (at the risk of losing the support of core groups)?

The literature suggests that in these regards legislators representing minority (or multiracial) districts exhibit stylistic variation. Writing about two of the most notable African American representatives of their day (Adam Clayton Powell and William Dawson) James Q. Wilson (1960) described in the 1950s: "One is militant on the race question, the other is moderate. . . . One raises the race issue on every occasion; the other goes out of his way to avoid discussing race or race questions" (347). Fenno's Congressman F exhibited a home style based around his status as a national celebrity and civil rights activist (1978), but his profiles of four African American legislators indicate that some younger representatives engage in more inclusive home styles, sometimes downplaying race (Fenno 2003); see also Swain (1993) who examined representation in solidly African American as well as multiracial districts.

More recently, David Canon (1999) has provided a systematic attempt at understanding some of this variation. He has taken a useful distinction developed in the literature of political theory and has applied it to the representational styles members of Congress use in order to relate to constituents. Thus, as articulated by former Rep. William Clay (first quote, top of chapter), some members highlight the "politics of difference." Believing that descriptive representation is important and that the members of racial groups differ in experience and identity from non-group members, some minority legislators will represent their constituents by highlighting differences, group identity, and the concerns of a primary constituency. In contrast, other members, for instance, John Lewis (second quote top of chapter), practice a "politics of commonality," seeking to forge multiethnic or multiracial coalitions. Such members seek commonalities (constituency service, partisanship, etc.) against a background of diversity. As Cannon (1999) argues, for these representatives racial (or other) differences reflect only different interests and not fundamental differences in identity or shared experience. Such representatives, then, believe in the pluralism of the American political system or the all-inclusive nature of the American dream. As Streich describes this view, "[D]ifference is a problem and a source of conflict in community that threatens to undermine our communities, and commonality is the cure" (qtd. in Cannon 1999, 35). Thus, "commonality" members treat everyone as equal and work to include all citizens in the political process.

An additional issue remains: What does this discussion about alternative strategies for representing multiracial congressional districts have to do with the local-national distinction at the heart of this book? The answer is thought provoking. As if it weren't enough to balance the concerns of a primary and reelection constituency within a member's district, legislators representing diverse constituencies may be faced with equally important questions about how to balance the needs of group members not only from within but beyond the borders of their constituencies. Regardless of gender, ethnic, or racial affiliation, legislators representing constituencies including underrepresented groups may find their lives closely connected to groups and events outside their individual congressional districts:

> Three hundred people have been killed, shot—men, women and children—in Soweto. And you know, those people look just like you do. Our roots are in that part of the world. And we, as church people, have an obligation to be concerned about our brothers and sisters in that part of the world. (Congressman F, qtd. in Fenno 1978, 114–15)

More generally, "Surrogate representation" involves advocacy for individuals and groups outside the boundaries of a representative's district (Mansbridge 1998). And indeed, the literature provides some poignant examples:

> Before [Rep. Mickey] Leland's death, his district administrator told me: "What people don't understand is that Mickey Leland must be the congressman for the entire southwest. There isn't another black congressman in this general vicinity unless you go to the Deep South or the Midwest." (Swain 1993, 218)

> Upon arriving in the House, she [Rep. Lindy Boggs] discovered that "[c]ongresswomen are really surrogate mothers of congress for millions of women who feel they have no special voice in Washington." (Swain 1993, 178)

> Although every issue that affects the quality of life of Americans is of concern to the Congressional Hispanic Caucus, there are national and international issues that have a particular impact on the Hispanic community. The function of the Caucus is to serve as a forum for the Hispanic Members of Congress to coalesce around a collective legislative agenda. (http://www.house .gov/reyes/CHC/AboutCHC.htm)

Obviously, these issues and choices signify some of the most highly charged political questions of modern times. Thus, when in this chapter we compare the home styles of two New York representatives from multiethnic and multiracial congressional districts, we do so in hopes not of solving all or even most of the difficult issues considered above but, perhaps more importantly, of raising these increasingly common concerns in a modern context. As was true of earlier chapters, here we have several goals: in the context of commonality and difference, as well as choices about balancing local and national constituencies, we seek to understand both the home styles of 1990s members of Congress and the constituency and background factors contributing to those styles.

We compare and contrast the home styles of two congress people representing two of the "most multiracial and multiethnic districts in the nation." Eliot Engel, a "white" representative from the Bronx and Nydia Velazquez from Brooklyn, the first Puerto Rican native to be elected to Congress, both serve urban (New York City) districts. Both districts are overwhelmingly Democratic and both reflect racial politics, not only in their demographic makeup (see below) but also in their political experiences. Both members represent specially created majority-minority districts. Engel's district was dramatically altered in 1992 to satisfy court-ordered mandates, and Velazquez's district was explicitly created the same year to ensure Latino representation. Thus, though of differing ethnic backgrounds, both congresspeople must grapple with similar issues. The following descriptions illustrate how each congressperson's unique perspective has impacted the development of his/her home style.

Constituency

The geographic dimensions of both the 12th and 17th Congressional Districts grew out of the 1990s national redistricting. Many states were expected to observe the federal mandate to comply with the 1982 Voting Rights Act amendments with the goal of increasing the number of minority officeholders. Thus, state legislatures were required "to maximize the number of majority-minority" congressional districts (Saffell 1992). To meet this requirement in New York City, both the boroughs of Brooklyn and the Bronx underwent extensive redistricting. Plans were submitted that transformed the 12th district, changing it into at least "a 51 percent Hispanic majority by combining pieces of Brooklyn, Queens, and Manhattan" (*TU* 9/18/91), as well as redrawing Engel's overwhelmingly "white" district in the Bronx (see Map 4).

Such radical redistricting led to rather unusual district shapes. For example, Velazquez's 12th has been commonly known as the "Bullwinkle" district due to its resemblance to a moosehead (*PIA* 2000, 939; see Map 4). The 12th has thus been characterized as an example of ethnic gerrymandering at its most precise. "One in five Democrats in the district are in Queens, including largely Colombian and Dominican Corona and Elmhurst, and pieces of Maspeth and Ridgewood. Almost three in five are in Brooklyn, including Latino sections of Bushwick, Williamsburg and Sunset Park. The remaining fifth are on Manhattan's Lower East Side" (*Newsday* 8/27/92). "Stitched together, often by the thinnest of threads, were the heavily Puerto Rican Sunset Park neighborhood in Brooklyn and on the other side of the borough, Bushwick . . . the district is connected by cemeteries or parks in at least three places" (*Almanac* 2002, 1075).

Representing what turned out to be a 58 percent Latino area, Velazquez is also faced with one of the poorest (the 12th has a median income of $20,782, the state's third lowest, bottom third nationally) and least educated (12 percent college educated, twenty-ninth of of thirty-one in the state, bottom third nationally [*PIA* 2000, 939; see Table 5.1]). It is no surprise, then, though perhaps a bit of an exaggeration, that *Newsday* referred to the district as "probably the poorest congressional district in the nation" (*Newsday* 7/5/92). The basic concerns of this constituency, most of whose residents cannot even afford their own housing, as 84.7 percent are renters (*1992 House Races*), center around increased economic opportunities.

Representing such an impoverished district is challenging enough, but it becomes even more so when one considers the racial diversity of the 12th. In addition to the large (58%) Latino community—actually a mix of Puerto Ricans, Dominicans, Colombians, and Panamanians—the 12th also consists of an Asian population of 19.7% (actually the eighth largest in the nation [Takeda, 2001]), a Caucasian population of 14%, and an African American population of 9% (*PIA* 1994, 1056).[1] To make matters more confusing, the 12th was re-redistricted in 1998 so that its Latino population is now just under 50%. (Table 5.1)

In contrast, Engel's 17th covers the north Bronx and lower Westchester County; though the constituency lacks a name or a shape as colorful as "Bullwinkle," its character is every bit as interesting. "A middle- to working-class district where New York City runs into nearby suburbs, the 17th district covers the North Bronx, with tentacles reaching into the South Bronx and Westchester County" (*PIA*

TABLE 5.1 Constituency Characteristics and Election Results for Reps. Engel and Velazquez*

	Eliot Engel 17th(19th) District				Nydia Velazquez 12th District			
Ethnic Make-up	White	African American	Hispanic	Asian	White	African American	Hispanic	Asian
1998	29%	38%	28%	3%	26%	12%	49%	14%
1992**	40%	42%	29%	2%	14%	9%	58%	20%
1988	77%	13%	16%	—	—	—	—	—
Other Characteristics								
Pop./Sq. Mile	26,917				42,156			
Median Household Income (in thousands)	27.23				20.78			
Rank	22 of 31 in NY/Middle Third in US				29 of 31 in NY/Bottom Third in US			
College Educated	17%				12%			
Rank	23 of 31 in NY/Middle Third in US				29 of 31 in NY/Bottom Third in US			
White Collar Workers	60%				53%			
Rank	18 of 31 in NY/Middle Third in US				28 of 31 in NY/Bottom Third in US			
Blue Collar Workers	20%				31%			
Rank	18 of 31 in NY/Bottom Third in US				1 of 31 in NY/Bottom Third in US			

*Data found in CQ's *Politics in America*; years 1990, 1992,1994,1996,1998, and 2000.

**Totals greater than 100%. Numbers for %White in New York City were inflated because many Latinos chose to self-classify as White rather than Hispanic.

TABLE 5.1 *(continued)*

Election Year	Eliot Engel 17th(19th) District			Nydia Velazquez 12th District		
	Engel General	Primary	District Vote for President Democrat	Velazquez General	Primary	District Vote for President Democrat
2000	89%	49%	71%	86%	77%	81%
1998	88%	85%	—	84%	Unopposed	—
1996	85%	77%	85%	85%	Unopposed	85%
1994	78%	61%	—	92%	82%	—
1992	80%	74%	76%	77%	33%	68%
1990	61%	72%	—	—	—	—
1988	56%	48%	—	—	—	—

2000, 953). To appreciate the impact redistricting has had on district politics, we need only consider the constituency's makeup at the time of Engel's first election in 1988. To say the least, the old 19th reflected an interesting mix: "Different ethnic groups were clustered here and there, Irish in Kingsbridge, Italians in Bedford Park, well-to-do WASPs and Jews in Riverdale" (*Almanac* 1996, 948). (For homemade pasta and freshly baked pastries, head to the Bronx's Little Italy on Belmont and Arthur Avenues).[2]

Interestingly, the district also includes other ethnic groups such as Albanians and additional Eastern Europeans. Finally, though a distinct minority, concentrations of African American and Latino neighborhoods rounded out the picture in the old 19th. As one might expect from the segregation of the neighborhoods, community ties among these groups have been described as unusually strong (*PIA* 1998, 1011).

The 17th is still diverse but the district has taken on a different character. The ethnic diversity still remains among whites, but the racial and ethnic proportions have changed dramatically; where the district was formerly 77% white, it is now approximately 30% white, 30% Latino, and 40% African American. To preview the upcoming profile, imagine what these changes might mean for Representative Engel, who is both white and Jewish.

As with Velazquez, Engel's district is largely urban with upward of twenty-six thousand people per square mile. However, as the much lower population density indicates (Table 5.1), the district includes areas that could more accurately be described as suburban on the northern edges (see Map 4). With a median income of $27,227 (twenty-second of thirty-one in the state, middle third nationally), and a college graduation rate of 17 percent (twenty-third of thirty-one in the state, middle third nationally), constituents are notably better off.

As a consequence of these demographics, both Engel and Velasquez have extremely solid Democratic reelection constituencies. Indeed, to say that both the 12th and 17th districts are Democratic is an understatement. For instance, over the last decade, the lowest percentage of votes that a Democratic candidate for a major electoral position— whether the presidency, the House, the Senate, or the governorship— has received from the 12th district was 58.7 percent in 1986. Even more striking is the fact that most of these voting levels are upward of 70 percent (*CDs in the 1990s*, 515). Similarly, "Long a Democratic-voting district, the 17th consistently elects Democrats to all levels of government" (*PIA* 2000, 953). So, Engel has won his last several general election contests by upward of 80 percent of the vote. President Clinton's winning percentages were 76 percent and 85 percent in 1992 and 1996 respectively, and Gore's 2000 winning percentage was 71 percent (*PIA* 2002, 667).

In sum, perhaps as an indication of a future America, it is apparent that unusual ethnic and racial diversity reflect the predominant characteristic of these congressional districts. Both are urban and Democratic. However, Engel's constituents are economically somewhat better off and, if possible, are more ethnically and racially diverse. As we consider the profiles of these representatives below, it will become evident how these constituency differences combined with the member's personal backgrounds have led to the development of substantially different home styles.

Eliot Engel: Bringing Together Difference

> In a 1996 interview with National Public Radio, Representative Engel recalled an incident that occurred the day after his initial election to the New York State Assembly in 1977. He explained: "My phone rang—in fact, it was very early in the morning, and it woke me up—and it was a woman who told me that she was having a problem with her landlord and she was told that I could help her, and the problem was that her toilet bowl was overflowing and nobody would come to help her, and I said to her, Would you like me to come over with a plunger?"
> —National Public Radio 10/13/96.

Although an amusing oversimplification, the above anecdote provides an initial view of the home style adopted by Eliot Engel, a home style that in large part deals with the major differences in his diverse district by treating all constituents equally. By focusing on issues, by highlighting partisanship and, most importantly, by engaging in frequent and very personal constituency service, he reaches out to large numbers of constituents, sometimes highlighting their differences, but more often seeking to find commonalities and assure equal treatment.

Background

As is true in most of the case studies of this book, Engel's prepolitical career would have a strong impact on what would become his home style. Born in 1947, he is a self-described "son of the Bronx" (*Almanac* 2000, 1145). This characterization would appear to be accurate. Growing up in an Eastchester housing project (*Newsday* 8/14/93), he attended Bronx public schools, obtained a BA in history from Hunter College, an MA in Guidance Counseling from Lehman College, and a law degree (1987) from New York Law School. In addition, he absorbed important aspects of the local culture, for instance expressing the lifelong love of baseball he acquired from growing up in proximity to Yankee Stadium. "To me, I'm still in awe of baseball players. It makes you feel like you're 10 years old again" (*AP Wire* 2/2/95).

Son of a labor leader, Engel got involved in politics early (*WSJ* 6/11/96). A "political junkie" (*Almanac* 1998, 1012), he could, even as a child, recite the names of all one hundred senators, and he paid attention to what was happening in Congress. For example, one of his political heroes, albeit an unlikely one for a New Yorker coming of age during the civil rights movement in the 1960s, was long-time Congress member Jamie Whitten "who spent 52 years papering his home district in Mississippi with federal projects" (*WSJ* 6/11/96). As we will see, such examples would come to influence the home style Engel would adopt later when he was elected to the House.

So, it is not surprising that as a young man, Engel worked as a union organizer and a Democratic leader in what would become his home base, the unique multiracial and multiethnic housing complex known as Co-Op City. This Bronx housing complex is composed of thirty-five, 35-story buildings (population over fifty thousand) (*Almanac* 2000, 1144), and it has been characterized as a racial and ethnic microcosm of the district (*PIA* 1994). Expanding on crucial backing from the Jewish community in the area and political mentors (including former Congress member James Scheuer [*The Hotline,* 5/6/92]), Engel developed his base. He became identified with the "reform" (rather than the "machine") wing of a sometimes notably factionalized and partisan Bronx Democratic Party (*Newsday* 10/31/88). Therefore, "In 1977, when a state assemblyman was forced from office by criminal charges, Mr. Engel—a high school history teacher—saw his chance. He risked his $7,000 life savings, won by 103 votes and absorbed a key lesson: 'I learned: every vote counts'" (*WSJ* 6/11/96).

Ironically, twelve years later, Engel would move up the political ladder and obtain his congressional seat by challenging another incumbent under criminal investigation. To understand the magnitude of Engel's 1988 effort, one has to appreciate the unusual stature and almost legendary status of his predecessor, incumbent Mario Biaggi, within the district. Biaggi had been a ten-term incumbent, a decorated police officer, a New York City mayoral candidate (*Almanac* 1990, 851) and even a nominee for the Nobel Peace

Prize in 1978 for his work on behalf of peace in Ireland (*Newsday* 9/6/88). However, in 1987, Biaggi was convicted of accepting "illegal gratuities" (*PIA* 2002, 703). His name remained on the ballot in 1988 even though he had actually resigned his office several months before the election (in August), following another conviction, this time for his role in the Wedtech scandal (*PIA* 1990, 1050). (After an early release from jail, Biaggi actually made another run in 1992.)

In addition, the factionalized nature of Democratic Party politics in the area played a considerable role in the election. Understandably, critics alleged that Biaggi's name was being purposely kept on the ballot in hopes of a Biaggi victory followed by a forced resignation. Bronx party "bosses" could then circumvent normal electoral procedures and could appoint his successor. Indeed, these unusual circumstances combined with his background in reform politics gave Engel a solid campaign theme, and Engel supporters argued that their candidate's "independence of the machine politics that are the trademark of the Bronx will be a refreshing change" (*Newsday* 10/13/88).

Thus, it is apparent that Engel is steeped in the culture of his district. In the capacity of a long-time professional politician, his career also reflects the factional politics of his district. More importantly, he seems to have learned from them the importance of each individual to ensuring favorable electoral outcomes. It is not surprising, then, that the home style he would adopt would place a premium on service to individual constituents and would prioritize district concerns.

Home Style

In the 1996 NPR interview quoted earlier, Engel elaborated:

> A traffic light for instance, a mailbox, help with social security or food stamps, someone buys something from a store and they won't give them a total refund; anything like that we roll up our sleeves and try to help. . . . I think that elected officials are really required to provide constituent services. That's what the people back home look for, and I think that if you've helped someone in your district with a personal problem or community concern, even if that person doesn't agree with your voting record a hundred percent, that person will overlook the issues on which you disagree because that constituent knows that you'll be there when they need help. (NPR 10/13/96)

Similarly, Engel's Web site is quite personal and constituency-oriented. It begins with a welcoming message:

> I have decided to call the page "Engel's Angle" because I would like to give you an idea of who I am and how the changes in Washington, DC are affecting the Bronx and Westchester. . . . The most common problems my constituents face relate to federal programs such as social security, Medicare, federal pensions, veterans benefits, student financial aid, small business loans and immigration visa assistance. . . . My district staff is trained and available to help you with these or other community or individual concerns. (www . . . engel)

Engel thus takes a personal approach with constituents. For instance, in his first term, he opened three district offices (Biaggi had two) and after the 1992 redistricting, he increased the number to five (*Newsday* 3/9/93).

Engel and his staff deal with "difference" by offering to help any constituent regardless of race or ethnicity. Indeed, the interactions Engel has had with constituents provide some surprisingly moving interchanges. For instance, Engel participated in a ceremony naming a neighborhood square in honor of a long-time local activist deceased at age thirty-eight (*Newsday* 9/10/92).

He also helped the family of an African American marine killed in Saudi Arabia obtain a more thorough investigation of the soldier's death. While initially blamed on the Saudis, the death turned out to be a racially motivated shooting by another American, and the family charged the government with covering up the incident (*Newsday* 1/16/91).

The plight of a noted AIDS physician forced to return to his Peruvian homeland led Engel to advocate for immigration reform (*Newsday* 6/5/92). Finally, over an extended period of time, Engel, along with other Congress members, led the effort to inquire into the fates of several Americans missing in Cyprus. He not only won the plaudits of Greek and Cypriot interest groups, but he also captured the affection of the families. Of Engel, a father of one of the missing persons said simply: "I love that man" (*Newsday* 3/15/98).

Yet, other constituent interactions are downright funny. For example, one of Engel's constituents regularly sends him alternate designs for the United States flag. An Engel staffer offered that these designs are always sent to the appropriate governmental office, although the staffer acknowledged that he did not always know what office this might be (*Newsday* 7/23/92).

Engel himself has found some novel ways to achieve constituent visibility. On "lobby days," he hangs out around ground floors of high-rise buildings, greeting constituents and handling their problems. For example:

> Mr. Engel seems sincere when, in a Bronx lobby, he spends 15 minutes with a woman and her disabled son who have been denied aid by a confusing federal bureaucracy. "Bring your W-2 form . . . and don't forget I'll be there until 2 o'clock," he says scheduling her for an office visit. (*WSJ* 6/11/96)

Also, since his freshman year in Congress, "political junkie" Engel has established a tradition and has made it a point to get an aisle seat for the presidential State of the Union messages. From that vantage point, he not only can achieve visibility but can be seen shaking hands with presidents. Though some constituents have complained that this is Engel's only congressional mark, he claims that any number of people remember him for this practice (*Newsday* 1/26/94).

Engel helps constituents on a larger scale as well. For example, he intervened with the Federal Communications Commission (FCC) when Fordham University, a beneficiary of public funds, was prohibited from broadcasting a popular Catholic mass on grounds of separation of church and state (*Newsday* 10/18/93). He arranged funding for the distribution of drug prevention booklets throughout the Bronx school system (*Newsday* 12/2/92). At the height of a nationwide rash of arson attempts on African American churches, Engel sponsored a conference educating his Bronx constituents about arson prevention (*Newsday* 2/30/96). "'The people of goodwill will make sure these acts of violence don't rear their ugly heads anywhere here,' Engel said" (*Newsday* 7/30/96).

All in all, by 1994, Engel claimed to have brought $365 million in federal funds and grants to his district (*Newsday* 9/8/94). As he expressed it, "I've been bringing home the bacon for a long time" (*Newsday* 9/8/94).

A second element of Engel's home style involves his issue focus. He proclaims an "unabashed interest in international affairs" (*PIA* 1996, 925). Given this interest, it is not surprising that he takes positions on the gamut of concerns relevant to the needs of his multiethnic district and, in his voting record, he is described as reliably liberal (*PIA* 2000, 952–53; *Almanac* 2000, 1145).

Following from the needs of his ethnic constituency and his own predilections, Engel is a foreign policy activist and a "liberal interventionist . . . [on] humanitarian tragedies" (*PIA* 2002, 702). Most notably, he has become a leader in advocating for the human and political rights for the Albanian minority in Kosovo (*Newsday* 3/5/98). He explained in an editorial:

> Kosovo is a region of the former Yugoslavia populated by an overwhelming majority of ethnic Albanians, yet dominated by the Serbian government in Belgrade. Although the Dayton accord ended the armed conflict in Bosnia, it did not address Kosovo—and now tensions are rising. Human rights groups describe the situation there as desperate. (*Newsday* 5/17/96)

Thus, he is one of the founders and co-chairs of the congressional Albanian Issues Caucus and has traveled extensively throughout the region. Indeed, in addition to his normal travels, an unusual incident took place. A Congressional delegation that he was leading was stopped at the border and was barred from entering Kosovo. "It's an absolute disgrace. If you are not letting three American congressman come to your country, it must mean that you have something to hide" (*Newsday* 3/22/98).

One newspaper summarized Engel's advocacy: "The Kosovo issue has been kept alive in Washington by a small group of congressmen led by Rep. Eliot L. Engel" (*Washington Post* qtd. on www . . . engel).

Similarly, Engel was an "early advocate for United States intervention in the civil war in Yugoslavia" (*PIA* 2000, 953), and he has co-chaired the Congressional Peace Accord Monitoring Group for the Dayton treaty.

As Engel's interest in Albanian concerns stems in part from the Eastern European populations in his district, other of his foreign policy interests also fit with the diverse character of the 17th. Indeed, one may come to appreciate what it means to represent such a diverse constituency by considering his foreign policy concerns. Thus, Engel has been a consistent supporter of the State of Israel and an advocate for Jewish interests. "He was the prime sponsor of the 1990 resolution to recognize Jerusalem as the capital of Israel" (*Almanac* 2000, 1145). A few years later, like many supporters of Israel leery of a U.S.-Palestinian relationship in Jerusalem, Engel was "concerned at the idea of having an office dealing with Palestinians anywhere in Jerusalem. Congress views Jerusalem as the undivided capital of Israel, and an AID [Agency for International Development] office there would have a negative impact" (*Newsday* 6/25/94). In addition, he attended the funeral of Yitzhak Rabin (*U.S. Newswire* 11/6/96) and has been a member of several other congressional delegations to Israel (*U.S. Newswire* 11/6/96; *Federal News Service* 9/4/97). He has focused on Nazi war criminals and repayments for thefts occurring under the Nazi regime, and he has spoken out against a proposed shopping mall on the outskirts of the site of the Auschwitz concentration camp (*Newsday* 2/22/98). Most recently, Engel responded to what he termed the "show trial" of several Iranian Jews accused of espionage in Iran. "I am outraged . . . the only 'crime' that these people have committed is the 'crime' of being Jewish . . . the Iranian government must understand that there is a price to pay for . . . these phony trials" (www . . . engel).

Engel has also supported the rights of the Catholic minority in Northern Ireland and has shown concern for Irish illegal aliens in his district (*Almanac* 2000, 1145). He attended Nelson Mandela's inauguration in South Africa. Along with other New York members of Congress, he has publicized the internment of Italian Americans during World War II (*Denver Post* 6/28/97) and, as had his predecessor, he has regularly sponsored a bill designating October as Italian American Cultural Heritage Month (*Almanac* 2000, 1145). He has been concerned about human rights violations in Haiti (*PIA* 1996) and has sponsored a Cuban Democracy Act (*Federal News Service* 2/5/92).

From this, one can see that there are clear advantages to representing such a multiethnic district. Diversity can cause problems, but the above list of foreign policy concerns demonstrates that ethnic interests can be quite segmented. Standing up for the needs and concerns of one group does not conflict with championing other causes. Engel's liberal ideology provides the glue to these diverse positions, and the segmented concerns of his constituents make his job easier.

Though retaining his foreign policy focus after redistricting in 1992, Engel has also begun to emphasize domestic concerns. Consequently, he has had a somewhat unorthodox committee career within Congress. While many freshmen begin with a bread-and-butter domestic committee, Engel was initially assigned to his first choice, Foreign Affairs. Soon after, he tried for assignment to the then–Post Office and Civil Service committee to serve the large number of government employees in his district. Because he voted against a 1989 congressional pay raise considered by the committee, he was denied a seat on this otherwise low-prestige panel (*Newsday* 3/5/90). However, in 1993 he received a seat on Education and Labor (*PIA* 1996, 925), and four years later he was assigned to the prestigious Energy and Commerce Committee—this "reward" coming because of his high degree of party loyalty in the 104th Congress (*PIA* 2000, 952).

In general, "His record on behalf of labor, civil rights and children reflects the concerns of his district" (*Newsday* 9/9/92). He has been described as "pro-choice all the way" (*Newsday* 8/22/92), has advocated for prescription drug plans ("When the Medicare program was put into affect 35 years ago, people weren't living as long, so people didn't think of prescription drugs. Now it's important. So we need to do that" [NPR 9/3/00]), and has been a consistent supporter of public broadcasting. He advocates for "protecting the health rights of New Yorkers and all Americans," and he also supports "safe, affordable housing for New Yorkers" (www . . . engel). ("It is also vital that affordable rental property be made available for lower-income families and that those families are empowered to move toward home ownership—one of the foundations of strong families and healthy communities in the United States" [www . . . engel]).

As he provides fairly detailed statements of issue positions and accomplishments on his Web site, he presents himself as a member up-to-date on constituency concerns. For instance, when the much-publicized trial of four white police officers accused of killing who turned out to be an unarmed African American male in his apartment doorway was moved out of the Bronx, Engel responded: "Moving the Diallo trial out of the Bronx is offensive to both the Bronx and its people and to justice. . . . In a borough of over 1 million citizens, or if necessary, a City of more than 7 million, it would not be so difficult to find 12 fair and honest people" (www . . . engel).

Similarly, he has supported providing intravenous drug users with clean hypodermic needles to prevent the spread of HIV/AIDS. "I am as opposed to drugs as the next person, but I also live in the real world. I represent an area of New York City—Bronx—where AIDS has just gone sky-high, and we need to use every available resource that we have to try to combat the scourge of AIDS" (*PIA* 2000, 952).

Finally, the bills Engel has sponsored also reflect the needs of his district. Included in the approximately twenty bills he sponsors each congress are such issues as:

Social Security:
- expanding nursing facilities and coverage
- hospitals with a high number of Medicaid patients should not lose a disproportionate share of reimbursement

Education:
- flexibility for counties in spending federal funds

- training of qualified veterans to take on positions of responsibility and serve as role models in public housing projects

Transportation:
- noise limits on airplanes
- equal pricing on rental cars regardless of location (inner city or suburbs)

Unemployment:
- extending the number of weeks of eligibility for emergency unemployment

Broadcasting:
- more bilingual and multilingual programming
- an office for diversity within the FCC

Consistent with his liberal issue positions and a focus on commonality, strong Democratic loyalty has additionally been a hallmark of Engel's home style. He was elected president of his Democratic House freshman class in 1988 (*Newsday* 9/9/92). His party unity scores generally range from the middle eighties to low nineties and achieved their high of ninety-six at the height of the 104th Congress in 1995. His rhetoric, too, at times can be quite partisan. For example, he has labeled Republicans "mean-spirited extremists who are bent on destroying Medicare and Medicaid" (*Almanac* 1998, 1012). He labeled Republican proposals for school vouchers and private education savings accounts "a hollow choice" weighted to subsidize private and religious schools with taxpayer dollars (*DN* 10/28/97). He expressed extreme crankiness with the partisan politics in 1995: "We all were very tired. . . . I haven't spent much time with my family or my constituents. Doing that is better than going to work at 8 A.M. and knocking off at 12 midnight with the Republicans setting the agenda" (*Newsday* 8/17/95).

Finally, Engel has expressed his party loyalty in the face of happier circumstances. He joked about the wedding announcement of then-Republican representatives Susan Molinari and Bill Paxon (both New York): "The Bible says be fruitful and multiply . . . I wish them in the future many healthy happy children. And may they all grow up to be good Democrats" (*TU* 8/6/93).

The Clinton impeachment hearings provide a final example, not only of Engel's party loyalty, but of the reinforcing effects of the elements of his home style. As we might expect, Engel was a staunch Clinton supporter, and his tradition of taking a seat on the aisle for the State of the Union message took on additional significance in light of the impeachment controversy: "Today, more than ever, I find it important to take my seat on the aisle, as I have for nine years," Engel said before the speech in 1998. "I think Bill Clinton has been a good president; he's a friend of mine, and I stand by him" (*PIA* 2000, 952). As we might expect, too, he traced this support in part back to the opinions of his constituents:

> I attended many, many barbecues and parades yesterday myself because I have a primary on Tuesday, so I'm running for re-election, and all the people in my district think that the president ought to stay in office. They don't like the Ken Starr witch hunt against him and they really think he's doing a good job as president and they support him. (CNN 9/13/98)

Discussion

Engel's home style, then, is forged on the basis of his own roots and personal identification with the Bronx, constituency service, issue positions, and partisanship. The elements of his home style have not only helped him win and retain his congressional seat, but they have far-reaching implications as well for modern politics. In this district, emphasizing constituency service and accessibility to all implies equal treatment for a broad spectrum of Americans. Taking issue positions also implies equal treatment for all as it entails taking the concerns of diverse groups, treating them equally, and representing them in Washington. Identification with the district means embracing differences and looking to find commonalities that transcend them. In that sense, Engel and representatives like him are covering new ground. With the increased impact of minority groups in politics, Engel is faced with the challenges of bringing these groups together and of forging sometimes-unusual coalitions. "Even if they disagree with me on the issues, if they meet me, they'll vote for me. I want to meet people all the time" (*Almanac* 1998, 1012).

However, in this heterogeneous district, Engel is simply at a descriptive disadvantage. He has faced a primary challenge in all six of his reelection runs (Table 5.1), squeaking by in 2000 with 49 percent of the vote. In

1994, Latin music icon and Latino advocate Willie Colon ably summed up the argument for demographic representation: "The people of the district need someone who is going to represent them a little more actively—somebody who knows who they are, who can see they are not invisible" (*Newsday* 7/24/94). In 2000, well-credentialed state senator and African American advocate Larry Seabrook extended the argument: "Our community needs real leadership on the pressing, urgent issues of education and job training and affordable housing and affordable health care" (*DN* 9/27/00). "The incumbent believes himself to be associated with our community. I think a representative should be a part of a community. But he is not" (*NYT* 5/12/00). "He's making it [race] an issue. This isn't about race. It's about new leadership," Seabrook said (*NYP* 6/19/00).

The fact that Engel received strong local and national financial backing from labor and Jewish groups in his 2000 primary (*DN* 6/2/00) substantiates this point: as much as a member of Congress might expand his or her base and attempt to treat all constituents equally, demographic loyalties can still counteract these pressures.

Too, as is clear from the Biaggi elections, politicians in the 17th district appear to be identified with one or more Democratic Party factions. Thus, Engel has often become embroiled in local political controversies. He has taken sides in party nomination contests in both Co-Op City and the Bronx (*DN* 5/7/96; *Newsday* 6/28/94). In some cases, his electoral fortunes have even been tied to political trends in and around the larger New York City area (NPR 9/3/00). Therefore, the 17th is a difficult district due to race and ethnicity but also due to factionalized politics.

There is evidence, too, that Engel may have contributed in small increments to the numerical disadvantages he faces, and, over time, critics of his home style have been quite vocal, perhaps more vocal than appears warranted in the face of objective evidence. For instance, he has made a decision to move his family to the Washington area and has purchased a residence in an upper-class Maryland suburb; critics charge this environment keeps him out of touch with the needs of his urban district (*Yonkers Herald Statesman* 6/14/94). Even more, Engel may leave (or may be perceived as leaving) too much to others. As we have seen, his Web site offers that he and his "trained staff" are available to constituents, and staffers often serve as Engel spokespeople in news clippings. To the extent that constituents (particularly members of excluded groups) need to interact with their Congress members at a more personal level, such reliance on staff may be counterproductive.

In addition, though Engel's concerns have broadened to include domestic matters, he remains focused on foreign policy. While such a focus may meet the needs of some ethnically oriented constituents and may enhance his personal interests, such a focus may nevertheless prove less satisfactory to his minority constituents.

Despite these difficulties, it should be clear from this profile that Engel has achieved a pretty good fit with his multiethnic district. His willingness to interact with and to stand up for constituents has led to a loyal following and to a reasonably successful home style.[3]

Thus, what lessons do we take away from Engel's home style? First, we see modern politics at work; a multiethnic, multiracial district such as the 17th would have simply been less likely to exist in the 1970s, the time of Fenno's initial work. Even a few short decades ago, minority constituents would have had less of a voice. Consequently, the 2000 primary highlights inevitable tensions between descriptive and substantive representation—Engel doesn't "look" like a majority of his constituents. While he seems able to provide adequate substantive representation, the need of many to be represented more symbolically is an existing tension in the district.

Second, the 1990s have allowed Engel to take advantage of new opportunities within Congress: in this day and age, a relatively junior member can be a leader on the foreign policy issues he cares about. When those issues come to the fore, Engel's visibility increases. His particular slant on foreign policy is a concern for human rights and the rights of minorities, and these, again, are new issues.

A final example sums up Engel's efforts to bring constituents together. His Web site features an interesting photo gallery. Engel is pictured with a variety of national and international leaders: President Clinton, Yitzhak Rabin, Nelson Mandela, and Coretta Scott King. He is also pictured with multiracial groups of his own Bronx constituents (www . . . engel). He is clearly attempting to show all his constituents that he appreciates their concerns and that he makes room for them in his efforts.

Nydia Velazquez: Latino Culture Drives the Politics of the 12th

Upon her initial election in 1992, Nydia Velazquez stated that she was going to go to Congress with a "double mission": first, to represent the constituents of her newly created 12th district of New York and, second, to speak for the interests of the larger Latino/Puerto Rican community, which needed a greater voice in the national legislature (*Newsday* 9/25/92). The fact that a local paper described the victory celebration as "Latinos, Asians, Muslims, and Whites sitting around drinking black coffee, Cerveza Corona and eating arroz con gandules" is indicative of her efforts on behalf of a large and diverse local community (*New York Amsterdam News* 9/19/92). However, the welcoming banner opening her Web site, "BIENVENIDOS," highlights her Latino heritage and the broader focus of a national movement. Thus, the story of how Velazquez perceives herself as fulfilling this double mission not only raises interesting dilemmas about the representation of minorities but also highlights the importance of a primary constituency, the connections between local and national concerns, and the challenges facing a female representative in a male-dominated culture.

Background

In some respects, Velazquez's route to political office is not unlike that taken by many other politicians. She had been a legislative aide to Representative Ed Towns in the early 1980s, had filled out the unexpired term of a New York City Council member (1984), and had subsequently worked in the political arena as director of the Department of Puerto Rican Community Affairs in the United States, a cabinet-level post under then–Puerto Rican Governor Rafael Hernandez Colon (Web bio). In that capacity, she coordinated the work of several regional offices, turned the organization "into a one-stop cultural, social, and legal assistance center for Puerto Ricans in the States" (www.hisp.com/oct95) and conducted a major voter registration drive ("Atrevete") of an estimated two hundred thousand voters prior to the 1992 campaign (*PIA* 1994).

However, Velazquez's career takes on added significance when we appreciate that very few Latinos, let alone Latinas, rise through these political ranks. In fact, Nydia Velazquez was used to being "first" (Margolies-Mezvinsky 1994, 14–16). Born the first of twins (*Newsday* 9/26/92) in the poor, sugar cane community of Yabucoa, Puerto Rico, she begged her parents to let her start school at age five, two years before the required age (*NYT* 9/27/92). After skipping several grades, she became the first member of her family to graduate from high school, the first to complete college (Magna Cum Laude from Puerto Rico University in Rio Pedras at age sixteen) and taught in Puerto Rico (*NYT* 9/27/92).

Recalling that conversation at the family dinner table revolved around issues including Puerto Rican Statehood and workers rights, Velazquez acquired a passion for politics early. "I always wanted to be like my father," she explained, noting that the elder Velazquez was something of a political activist, making speeches from the back of a truck and even founding a local political party (*NYT* 9/27/92).

After persuading the family that she should take advantage of a scholarship and go to New York City (*NYT* 9/27/92), she earned her master's in political science from New York University (1976), subsequently teaching as an adjunct professor of Puerto Rican studies at the City University of New York at Hunter College.

Thus, Velazquez's interest in politics and the name recognition she acquired through her work as an activist and the voter registration drives made her a natural candidate for the congressional seat in the newly created 12th district. However, as some scholars have argued, and as is true of many new majority-minority districts (Canon, Schousen, and Sellers 1996), the race would be a hard-fought one, raising pertinent issues about demographic representation. For instance, does the demographic character of majority-minority districts mean that a member of the "majority" race or ethnicity is best able to "represent" the district? What credentials might an "appropriate" Latino candidate have to "qualify" as a representative, and how should divisions among Latino candidates be taken into account?

Further, it was by no means a foregone conclusion that Velazquez, or for that matter any other Latino candidate, would come to occupy the seat. Velazquez competed in the primary not only against other credible Latino candidates but also against nine-term incumbent Stephen Solarz, who had been redistricted and who decided to run as an outsider in the 12th. As observers described him as one of the most effective leaders in the 102nd Congress, as a prime sponsor of the Gulf War Resolution, and as an active contributor to the worldwide movement toward emerging democracies (*Almanac* 1994), his candidacy had to be taken seriously. Interestingly, Solarz argued that he would provide important substantive representation for the district. Thus, although he didn't actually speak Spanish (he said he would learn if elected), he argued that "down in Washington they speak English" (*Newsday* 8/27/92). But Solarz had obvious weaknesses in the Latino community, and the term "carpetbagger" was thrown at him quite frequently (*PIA* 2000, 940). Velazquez countered, "You don't know our language, and I don't mean Spanish, but the language of oppression" (*PIA* 2000, 940).[4]

In addition, other Latino candidates, including Elizabeth Colon of the Association of Puerto Rican Executive Directors and Reuben Franco, President of the Institute for Puerto Rican Policy, were interested in the seat, clearly providing a source of concern as well as an opportunity. The concern, of course, was that a large field of candidates would dilute the Latino vote, giving the "carpetbagger" the victory. The opportunity was the field of very credible candidates, all of whom received endorsements from influential politicians (*Almanac* 1994; *Newsday* 8/27/92; *NYT* 9/25/92; *Newsday* 9/16/92). Most particularly, Velazquez was described as following a progressive agenda, with a desire to bring more federal funds to enhance economic development (*NYT* 9/17/92) and a willingness to take controversial positions on the Left (supporting a strike of *Daily News* workers and opposing Mayor Dinkins's plans for an incinerator at the site of the now-defunct Brooklyn Navy Yard [*NYT* 9/17/92]).

The highly charged nature of the ethnic tensions surfacing during the campaign can be appreciated from an analysis of one candidate debate (*Newsday* 8/27/92). From *Newsday's* description, it is clear that this was not a normal unemotional recitation of issue positions. Members of the audience engaged in pushing matches, the candidates had to shout at each other to be heard, and the moderator had to repeatedly call for quiet. While Solarz, speaking through an interpreter, touted his experience, hecklers shouted at "the Jew" to go home. The Latinos, in turn, disagreed on a number of issues that would be, to say the least, unusual political topics in other congressional districts, such as which candidate's ties to the Island of Puerto Rico were too close and which candidate spoke better English (*NYT* 11/2/92).

A final matter that surfaced in the campaign involved a personal attack on Velazquez's character. Shortly before Election Day 1992, medical records were anonymously faxed to a local newspaper indicating that Velazquez had almost done the unthinkable and had attempted suicide a year earlier. The pressures accruing from all these "firsts" and from being a doubly disadvantaged minority took their toll, and she had taken an overdose of pills (*Newsday* 10/10/92). Surprisingly, instead of ending her life and/or her political career, this act gave her the strength and conviction to push forward:

> After it happened, when I woke up in the hospital, I realized that I was still alive. The first thought that came into my mind was, God wants me here, and he wants me here for a reason. And that day when I woke up, I knew that I was coming here, that I was coming to Congress. (Margolies-Mezvinsky 1994, 39)[5]

Even more, observers point to Velazquez's use of a grassroots-style campaign—a type of campaign we might expect to be most successful in a newly majority-minority district. Thus, Velazquez's campaign concentrated on "door-to-door organizing and coalition building" (*Newsday* 9/17/92). She even visited residents in extremely poor housing projects who probably were not used to meeting congressional candidates (*Newsday* 7/5/92). Dennis Rivera of the Coalition for a New New York probably sums up the flavor of the campaign: "In this most important congressional campaign (Velazquez) in the United States we put together the most massive get-out-the-vote campaign New York has seen in a very long time" (*Newsday* 11/9/92). Ultimately, Velazquez won the primary with 33 percent of the vote to Solarz's 27 percent and Colon's 26 percent. She was subsequently victorious not only in the 1992 general election (with 77 percent of the vote) but has gone on to win all later contests handily, with upward of 80 percent of the vote.

Home Style

Velazquez's strategies for representing her constituents and for pursuing her "double mission" reflect her background as a community activist and as a practical politician. Through her general philosophy, she perceives herself as advocating for the Latino community, other minorities, and women. However, and perhaps somewhat surprisingly for a former academic with such a philosophical bent, she also prides herself on the wide array of tangible federal benefits she has brought to the residents of New York's 12th and on her accessibility within the constituency.

Partisan Advocate. To begin, for Velazquez, "her biggest commitment is to her district and her 'pueblo'—the Latino community she says has historically been shut off from access to power and information" (*Newsday* 12/17/92). Therefore, it is not surprising that she began her speech after the 1992 primary win (in Spanish): "My first words are going to be in our language. . . . Are you ready for a new era in politics? Today we write a new page in the development of our community" (*Newsday* 9/16/92).

Subsequently, she has been a sought after speaker by Latino groups at the local, state, and national levels (*NYT* 2/9/98). ("We know that we've got the numbers and we can take the power. . . . Decision makers who ignore us do so at their own risk" [*NYT* 3/23/98])

As a member of Congress, it would be a rather large understatement to suggest that Velazquez has given voice in support of issues facing Latinos in the 1990s. In fact, the list of illustrations presented below not only provides a sampling of her activities in this regard but also informs non-Latino "outsiders" of some important Latino concerns.

Thus, Velazquez urged Latinos to take part in the 2000 census (PR 3/30/99), helped a Colombian woman obtain a visa to be with an ailing family member (*Newsday* 7/8/93), and worked for a memorial to the Puerto Rican 65th Regiment, who fought in the Korean War (www . . . velazquez). She has consistently worked on immigration issues and, in fact, considers her most important accomplishment to be the "naturalizing of more than 1,700" Latinos through citizenship workshops (*Newsday* 1/19/97; 3/6/96). In addition, she has sponsored legislation requiring the Immigration and Naturalization Service (INS) to use discretion before deporting immigrants accused of committing minor crimes (*Newsday* 11/6/97), and she has argued that illegal aliens should not be forced to return to their homelands while applying for citizenship (*DN* 10/30/97). She has also sponsored her own immigration bill, in response to a very unusual incident, to prevent the deportation of fifty-six deaf Mexicans who were allegedly brought to the United States and forced to peddle trinkets on the subways (*Newsday* 9/16/97). Finally, she has even been arrested for protesting the efforts of the Clinton administration to repatriate Haitians *(Los Angeles Times* 5/6/94).

What other issues have confronted Latinos throughout the 1990s? Velazquez has been described as a "major player" in debates over Puerto Rican statehood. A former proponent of independence, she now advocates for preservation of the Commonwealth (*PIA* 2000, 939). She has co-sponsored a bill to open up trade relations with Cuba (*Newsday* 12/20/93), and was a citizen observer during the 1994 elections in El Salvador (*NYT* 4/13/94).

In a controversial move, she supported President Clinton's plan for clemency for sixteen members of the Fuerzas Armadas de Liberación Nacional Puertoriquena (FALN). These terrorists were jailed for almost two decades for various bombings, including one in the United States Capitol. She not only sided with the president, she also openly defended her stand. When then-senatorial candidate Hillary Clinton took the opposing side, Velazquez, acting very much in character, chided: "Regarding Mrs. Clinton, she is on a listening tour, isn't she? I would advise her strongly to continue, and to come to (the Puerto Rican) community to see what the issues are" (AP 9/8/99).

As might be expected, Velazquez strongly opposes English-only laws. So, when Republican Peter King sponsored a bill making English the nation's official language, she responded: "I want him to show me how a non-English student can receive equal educational opportunity if that student is immersed in English-only classrooms where he cannot understand the teacher, where he cannot understand the textbooks" (*Newsday* 2/22/95) "With all the important things to focus on why are we wasting time on this nonsense? . . . Peter, you are a better person than that" (*DN* 8/2/96).[6]

Finally, Velazquez has been a leading advocate for hurricane relief funds for areas in Central America and the Caribbean (*DN* 9/11/96; *Newsday* 10/1/98; 11/6/98),[7] was critical of what she saw as the Clinton administration's failure to appoint more Latinos to high federal office (*Newsday* 5/15/94), and has been active, most recently, in the Vieuqez naval base controversy.[8]

Even though Velazquez is generally a strong supporter of President Clinton, she also criticized the administration for what she saw as its failure to appoint more Latino officials to high federal office (*Newsday* 5/15/94), lobbying for the nomination of Judge Cabranes to the Supreme Court:

> I take great pride in standing before you today, both as the first Puerto Rican woman elected to the U.S. House of Representatives and as a Latina . . . proud because as a Latino—this time a son of Borinquen—is a front-runner in the candidacy to one of this nation's most important posts. (*CR* 4/15/94).

Clearly, some of Velazquez's activities—encouraging citizenship, memorializing soldiers, and requesting humanitarian hurricane relief—are not particularly controversial. In other areas, however, Velazquez is definitely challenging the status quo. Nor does she necessarily minimize the challenge. So, there is sometimes a strong partisan and ideological edge to her presentation of self:

> Her notions about what government should do differ markedly from the policies espoused by the House's conservative Republican majority. Like her New York City liberal Democratic colleagues, Velazquez spends a good portion of her time simply trying to stop the GOP from enacting what she sees as bad ideas. On abortion, welfare, immigration, public housing, gun control and a long list of other issues, Velazquez's liberal views conflict with Republican dogma. (*PIA* 2000, 938)

Consequently, her party unity scores consistently rank above 90 percent while her Conservative Coalition ratings score only as high as ten. Where some Democrats advocated for finding common ground at the height of the Republican revolution in 1995, Velazquez certainly did not. "Job no. 1 is fighting for my district, which has some of the most dire needs in the country. I don't believe in labels, I believe in action. There is no way I can relinquish my convictions to accommodate politically" (*DN* 6/18/95).

In the context of the 1996 debate on raising the minimum wage, Velazquez used strong language to argue:

> Eighty five percent of Americans are in favor of raising the minimum wage. I will say to my Republican colleagues, they have lost the battle in the court of public opinion. So what does the Republican leadership now plan to do? Instead of following the will of the American people, they are following the will of corporate America and the fat cats who have funded their campaigns. That is immoral. (*CR* 4/24/96)

Similarly, Velazquez did not hesitate to compare Speaker Newt Gingrich and his fellow Republicans to "schoolyard bullies . . . [who] want to steal our poor children's lunch money" (*TU* 2/28/95) or to blast Republican opposition to statistical sampling (*PIA* 2000, 939).

As a consequence of her partisanship, Velazquez was generally a loyal supporter of President Clinton (her presidential support scores averaged in the high seventies). However, at strategic times, she was quite critical of administration actions. Thus, early on in her congressional career, she was part of a Jesse Jackson–led group encouraging the new president to promote a liberal agenda rather than a move to the center (*Newsday* 2/13/93).

She was particularly critical of Clinton in cases dealing with international trade agreements, which clearly pose a very real conflict for a representative whose district exhibits such severe unemployment. As Velazquez explained, "They said it was going to mean more jobs, to the people I represent—my district has a 12 percent to 14 percent unemployment rate—it's an abstraction. They want jobs now, not five years from now" (*Newsday* 10/26/97).[9]

Practical Politician. Her partisanship notwithstanding, Velazquez's presentation of self as a role model and advocate on behalf of Latinos can easily extend to other ethnic groups and women. Such efforts begin with genuine identification and support. For example, on the occasion of a celebratory trip to Puerto Rico after her 1992 primary victory, "Velazquez said she hoped her all-but-certain election in November would embolden Puerto Rican women to challenge the island's male-dominated politics"

(*Newsday* 9/27/92). "'You will have to forgive me, my father, for what I am going to say. I want to dedicate my victory to my mother and to all the women of Puerto Rico,' Velazquez told cheering Yabucoenos, as her seventy-nine-year-old father beamed in approval" (*NYT* 9/27/92).

Thus, Velazquez uses her position as member of Congress to raise concerns about women's issues. Calling them the "heart and soul" of the facility, she attended a rally on behalf of striking nurses at Maimonides Hospital (www . . . velazquez), was an outspoken critic of the Mitsubishi "sexual harassment" case, which she claimed illustrated a "crisis" of sexual harassment in the workplace that "society has largely ignored" (*Newsday* 5/6/96), and was upset by NBC's minority hiring practices (*Newsday* 5/15/94). She has spoken out to protest violence against women ("This national tragedy affects women from all socioeconomic groups. However, poor immigrant women with children face unique challenges and bureaucratic hurdles" [*CR* 3/27/96]) and has promoted Women's Development Centers to encourage business opportunities.

As has Maloney, Velazquez herself has had to respond to discrimination due to gender even on the floor of Congress. As a freshman, she was actually asked by another representative if she had come to Washington to find a boyfriend. Velazquez snapped back, "Now why would I have to come to Washington to find a boyfriend? I'm here, just like you are, to work for my constituents" (*Newsday* 12/17/92).

As well, Velazquez stands up for her Chinese constituents. Velazquez is one of the few representatives who voted "yes" to renew normal trading status with China (*Newsday* 7/26/98). She has been active in the fight to prevent the abuse of labor in Chinatown ("We will not allow exploitation of immigrant communities" [*Newsday* 8/19/95]) and she has worked with the American Fugian Association of Commerce and Industry (*CR* 5/12/99). That these efforts have not gone without recognition is evident by the fact that Asian Americans for Equality honored Velazquez at its twenty-second annual Lunar New Year Banquet (*Newsday* 2/28/96).

Often, the links Velazquez makes on behalf of minority interests come not only through her status as a role model but also through her belief in the importance of the need for economic advancement. For instance, she sometimes frames women's concerns in economic terms. Thus, in the context of a congressional debate on the importance of parental notification for abortions, she argued that such requirements would be felt most keenly by low-income teenagers needing to use federally subsidized clinics. "It becomes an issue of the haves and the have-nots, and the have-nots, as usual, lose" (*Newsday* 3/26/93).

Similarly, during the very partisan 104th Congress, members of the Congressional Caucus on Women's Issues were advocating for a Paycheck Fairness Act, aimed at closing the gender gap on wages and stiffening penalties for noncompliance with the 1963 Equal Pay Act. What was Velazquez's take on the matter? She responded: "If we are really honest about reforming welfare, you could get one answer by passing this [act]" (*Newsday* 6/15/97).

In addition, this emphasis on economics, and by extension infrastructure, has led to practical and hands-on aspects of Velazquez's home style. Perhaps surprisingly, given her passion for philosophical empowerment, she supplements her broad advocacy work with a focus on bringing real benefits to her constituents. She explains:

> The only way to pump up the economy is by investing in its greatest resource—people. We need the kind of government where people are contributing to economic life, not being excluded from it. We need to create jobs, train people to fill those jobs, develop more childcare services and expand and strengthen our education system. *(Newsday* 6/25/95)

With this in mind, Velazquez has used her position in Congress not only to provide voice to abstract ideas about representation but also to bring tangible benefits to her constituents. Her committee assignments include Banking and Financial Services and the Small Business Committee (*Crain's New York Business* 11/15/99). As such, she was the first Latina to be ranking member or chair of a full House committee (Small Business) (*Almanac* 2000, 1129).

In this regard, and arising from concerns in her district linking areas of drug trafficking to money laundering, Velazquez has publicized these concerns by introducing The Financial Crimes Strategy Act of 1996. The act mandated a national strategy to fight money laundering and bank and credit fraud (*Newsday* 7/30/96). Velazquez pointed out, "There's hundreds of these criminal operations in Queens. That brings guns and fear into the community" (*Newsday* 1/19/97). She has also worked to block bills that would "curb the reach of the Community Reinvestment Act," which has brought approximately $2.3 billion in loan commitments to New York State (*Newsday* 6/4/95).

Appreciating the problems her father had working a small construction business ("He didn't have the capital, the equity or the sophistication of information to be successful" [*Crain's New York Business* 11/15/99]), "on Small Business she has pushed to promote economic development in low income areas and to increase the share of government business that goes to small firms" (*PIA* 2002, 692). "In the 106th Congress, Velazquez introduced a number of bills with that goal, including a measure to help women-owned businesses win a bigger piece of the government procurement pie" (*PIA* 2002, 692) and argued against the practice of bundling (the tendency of government agencies to combine small contracts into one big one for purposes of efficiency over inclusion), which notably advantaged large contractors.

She has also used her committee positions to bring "hundreds of millions of dollars in federal grant funding to a variety of organizations in the 12th" (www . . . velazquez). To appreciate this, all one has to do is look at the newsletters and press releases on her Web site. A recent newsletter ("Bringing Funding to the 12th District") included the following impressive list:

> $5,000,000 Family Health Grant, $150,000 Federal Grant to Train Women Entrepreneurs, $93,000 HUD Grant to Assist Residents of Bushwick Houses, $94,000 HUD Grant to Assist Residents of Rutgers Houses, Helped Secure Federal Grant of Computers to St. Peter and Paul School, $75,000 Federal Language Education Grant, $500,000 Federal Grant for Early Intervention Services for People with HIV/AIDS. (www . . . velazquez)

Judging from this presentation of self, Velazquez certainly wants to be perceived as someone who has helped her constituents in very concrete and practical ways. In addition, she has held innumerable workshops on grant writing and small business opportunities and advertises a special "federal grant" program on her Web site (*Newsday* 7/15/94).

In addition, Velazquez engages in other traditional activities encouraging representative-constituent interactions. She holds regular town meetings on topics such as the cost of prescription drugs for seniors (*DN* 11/11/99) and the census (*DN* 4/15/99). She has also taken note of the accomplishments of individuals in the district. For example, after making "a very passionate plea to President Clinton himself" (*DN* 8/26/98), she helped veteran Tony Galdi obtain his long-awaited Bronze Star. She has inserted in the *Congressional Record* the accomplishments of notable constituents, for example, acknowledging the retirement of a local reverend (6/28/99). She also recognized a policeman who had "gained the confidence of the east New York community who had lost faith in those who were supposed to protect and defend them" (*CR* 5/16/95), and paid tribute to a physician ("It is with great honor and pride that I rise to congratulate and recognize a fellow Puerto Rican, Dr. Antonia Pantoja, for receiving the Presidential Medal of Freedom, the highest award a President can bestow on a citizen" [*CR* 9/12/96])

Even more than one-on-one connections, she takes on the role of community leader, serving as an ombudsperson helping to solve problems in her district. Thus, when a multiplex theater/development was being planned, she publicized constituent concerns to make sure adequate study would be given to changing neighborhood traffic patterns (*NYP* 7/17/98). She led a delegation to meet with officials of the Federal Highway Administration in support of a plan to replace what the group perceived as an out-of-date expressway with a tunnel system (*DN* 11/4/97) and, in a somewhat unusual incident, she helped mediate between aggrieved families and a cemetery whose graves had been contaminated by construction debris (*DN* 6/2/95).

Even more, she has marched with residents protesting gang slayings (*Newsday* 4/11/93), has worked with Jesse Jackson and Toys for Guns to decrease school violence (*Newsday* 3/3/94), and has mediated disputes between Hasidic Jews and Latinos *(Newsday* 9/21/92). She has (successfully) been among those lobbying for a Lower East Side tenement museum to preserve district history (*CR* 7/17/97), and has expressed understandable displeasure with a plan to relocate a Social Security office out of the district (*Newsday* 3/27/95).[10] As one obviously well-satisfied constituent poignantly summed up her efforts: "In the past, our community was never approached for political involvement. Now, we are never left out" (*Newsday* 3/3/97).

Discussion

Though representing the 12th district is in and of itself of obvious political significance, Velazquez's home style has its critics. As we have seen, in many ways, controversy has been a part of her entire political life. Representing a racially and ethnically diverse district is difficult at best and is made even more so by the charged racial politics of the 1990s. Thus, in attempting to fulfill her "double mission" to give voice to the constituents of the 12th district and the larger Latino community, Velazquez, as well as the growing number of legislators in similar positions, must balance sometimes-conflicting demands.

On the one hand, Velazquez has been criticized for overrepresenting her primary constituency, defined either narrowly as the Puerto Rican community of her origin or the larger Latino population (*Newsday* 8/27/92). Others have charged that despite her rhetoric, though she represents Latino interests well, she has failed to forge solid enough relationships with other minority groups. Despite clear examples of her support for the Asian interests in her community, those examples certainly do not form the defining characteristic of Velazquez's home style. A cynic might wonder: If there were fewer Asians in the district, would Velazquez pay much attention to their interests? Similarly, at least one African American constituent observed: "A lot of black people live in this area, and they feel they don't get any representation because it's a Puerto Rican district" (*Newsday* 1/17/95).

But, in some respects, given her efforts on behalf of small business, it might be argued that Velazquez is paying undue attention to a wider reelection constituency. Of course, in her view, her efforts in this area represent increased community empowerment and are even more significant because they are helping to empower a particularly impoverished and excluded community. There are more negative interpretations as well. An increased focus on small business is clearly a less controversial strategy to develop a wider appeal to a more diverse constituency. In addition, though she might disagree, Velazquez's work in support of small business provides a conservative element to her home style. The article in *Crain's New York Business* (11/15/99), cited earlier, provides an assessment of Velazquez's actions on her committee. For example, her support scores from the Chamber of Commerce, though not high, increased in the 105th Congress to 33 percent, over a career average of 14 percent. Similarly, some of the positions she has taken might be seen as out of character for someone who is such a staunch liberal Democrat. Thus, she has been described as "the most significant Democratic supporter" in opposing President Clinton's plan to cut back the SBIC (Small Business Investment Company) program and has supported reductions in estate taxes and increases in deductions for business meals and health coverage (*Crain's New York Business* 11/15/99). She also voted in the 105th Congress for an overhaul leading to a more restrictive bankruptcy code (*PIA* 2000, 939).

Consistent with her determination to represent all constituencies to which she is responsible, Velazquez again took note of her "double mission" and defended her record: "As a ranking Democrat on the committee I understand I have dual responsibilities—to defend my district but also to be responsive to a national constituency of small businesses" (*PIA* 2000, 939).

These criticisms, raising the potential for serious challenges to Velazquez's representation, take on additional weight in the context of recent events. In 1995, the Supreme Court ruled, "Congressional district lines are unconstitutional if race is the predominant factor in drawing them" (*TU* 6/30/95) and ordered the state legislature to redraw district lines (*Almanac* 1998). The upshot was a redrawn 12th district where the Latino population amounted to only about 45 percent (*TU* 10/11/97). Yet, a final appreciation for the significance of Velazquez's work can be seen from the support she received thereafter. While participating in meetings of the New York State Hispanic Task Force of the State Assembly, "[a]t every turn, Ms. Velazquez has been besieged by well wishers expressing hope that her appeal will be successful" (*TU* 10/11/97). However, Velazquez's home style— a combination of general philosophy and practical politics—is perceived as a successful effort at integrating the interests of the residents of her district with national and international concerns.

Conclusion

Focusing on the increasingly common "phenomenon" of multiracial/multiethnic congressional districts, this chapter has documented two very different home styles; home styles that happen to correspond to Canon's categorization of representation by highlighting "commonality" or "difference." Thus, while Rep. Velazquez has chosen to place more weight on her Latino primary constituency, Engel remains an expansionist, opting to appeal to a wide range of groups. While Velazquez can be seen as an advocate with a "double mission," including helping to give voice and empowerment to the Latino population, Engel takes a more practical approach, emphasizing services to individual constituents, regardless of race or ethnicity. In so doing, his representational style embraces difference and treats all constituents on equal terms.

This chapter has also shown that the combination of constituency and background factors so important in explaining the home styles of other representatives goes a long way toward explaining the differences between these legislators. Even though both represent multiracial districts, as we have seen, those districts have a very different ethnic character. Given that the 12th was explicitly drawn with the purpose of creating a Latino majority (58 percent in 1992), Velazquez's advocacy style fits nicely with the district's raison d 'être. In turn, given that there simply is no majority group in the 17th, a representational strategy highlighting commonality (partisanship, service) makes political sense. In addition, the redistrictings over the 1990s also figure in the story. As Engel saw his district change from a multiethnic but overwhelmingly Caucasian constituency, he augmented his foreign policy focus with more attention to domestic affairs, obtaining a seat on the Commerce Committee and increasing his sponsorship of domestic legislation. As Velazquez found her district reshaped to a just fewer than 50 percent Latino majority, she appears to have increased her focus on small business activity and economic empowerment, perhaps shifting somewhat toward a "politics of commonality."

At the same time, the profiles make it very clear that these members of Congress have certainly put their individual stamps and personalities on their representational styles. Velazquez, a lifelong activist from a political background, has chosen to represent her multiethnic constituents by advocating for the disadvantaged. In turn, as a long-time state legislator/professional politician with a reputation for not being a risk taker, it is not surprising that Engel has chosen a more traditional path: to represent constituents on the basis of commonality. So, factors in addition to constituency help explain home styles. Thus, even in the face of substantially altered districts (Engel's in 1992 and Velazquez's several years later), somewhat to his detriment, Engel has, in large part, maintained his foreign policy focus, and Velazquez has never lost her passion for the disadvantaged.

How does the local-national distinction figure in the picture? At bottom, localism comes first in both districts and in both home styles. Both legislators highlight accessibility and service, Engel is a "son of the Bronx," and Velazquez's fortunes can be linked to her roles as a local party and community leader, but national elements set the context underlying local politics. At the most basic level, Velazquez and Engel have responded to the challenges of the 1990s in traditional "Fennoian" ways: by simply interacting with constituents, by "servicing" the district and by focusing on issues of concern to the district.

Yet, for both members the local and the national are very much interconnected. Velazquez makes the link when she articulates her "double mission" to represent not only constituents of the 12th but also the national and even international Latino community. In turn, national and international factors clearly impact her district, and the local concerns of her constituents have implications extending well beyond the borders of the 12th. Indeed, it is difficult, in Velazquez's case, to separate out exactly what is local and what is national.

On the one hand, Engel's style is more local. After all, he is at bottom a "son of the Bronx" who thrives on providing constituent services. But even for Engel, the diverse national concerns of the racial and ethnic minorities of his district, in conjunction with his own predilections, thrust him into a broader arena. He has been led to actively pursue foreign policy goals with obvious national and international implications. In addition, with the bills he has sponsored, he has taken constituent concerns to Washington, and he has also, as we have seen in the case of arson prevention, attempted to localize a national problem. Thus, although the linkage is slightly different, Engel's local style has been influenced by national factors and, as with Velazquez, the local politics of his district have had national implications.

Finally, the larger sociopolitical context can impose opportunities and constraints on legislators. Considering the greater political clout of African Americans and Latinos, the push in the early 1990s for majority-minority districts, and the demands of an increasingly diverse society, the 1990s appeared to offer opportunities for legislators such as Engel and Velazquez. The individualistic nature of Congress would similarly appear to enhance these opportunities as it has allowed these legislators to expand the issue agenda, voice concerns on behalf of issues ranging from Kosovo to a broad array of Latino matters easy to ignore in the larger society, and provide a platform of institutional power (consider Velazquez's position on the Small Business Committee). For instance, had Solarz won the 1992 primary, an experienced and able legislator might have (as he claimed) represented the district equally well. However, important Latino concerns would likely not have been placed as highly on the political agenda.

In conclusion, the profiles presented here lead to a practical illustration of the advantages/disadvantages of commonality and difference representational strategies. Velazquez has chosen to represent the minority interests of the Latino community by directly voicing its concerns while Engel is less likely to give direct voice to minority issues. His focus on a broader range of issues of concern to urban communities and particularized benefits, however, may mean that he better serves the needs of more of his constituents. The judgment about which style is more effective or appropriate (Velazquez's emphasis on the politics of difference or Engel's efforts at commonality) leaves the reader with a thought provoking set of questions.

In the end, too, an understanding of the home styles of both Velazquez and Engel expands our appreciation of how interconnected the local and the national can be in an era marked by a diverse American society. In light of changing demographics across the nation, this chapter has sought to examine the local-national connection in the context of multiethnic or multiracial congressional districts.

Chapter 6

BALANCING CONSTITUENCIES: FENNO'S BULLS-EYE MODEL IN THE 1990S

A forceful advocate for families, children, consumers, the environment and her State of California, Barbara Boxer became a United States Senator in January 1993 after 10 years of service in the House of Representatives. She was elected to a second six-year term in 1998.
—http://boxer.senate.gov/about/index.html

As California's senior Senator, Dianne Feinstein has built a reputation as an independent voice, working with both Democrats and Republicans to find common-sense solutions to the problems facing our State and our Nation.
—http://feinstein.senate.gov/biography.html

As should be clear by now, Fenno's bulls-eye model, with its concentric circles of geographic, reelection, and primary constituencies, has been at the heart of the descriptions of previous profiles. Many of the congresspeople considered have made crucial choices about balancing within-district constituencies. Engel's focus on service/ethnic issues and McCarthy's nonpartisanship clearly reflect broad-based strategies encompassing a wide-ranging reelection constituency, yet they contrast with Houghton's moderate Republicanism or Maloney's push on women's concerns, strategies that in turn highlight the needs of smaller constituent groups.

For a number of reasons, it seems appropriate to conclude the profile chapters of this work by bringing Fenno's bulls-eye model front and center. As should be clear, one purpose of this book has been to emphasize the alternative choices and dilemmas faced by modern representatives; highlighting which constituents get represented is obviously a

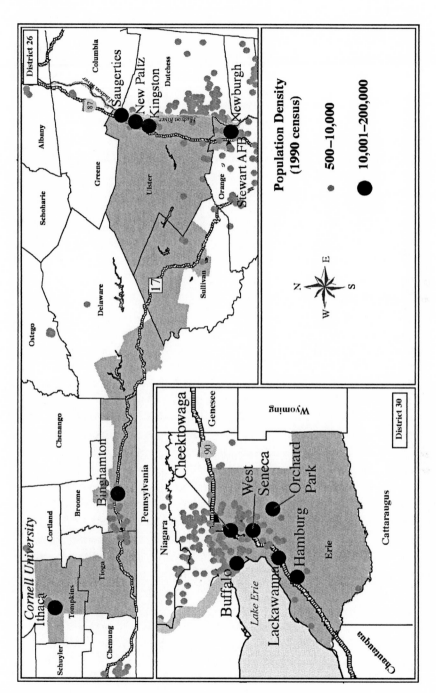

Map 5. Congressional Districts for Reps. Quinn and Hinchey.

fundamental representational concern. As Fenno described it, even in the best case, "[a]ll our observations and, hence, all our generalizations about congressman-constituent relations involve a set of constituents far smaller than the total number in the district" (Fenno 1978, 237). Thus, the geographic constituency is only the beginning of the story. Therefore, "as they move about the district, House members continually draw the distinction between those people who vote for them and those who do not" (Fenno 1978, 8). In short, though congresspeople are, of course, legally required to take all their constituents into account, in reality, some legislators have hard choices to make about which of their now almost six hundred thousand citizens will receive their focus.

In the context of the larger bulls-eye model, Fenno asked: How do representatives balance the sometimes-conflicting demands of constituents? When does it make sense to tailor a home style toward the needs and interests of a particular partisan, ideological, or economic group, and when would the choice of a more broadly based strategy work better? What role does a member's prior background play in answering these questions, and how does the makeup of a constituency impact these choices?

As the two quotes above this chapter indicate, these questions pose strategic dilemmas for representatives. There are obvious advantages to developing a broad-based reelection strategy. Members may ensure themselves enough support to increase their electoral safety, may genuinely believe in the need to stretch out and build cross-group coalitions (Senator Feinstein), or may have a background and life experiences that help them do so. Yet, there are equally obvious risks: in stretching across constituent groups, a legislator takes the chances of alienating core and intense supporters or of simply pleasing none a lot.

On the other hand, "strong supporters display an intensity capable of producing additional political activity, and they tender their support 'through thick and thin' regardless of who the challenger may be" (Fenno 1978, 18). Consider Senator Boxer's efforts on behalf of consumer groups and environmentalists (first quote, top of chapter), or witness Fenno's (1996) interesting description of three consecutive senators serving the state of Iowa. Sen. John Culver (1974–1980) was the policy wonk able to satisfy his primary constituency. In contrast, Sen. Dick Clark (1972–1978) used a walk across the state to ensure broad-based name recognition, yet he was unable to translate that "weak" support into a high degree of intensity when he needed it. Learning from the history of both his Democratic predecessors, Senator Tom Harkin (1984–present) was able to win election on the basis of a coalition incorporating the best of both worlds: a strong group of core supporters along with the goodwill of a larger reelection constituency.

So, at one level, highlighting the bulls-eye model is important because it speaks to a fundamental dilemma with implications for which citizens receive the "best" representation. Such a focus has additional advantages: it highlights the importance of the local. Following from the research question of this book, the argument thus far has quite naturally emphasized how the changed political circumstances characterizing the 1990s have contributed to a more national politics. Yet, it is time to reiterate a finding becoming clear from earlier chapters: even in a book focusing attention on national elements, it is important to highlight how local politics still is. Witness the innumerable examples of constituency service performed by each and every one of the congresspeople thus far considered. Witness, too, the strong roots that many have in their districts and the many ways their Washington activity derives from a constituency focus. In short, in an era where the national matters, these profiles provide an important reminder that the local is not only alive but is actually thriving.

Yet, also consistent with the focus of this book, it appears as though today the local and the national are often interconnected. Though this chapter concentrates on local-level politics, the title "Fenno's Bulls-eye Model in the 1990s" suggests an additional twist: even where politics is fundamentally local, national factors can impact home styles. Thus, even when the central question for a representative is which of his/her constituents to allocate most attention to, the national factors we have already discussed—partisanship, issues, minorities—play a role in local politics. Put another way, we might consider: Do national factors have an impact even in congressional districts where local concerns predominate? How national is it possible to be in light of important local circumstances (in this case, severely depressed local economies)?

In short, this chapter will provide an additional demonstration of the interactions of the local and the national. Even where home styles are at bottom dependent on local conditions, the two profiles below demonstrate that the national environment enters in, impacting election contests, presentations of self, and Washington activity.

Finally, this chapter will focus attention on the local-national connection in an additional way. Fenno, as we have seen, considered the politics of each of the congressional districts he examined in isolation; what a member did in his/her particular district had little to do with the activities undertaken by another congressperson even in a nearby constituency. In contrast, the argument of this book has been that the larger national environment has the potential to impact local arenas, thus implying a common backdrop to otherwise diverse congressional elections. In this regard, the two districts that will be considered below have in common the undeniable fact of the declining economy that has characterized the modern life of New York State. This shared characteristic of the two geographic constituencies in turn sets the boundaries for the home styles of these two members of Congress serving as another reminder of cross-district commonality.

Thus, below, I examine the home styles of two representatives. Jack Quinn, Republican representative from the 30th district in and around Buffalo, must win the support of a largely Democratic constituency. He has chosen to tailor his home style to a fairly broadly defined reelection coalition. In turn, perhaps more liberal than many of his constituents, Rep. Maurice Hinchey is an issue activist representing a heterogeneous area. He likely weights his home style toward those core supporters who share his policy preferences. In short, these two representatives have made alternate choices about home styles. Both styles have been electorally effective, and both legislators implement their alternative strategies well. From these two members of Congress, we can get a real-world sense of the tradeoffs involved in balancing constituencies, can examine the impact of national politics even on local styles, and can consider the importance of the common circumstance of economic downturn on the development of legislator home styles.

Constituency

In an era marked by strong incumbency advantages and noncompetitive congressional elections, the two constituencies under examination in this chapter stand out as particularly intriguing. While Congressman Quinn faces the challenge of representing a district composed largely of constituents of the opposite party, Rep. Hinchey must build and hold the support of citizens in a notably competitive area. Thus, as will become clear, in contrast to the descriptions of the members from safe districts described in the last chapters, the profiles of the two legislators depicted below reflect the rough and tumble of partisan and political struggles.

Before describing the character of these two constituencies in detail, it is important to set the context. As was hinted at in the introduction to this chapter, the backdrop for the two profiles below is the seriously declining economy that has marked upstate New York over the past few decades (*Almanac* 1998, 961; AP 10/28/00). For starters, the effects of this declining economy have been particularly devastating to the Buffalo area. So, though "Buffalo should also be credited with building a heavy industrial base in the late 19th and early 20th centuries, as America's number one grain-milling center and as a major steel producer" (*Almanac* 2000, 1178), in the later twentieth century, deindustrialization brought significantly harder times. The loss of forty-five thousand jobs between 1980 and 1991 in Quinn's district has created a new service-based economy (*PIA* 1996, 961). "The unemployment rate [in the district] was as high as 15% in the early 1980s and then dipped to nearly 6% at the end of 1992; it was 9% in early 1997" (*PIA* 1998, 1050). While steel was once a dominant industry in Lackawanna, employing thousands, today the buildings that once housed steelworkers lie still (*PIA* 1996, 961).

The economic decline has also contributed to a significant decrease in population. While still one of the nation's fifty largest cities (*PIA* 1994, 1107), Buffalo lost fully 29 percent of its population in the 1970s and another 9 percent in the 1980s (*PIA* 1996, 961).

Despite this genuine hardship, Buffalo and its surrounding areas have been attempting to regain their economy, so the U.S.-Canada free trade agreement (late-1988), the revitalization of the Buffalo waterfront, and the creation of a nineteen thousand-seat minor league baseball stadium (*PIA* 1996, 961) have been among the efforts at redevelopment.[1]

Today, the district is a solidly blue-collar area with major industries including pharmaceutical production, grain milling, and automobile parts, and the largest employers include Buffalo city government, Buffalo General Hospital, Buffalo Greater International Airport, and Ford Motor Company Stamping Plant (*PIA* 2000, 988). In addition, Buffalo is still cited as the "flour milling capital of the world producing an astounding 6.6 million pounds per day" (*PIA* 2002, 729).

Table 6.1 highlights these economic difficulties as Buffalo has a median income of $26,263, a college graduation rate of 15% (ranks twenty-sixth in the state, bottom third nationally), the proportion of white-collar workers of 55% (twenty-sixth in state, middle third nationally), and the proportion of blue-collar workers of 28% (ranks fourth of thirty-one in state, middle third nationally). As an indication of this high percentage of blue-collar workers, Buffalo has actually been cited as the most unionized city in the nation (Web bio).

Though Hinchey's constituents are doing somewhat better (median income $30,335 ranks nineteenth of thirty-one in state, middle third nationally), the effects of economic decline have also been felt in the 26th district. With plants throughout the area (including Kingston on the east, Endicott on the west; see Map 5), IBM (founded in Endicott) is a major employer (*PIA* 1994, 1095). But more recently, "IBM layoffs and cut backs have hit the area hard, rippling through virtually every aspect of the local economy" (*Ithaca Journal* 11/3/94).

These ripple effects are clear. Not only was the area around Binghamton hurt by IBM layoffs but major defense contracts decreased as a result of post–cold war budget cuts (*Washington Alert* 1998, 6). Thus, as a newspaper article has poignantly described it, "Binghamton is full of underemployed people, unemployed people, and retired people with nothing to spend" (*IJ* 11/3/94). This lack of jobs throughout the district has forced young people to seek other options. Similarly, in the eastern part of the district, "[o]nce known as the queen city of the Hudson, this historic community [Newburgh] has fallen on hard times. Many of its factories stand empty, and the old neighborhoods experienced poverty, layoffs and misfortune" (*TU* 4/3/94).

Though these two districts share a declining economy, they also exhibit important differences. Buffalo simply has an image problem. For example, prominently displayed on Rep. Quinn's Web site is a picture of the Buffalo sky line entitled "the Buffalo you don't see on the weather channel." The reference is, of course, to the stereotypically large amount of snowfall in the city, the butt of jokes to outsiders.

But, in reality, there is more to the area than makes it to TV. "Tucked on the shore of Lake Erie in western New York, the 30th contains most of the southern and eastern part of Buffalo and the portion of Erie County that lies South of the city" (*PIA* 2000, 988; see Map 5). Thus, the district includes a large portion of Erie County, two-thirds of the city of Buffalo (two hundred fourteen thousand in Quinn's part of the district [*PIA* 2000, 988]) and other small cities (Cheektowaga, population eighty-four thousand; West Seneca, forty-eight thousand; Lackawanna, nineteen thousand) as well as many (thirty-four) towns and villages (www . . . quinn). In total, the 30th is 83 percent urban, encompassing 725 square miles (801 people per square mile; Table 6.1).

As a relatively urban area, it is not surprising that the 30th reflects a notable ethnic and racial character. As Polish and Irish are the largest ethnic populations, the Catholic Church has been an important presence in the area, so despite "liberal" economic values (see below), many constituents have conservative beliefs (pro-life, pro-school choice) on social issues. Geographic concentrations (Polish in Buffalo and Cheektowaga and Irish in south Buffalo [*PIA* 1994, 1107]) enhance these ethnic ties, and

TABLE 6.1 Constituency Characteristics and Election Results for Reps. Quinn and Hinchey

	Jack Quinn	Maurice Hinchey
District #	30	26
Party	R	D
Yr. Elected	1992	1992
District Profile		
Land Area (square miles)	725	3,083
Population Per Square Mile	801	188
Percent Urban	83%	46%
Percent Rural		43%
Percent White	81%	91%
Percent White Collar	55%	61%
Rank (state)*	26	17
Rank (nation)**	2	2
Percent Blue Collar	28%	23%
Rank (state)*	4	12
Rank (nation)**	2	3
Percent College Educated	15%	23%
Rank (state)*	26	12
Rank (nation)**	3	1
Median Income (in thousands)	26.26	30.34
Rank (state)*	24	19
Rank (nation)**	2	2
Election Results		
2000	67%	62%
1998	68%	62%
1996	55%	55%
1994	67%	49%
1992	52%	50%
District Vote For President		
2000	D-59%	D-51%
	R-35%	R-41%
1996	D-59%	D-53%
	R-29%	R-36%
1992	D-46%	D-45%
	R-26%	R-35%

*Rank in state: 1 = highest, 31 = lowest.

**Rank Nationally is Expressed in Thirds: 1 = Top Third, 2 = Middle Third, 3 = Bottom Third the constituency includes large concentrations of African Americans in Buffalo (43 percent of the Buffalo section [*PIA* 1994, 1107]).

In contrast to the compact and urban Buffalo area, Hinchey's 26th district sprawls across part of the southern tier (the district is 43% rural [see Map 5] and includes a geographic area larger than the state of Connecticut (3,083 square miles, sixth largest in the state [*CDs in the 1990s*, 537]). The district is also characterized by an elongated "barbell" shape (*Kingston Daily Freeman* 11/6/94) that "reaches from high above Cayuga Lake's waters to the banks of the Hudson River. Most of the population is found in the pockets at the district's extremes: the Ithaca and Binghamton areas to the west, and the Hudson Valley Region—which includes the cities of Kingston, Newburgh and Beacon—on the eastern edge" (*PIA* 1994, 1095).

So, the largest population centers, Ithaca (population twenty-eight thousand; northwest part of district), Binghamton (population forty-eight thousand; central part of district), Newburgh (population twenty-six thousand), and Kingston (population twenty-three thousand) (both at eastern end of district), are scattered throughout the district (see Map 5). Rural areas and towns surround these medium-sized cities so that in total the district is an approximately equal mix of urban (46%) and rural (43%) areas.

In turn, this mix reflects a divided socioeconomic base. The area features many colleges, community colleges, and universities (Cornell, Ithaca College, SUNY Binghamton, and SUNY New Paltz) and the major industries include higher education (it is the educational base that has contributed to the district's economic recovery [*PIA* 2002, 721]), technology, manufacturing, and agriculture (*PIA* 2000, 978). It is thus not surprising that, on balance, residents are reasonably well-educated, 25% college educated (twelfth of thirty-one in New York State and in the top third nationally), 61% white collar (ranks seventeenth of thirty-one in state, middle third nationally), and 23% blue collar (twelfth of thirty-one in state, bottom third nationally) (Table 6.1).

These statistics come alive through a glance at the Web sites of the eight counties wholly or partly included in the district. For instance, given the rural and sprawling character of the area, features of the land and terrain are often noted—e.g., the Hudson River, many lakes, the Catskill and Taconic mountain ranges (see below Hinchey's concern for the environment)—as one quote beautifully expressed it, "Native Americans called it 'the lovely land' and 'land in the sky'" (www.co.ulster.ny.us).

In short, the two constituencies considered throughout this chapter reflect the economic hard times that have impacted the northeast generally. In addition, though it includes suburbs and rural areas, Quinn's district is largely urban, blue collar, and ethnic. In contrast, the character of Hinchey's district is sprawling, economically more diverse, and largely white.

These differences translate into alternative strategic problems for their representatives. The blue-collar nature of Republican Quinn's district combined with its strong ethnic traditions has meant that the area is "mostly Democratic" (*PIA* 1998, 988). Henry Nowak had handily won election to congress since 1976, and, despite a substantial Perot challenge (he garnered 28% of the 1992 vote, the largest in any "major central-city metropolitan county" [*Almanac* 1994, 933]), Clinton easily carried the district in both 1992 (46%) and 1996 (59%). In 2000, candidate Gore garnered 59% of the vote (*PIA* 2002, 667).

In turn, the economic divisions throughout the 26th imply partisan divisions; "Ithaca, home to Cornell and Ithaca College, remains a haven for liberal activists. The town elected a socialist mayor to three terms in the early 1990s, and it circulates its own currency, Ithaca HOURs, which is accepted in more than 350 locations" (*PIA* 2000, 978). On the other hand, the area in and around Binghamton (the Triple Cities) features a "mix of high tech employees and a traditional blue collar constituency" which "make Broome politically competitive" (*PIA* 1994, 1095). Ulster County, in the eastern part of the district, though solidly Republican, nevertheless elected Hinchey to nine terms in the state legislature. Clinton narrowly carried the district in both 1992 and 1996 (45 to 35 and 53 to 36), and Gore in 2000 received 51% of the vote. On balance: although the 26th, like most upstate districts, has a Republican heritage, its demographics have made it a political swing district.

To summarize, though they have different partisan makeups, both these districts are heterogeneous. Hinchey's district is politically split whereas Quinn actually represents a constituency of the opposite party. Both districts, though particularly Quinn's, have undergone severe economic downturns. Finally, while Hinchey represents a sprawling, somewhat sparsely populated constituency, Quinn's district is more urban and compact. As we shall see, all these factors impact the home styles of the two members.

Jack Quinn: Having Your Cake and Eating It Too

If President Ronald Reagan was the "Teflon politician," then Rep. Jack Quinn must be made of kryptonite. How else can you explain a Republican who gets reelected by wide margins in a vastly Democratic district, a politician who garners endorsements from the right wing National Federation of Independent Business and the AFL-CIO in the same year? (*Buffalo News* 10/29/01)

Similarly, a 1993 fundraiser for Representative Jack Quinn featured a guest list which its organizers described as unique, staunch Republicans mixed with Democrats and business executives sitting next to labor leaders (*BN* 10/18/93). As we shall see, Representative Quinn has received recognition from a wide range of political groups and has compiled a voting record satisfactory to constituents on many sides of the political spectrum. In recognition of this success, *Congressional Quarterly* has even ranked him among its most "effective" representatives: "In the breakdown of the list of 50, Quinn was listed as one of five 'political survivors'—members whose political affiliations seem to defy the makeup of the districts they represent" (*BN* 10/28/99).

So, illustrative of the themes of this chapter, Quinn's representational style involves not only satisfying a Republican primary constituency but also entails reaching out to Democrats and labor. In addition, the national political scene complicates matters for Quinn, as a more conservative Republican Party in Washington potentially makes more difficult coalition-building efforts at home.

However, the profile below is not just an account of political survival; in contrast, Quinn and his staff appear not to cringe at the political challenges inherent in representing constituents of the opposite party, but they actually seem to thrive on the difficulty. So, given the situation, it is not surprising that Quinn's representational style emphasizes some commonsense political strategies—constituency service, bipartisanship, and highlighting visible labor issues. These are, of course, tried and true methods of holding support among diverse constituencies. However, what is unique about this profile is that Quinn (and his staff) takes some of these strategies to a higher level, making real efforts at proactively stepping up to the challenge.

Background

The story is even more interesting as Quinn's election to Congress in 1992 had all the earmarks of a "minor" miracle and a political aberration (*BN* 11/15/92). "'We were the underdog from Day One, and in some people's minds, we were the underdog right up to yesterday,' said Quinn, the Republican supervisor from Hamburg. 'But when we announced back in June—June 17—we believed we really had a chance to win this race'" (*BN* 11/4/92).

The 30th district had been represented since 1974 by popular Democrat Henry Nowak who had focused much of his attention on local concerns (*NYT* 6/18/92) and whose seniority on the Public Works and Transportation Committee allowed him to help develop portions of Buffalo and to bring federal dollars (reportedly more than $1 billion [*PIA* 1994, 1106]) to the district for highway construction, a transit system, and waterfront development (*PIA* 1994, 1106).

The Democratic edge in party registration, Nowak's popularity, and the lateness (June 1992) of his retirement announcement left little time for candidates to mount a campaign. The advantage was clearly with any Democratic candidate, and Dennis Gorski the son of a former congressman, appeared to be advantaged in his own right (*BN* 11/4/92). As the County Executive from a county (Erie) contiguous with the 30th Congressional District, Gorski had a ready-made constituency and enjoyed widespread name recognition. In contrast, Republican Jack Quinn was a town supervisor (formerly a councilman, since 1981) serving in the small (but Democratic) suburban jurisdiction of Hamburg. While Quinn's name was out there, he was seen as having limited political experience in an area atypical of Buffalo proper (*BN* 12/28/92). Still, Quinn had numerous advantages and as it turned out, his apparent disadvantages turned into the factors that would not only help him win the congressional seat but would shape his home style as well.

First and most importantly, Quinn has deep roots in the Buffalo area, growing up Irish Catholic in a Catholic city (*BN* 11/15/92):

> My ties to labor go back to my early days growing up in a close-knit community in South Buffalo, New York. My entire family worked for the unions. In fact, my father, Jack Sr., spent more than thirty years as an engineer on the South Buffalo Railroad. During my late teens, I spent the summer months off from high school to work at Bethlehem Steel. (PR 4/16/99)

> After graduating from Siena College, Rep. Quinn taught English in the Orchard Park School District for 10 years . . . earned his Masters Degree in Education (SUNY Buffalo) and received his New York State School District Superintendent Certificate from SUNY-Fredonia. (Web bio)

In addition, Quinn's experience had taught him lessons in bipartisan politics that would serve him well as he would represent the larger and significantly Democratic 30th district. In fact, "Quinn says he became a

Republican almost by chance—his uncle, a local GOP elections official, happened to be the one who sent him his voter registration ballot" (*PIA* 2000, 989). Thereafter, "Quinn got into politics by accident when a friend asked him to help stuff envelopes. He thought that was the end of it. 'It was somewhere in the middle of that first term that I found I really enjoyed what I was doing'" (*BN* 11/15/92).

On the Hamburg Town Board (actually three-to-two Democrat), Quinn also exhibited a bipartisan style: "We have a split board out here, but I believe we've always made our decisions based on what's right, not on party politics" (*BN* 11/4/92). A Democratic colleague corroborated this by describing Quinn as a good consensus builder and a nice guy. "The 'nice guy' reputation Quinn has is real: 'He has a very sincere interest in the community, and that's not just a campaign thing . . . Unlike a lot of people in public life, he's real. It's no show or front'" (*BN* 11/15/92).

Quinn's district rootedness, bipartisan style, and "nice guy" image allowed him to communicate his understanding of the problems people were facing, sympathize with the economic and political disenchantment prevalent in the area, and reach out to Democrats. Thus, the difficult economy contributed to understandable unhappiness with not only government in general but incumbents in particular. As we have seen, Ross Perot received one of the highest (28%) vote totals in a central city (*Almanac* 2002, 1122). Emphasizing change, "Quinn got the Perot vote while Gorski ran basically even with Bill Clinton's 46% plurality" (*Almanac* 2002, 1122).

In all of this, particular note should be made of Quinn's relationship to the national Republican Party. Despite his bipartisan style, Quinn has generally been a loyal supporter, coordinating the 1988 Bush campaign in Erie County (*PIA* 1996, 960), speaking in 1998 on behalf of Senator D'Amato (*BN* 11/1/98), and appearing at his share of Republican Party functions. Partly because of a push from neighboring representative Bill Paxon (then member of the Executive Committee) (*BN* 11/7/92), Quinn received assistance ($51,000) from the Republican National Committee, assistance that he used to buy more than one hundred last-minute television ads. However, "during his campaign he (Quinn) sounded more like Clinton than President Bush, concentrating more on economics than 'family values'" (*BN* 11/15/92).

So, Gorski had campaign fodder: "Now (Quinn) runs away from the president every chance he gets, despite taking $50,000 from the National Republican Party to run his campaign. . . . Responding to Gorski's charge of 'distancing,' Quinn said late Saturday that he plans on 'rolling up my sleeves and working with whoever is president—whether it's President

Bush, President Clinton or President Perot—and doing whatever is best for the people of the 30th District'" (*BN* 11/1/92).

In the end, capitalizing on the economic disenchantment, downplaying partisanship, and running a "textbook campaign" (*BN* 11/15/92), Quinn managed an upset victory (52 percent of the vote) and became the first Republican to represent this area of New York State since 1950 (*BN* 11/4/92), winning all subsequent elections except one with well over 60 percent of the vote (*PIA* 2002, 728).

Home Style

As Jack Quinn took a three-mile "leisurely" jog ("I'm a Bill Clinton jogger") around his Hamburg neighborhood his first morning as congressman-elect, he was already developing his home style (*BN* 11/4/92). "I went out to get your newspaper just to make sure this is real" (*BN* 11/4/92). He let it be known that his style of representation would, at bottom, be the style that had propelled him into office. Thus, he would first and foremost focus on district interests by emphasizing local concerns and constituency service, by highlighting his accessibility, and by reaching out to wide varieties of constituents. And, of course, given the partisan makeup of the district, "reaching out" would involve not only keeping the support of his (Republican/business) primary constituency but would also entail attracting a (Democratic/labor) reelection constituency as well.

Some of Quinn's early decisions provide vivid illustrations of this constituency-oriented home style. He first held an unofficial swearing-in ceremony, not in his home suburb of Hamburg, but in the heart of the inner city at Erie Community College City Campus: "'There's no way we could take them all to Washington, so we had a local swearing-in ceremony. . . . As the supervisor of Hamburg, I found out this is a business where the people are put first,' and that, Quinn added, 'means all the people'" (*BN* 12/28/92).

Similarly, Quinn decided that his family would continue to reside in Hamburg and that he would make frequent commutes back and forth to spend weekends in the district (his Web site even provides detailed directions, short cuts included, for the trip from Buffalo to Washington). In addition, Quinn opened a satellite district office at 1490 Jefferson Avenue in the heart of Buffalo's African American community (*BN* 12/8/93). "Henry Nowak's office there was able to deliver services, and I want to continue to do that" (*BN* 2/8/93). Finally, in contrast to many representatives, Quinn opted to base his top staffers (an administrative assistant and press secretary) in the district (*BN* 12/6/92). "We want to make certain that constituent service is my top priority" (*BN* 12/6/92).

As the following will make clear, Quinn and his staff appear to have delivered on this promise. Years after coming to office, he advertised:

> Service to constituents has remained Rep. Quinn's top priority since first being elected to Congress. Whether helping a veteran in obtaining benefits, aiding senior citizens in acquiring their Social Security payments, or working on any other problems individuals may be facing in dealing with the federal government, Rep. Quinn has successfully opened and closed thousands of cases on behalf of the people in his district. (Web bio)

The operative and perhaps even innovative words in the above quote may be "open" and "closed." It is more than clear from the examples in this book and the larger political science literature (Fiorina 1977; Johannes and McAdams 1981) that members of Congress engage in constituency service and advertise their success at their ombudsperson abilities. As we have seen, it is not unusual to see member Web sites proclaiming this level of engagement. It is, however, a bit more innovative to focus on an overall success rate—so, Quinn is highlighting his actual performance rather than simply the potential to follow up with individual constituents.

It is thus easy to find examples of Rep. Quinn interacting with constituents, participating in community ceremonies, announcing federal grants to the area, and generally promoting district interests:

- Quinn To Help Kick Off Fund Raiser to benefit West Seneca Ameri-Corps Literacy Tutoring Program (*BN* 11/28/99)
- Quinn To Help Donate 24,000 Books In Drive For Children (*BN* 5/2/99)
- Rep. Jack Quinn Presents Scholarship to Hilbert College Student (PR 2/21/01)
- Quinn Announces Over $900K in Federal Funds for Children's Hospital Funding For Emergency Room and Research Study (PR 1/25/01)

More generally, Quinn and his staff have held regular town meetings in the district (*BN* 9/17/93; 7/30/93; 3/5/93; 6/4/94). More, Quinn organized a fairly unique group, a group of about twenty labor leaders who meet regularly and keep him up to date on their concerns:

"Our 'Labor Round Table' has been in existence since the end of my first term in Congress. It serves as a very helpful communications outlet. For years, I have suggested to my colleagues in Washington to organize similar committees in their own districts. It really works well," Quinn said. (PR 2/22/01)

In fact, a style of bringing diverse groups together to address local and national problems more generally has worked well for Quinn, as he has conducted similar roundtable-style meetings with agriculture groups, which "prove invaluable when important agricultural issues are discussed and voted on in the Capitol" (Web bio) and on crime/juvenile violence ("Rep. Jack Quinn, R-Hamburg, said he put the session together 'as an opportunity to present successful programs from all levels of law enforcement and create an awareness of these programs for possible inclusion in the crime bill under consideration by the U.S. Congress'" [*BN* 1/20/94]).

He was also involved in initiating the Call to Protect Program, a program to recondition deactivated cellular phones for victims of domestic violence. "Police departments from East Aurora, Orchard Park, Cheektowaga and Hilbert College collected phones for Quinn, as well as Respiratory Services of Western New York and numerous area residents" (*BN* 4/26/00).

As is true for the other representatives studied throughout this book, Quinn has worked on additional constituent issues, for example, promoting competition among local railroads, improving roads, and even telling "the EPA not to send his district the Hudson River's PCB-infected sediment" (*Almanac* 2002, 1123). He has worked to attract new and cheaper airlines to the Buffalo area (*BN* 2/24/98), "joined preservationists in their fight to delay the demolition of Transfiguration Catholic Church" (*BN* 4/3/94), and helped local veterans by getting phones into the rooms at the Veterans Administration Hospital on Bailey Avenue (Web bio). Additionally, Quinn participated in the selection of a local bishop to take part in a "summit" exploring provision of social services by faith-based communities (PR 3/15/01) and was involved in demonstrations of Operation Respond ("to improve efficiency of emergency personnel" [PR 6/4/01]).

Quinn is also in and around the district just plain having fun: "Quinn Bets 100 Wings On The Bills" (football team headed to the Super Bowl) (*BN* 1/6/96). And, "I told my wife, 'You can't believe how lucky we are: I got Springsteen tickets'" for the Buffalo concert reuniting entertainer Bruce Springsteen after a decade with the E Street Band (*BN* 11/19/99).

Finally, in keeping with the stereotypic view of Buffalo as one of the snowiest places in the nation, it seems appropriate to conclude the discussion of Quinn's district-oriented activities with note of the congressman's efforts to provide disaster assistance. On more than one occasion, including blizzards in 1993 and 2001, "Western New York was hit with record-setting snowfall. . . . Rep. Quinn was the first to call the White House (in 2001) and tell the president that 'the snow is over the Big Man's head,' referring to the President's nickname for him as the 'Big Man from Buffalo'" (President Bush authorized aid) (Web bio).

Quinn's Washington behavior reflects a continuation of his district work. "'I think Quinn has done a good job at playing the incumbency card,' said James Twombly, a political science professor at the University at Buffalo. 'He does the casework very well, and he votes with the constituency whenever he has to'" (BN 11/7/96). Consistent with his efforts to maintain a broad-based reelection coalition, he focuses on issues impacting the local area. In this regard, his record is interesting enough in itself. In addition, given the Democratic character of the 30th district, Quinn's efforts have crucial national implications, placing Quinn in a unique position within the national Republican Party.

To begin, much of Quinn's committee work—on Transportation and Infrastructure and Veterans Affairs—focuses on constituency-related concerns. As a newcomer, he lobbied hard to succeed Nowak for the former assignment (PIA 1994, 1106) "I'm absolutely delighted that the leadership in Washington was able to meet my requests. . . . There are a number of projects (including the 'Nowak Project' to boost tourism) in the pipeline" (BN 12/12/92).

In these capacities, Quinn has first highlighted constituency concerns, but he has also used these posts to "nationalize" and broaden the scope of his interests. For instance, "a fatal accident on the Niagara Thruway in late 1992, in which steel coils fell from the back of a truck and killed four people," prompted Quinn to advocate for additional regulation of these steel coils (BN 6/4/93). (He claimed credit and got his picture in the local paper: "Rep. Jack Quinn, R-Hamburg, stands in front of an 18-wheeler loaded with steel coils Saturday to announce new federal regulations for securing such loads" [BN 8/7/94.])

Similarly, Quinn has turned his district's connection to railroads into a more national commitment. He has thus been a loyal supporter of Amtrak, for instance, winning approval of amendments protecting employees during the transition to a private company in 1995 and placing restrictions on subcontracting (*PIA* 2000, 988). He even became involved in some internal politics in the 105th Congress when some "Western Republicans threatened to vote against reauthorizing Amtrak if Eastern Republicans, including Quinn, continued to vote against them on environmental issues" (*PIA* 2000, 988).

In addition, Quinn has become involved in broader aspects of national railroad policy. "Rep. Quinn has already taken action as Chairman of the Railroads Subcommittee. He is listed as an original co-sponsor and led floor debate two days ago on H.R. 554, the 'Rail Passenger Disaster Family Assistance Act of 2001'" (PR 2/16/01) and sponsored (with Bob Clement, D-TN and Spencer Bachus, R-AL) "The 'Railroad Track Modernization Act of 2001'" (PR 3/14/01).

Similarly, Quinn's work on the Veterans Affairs Committee is, on the one hand, closely connected to the active veterans' community in his district but also pulls him into areas of broader national policy. So, beginning with an idea from a *Buffalo News* columnist ("Bob Curran is a leader on these issues, and we respect his advice" [*BN* 3/11/99]), Quinn has repeatedly introduced legislation (105th-107th Congresses) "that would designate 'Pearl Harbor Day' a national holiday" (Web bio). "I think this is an opportunity to pay our respect to those who served . . . I've heard a lot about this idea from veterans on my travels, and from veterans at the Buffalo VA hospital. We want to give veterans recognition every chance we get" (*BN* 3/11/99). (However, when told that actually making Pearl Harbor Day such a national holiday would cost the nation fully $27 million Quinn's reaction was, "Holy jeepers" [*BN* 3/11/99]).

In the 105th Congress, Quinn became a subcommittee chair on Veterans Benefits. In this capacity, "he was credited for his effort to install phones at veterans' bedsides and legislation he introduced to establish quality standards for mammograms administered at our nation's VA Hospitals" (Web bio). In addition, he has advocated for social security benefits for Persian Gulf veterans who served in Israel or Turkey, for expanded eligibility requirements for veterans qualifying under the work-study program, and for employment rights clarification for veterans. (PR 4/28/99). And, "with the support of Congressmen Amo Houghton, R-Corning, and Thomas R. Reynolds, R-Clarence, introduced a bill (H.R. 2455) to convey the USS Sphinx (ARL-24) to the Dunkirk Historical Lighthouse and Veterans Park Museum" (PR 7/12/01).

Given this constituency focus, it is not surprising that the first bill Quinn introduced in Congress originated with a constituency problem. "In the wake of a series of bombings that claimed five lives in upstate New York in December, Rep. Jack Quinn is proposing a new federal crackdown on the sale of explosives" (*BN* 2/23/94). Quinn's Federal Explosives Control Act of 1994 "would prevent people from walking into an explosives dealer's office and walking out with dynamite. Instead, it would require a federal permit for explosive sales . . . [and] require a five-day waiting period before explosives sales" (*BN* 2/23/94). And, "Congressman Jack Quinn today has become the lead Republican on a bill that would help resolve the crisis of low-cost, poor quality steel imports being dumped into the United States" (*PR* 1/25/99).[2]

At the same time, it has been Quinn's consistent support of organized labor that makes his profile so interesting. Obviously, such support is consistent with the character of his constituency. But, this support has had national implications as well. It has helped propel Quinn, on occasion, into the national spotlight. But, it has also put him at odds with the mainstream of his Republican Party's policy positions.

His most publicized work in this regard involved his activity in the 104th Congress on behalf of a minimum wage increase. In 1996, a bill to increase the minimum wage by ninety cents over a two-year time period had been proposed by President Clinton and congressional Democrats. The bill was all but dead due the strenuous opposition of the Republican leadership (majority leader Armey even vowed to oppose it with every fiber of his being). It was Quinn and Christopher Shays (R-CT) who went head-to-head with party leadership (actually proposing a bill including a higher wage hike—one dollar per hour over a fifteen-month period, raising the overall wage to $5.25 [*BN* 4/17/96]) to bring the bill to a vote, despite the fact that their stance on the issue flew in the face of Republican philosophy of minimal government intervention in business (*BN* 5/24/96). A rank-and-file Republican even said to Quinn: "You're going to be the reason I lose my re-election this fall. You're going to make me vote against minimum wage" (*BN* 5/25/96).

But, "Rep. Jack F. Quinn has fought skirmish after skirmish over the past few weeks, trying to win congressional approval for a hike in the minimum wage" (*BN* 5/18/96).

When the leadership backed down, Quinn added that:

[h]e was happy with the change in the leadership's tone. "Two weeks ago, the Republican leadership didn't even want to talk about the minimum wage. . . . And here we are today talking about scheduling a vote. It's unbelievable that we've been able to move the leadership that far in two weeks." (*BN* 5/2/96)

It is worth noting, in the context of Quinn's bucking the party line, that despite Quinn's obvious leadership, another party member (Rep. Frank Riggs, R-CA) was named official sponsor and leader of floor debate (party leadership argued that Quinn was not a member of the reporting committee, but other Republicans saw this as a slap at Quinn's efforts) (*BN* 5/24/96).

District press was more favorable. The *Buffalo News* printed the following headline on May 24, 1996: "Quinn Finally Gets His Place in the Sun After Minimum Wage Vote." More than the title, one passage from the article indicated how deeply Quinn was involved:

> About a dozen moderate House Republicans crowded in a news conference Thursday afternoon about their victory on the minimum wage increase, but they refused to begin it until the Hamburg Republican arrived. Then let Quinn do most of the talking. . . . Jack believed in it, crafted it, and, most importantly, wouldn't let it be sidetracked by the naysayers. (*BN* 5/25/96)

On another difficult vote, Quinn again broke ranks with most Republicans to support labor's opposition to the North American Free Trade Agreement (NAFTA).

Of course, the issue of free trade directly pits elements of his primary constituency (Republicans with a business orientation) against his reelection constituency (labor). Due to the 30th district's proximity to the Canadian border, the NAFTA controversy was particularly relevant to Quinn's constituency. The Canadian Free Trade treaty of 1989 had been seen as beneficial to the economically troubled area in making it more advantageous for business to locate on the Canadian border (*PIA* 1996, 960). However, the inclusion of Mexico with NAFTA heightened concerns among blue-collar constituents that free trade would mean losing jobs.

In 1993, the image of jobs again moving away from Erie County to low-wage locations seemed real (*BN* 11/21/93), so constituents were attentive. Some supported NAFTA and "an Orchard Park firm . . . was among the companies that exhibited their wares on the White House lawn Wednesday in a quickly organized exports 'Product Fair' designed to generate congressional support for the North American Free Trade Agreement" (*BN* 10/21/93).

But anger was more indicative of public sentiment. So, when Representative Quinn (who had opposed NAFTA throughout the 1992 campaign) was mistaken for one of Vice President Gore's pro-NAFTA aides, both

Quinn's office and the local paper were flooded with irate telephone calls
(*BN* 11/21/93).

In the end, the issue though wasn't really a difficult one for Quinn. "On
issues such as NAFTA, Quinn said he spends a lot of time finding out what
his constituents want" (*BN* 12/15/93). He did, however, acknowledge at a
local meeting:

> Once you're elected, whether it's town supervisor or U.S. congressman,
> you're faced with a balancing act: Well, I was elected. Do I do what I want
> to do, or do I do what the people ask me to do? And no matter what office
> it is, you are faced with that. (*BN* 12/15/93)

In recognition of these and other efforts on behalf of labor (including his
vote against a striker replacement bill, his work arranging a meeting
between Republican members of Congress and the AFL-CIO president,
and his sparring with "President Bush over his decision to ban project
labor agreements" [*Almanac* 2002, 1122]), Quinn was named the local
AFL-CIO's 1994 "Man of the Year" (AP 7/12/00) and AFL-CIO's International Brotherhood of Boilermakers, Ironship Builders, Blacksmiths, Forg-
ers and Helpers "Man of the Year" for his work.

Later, Quinn was treated to "one of my biggest days since I've been in
Congress" (*BN* 4/22/98). He followed minority leader Richard Gephardt
to the podium at the annual conference of the AFL-CIO Building and Construction Trades Council. "Both sides (Democratic and Republican) have
good ideas and ideas that will work. What seems to scare some people is
the idea that the two sides can work together" (*BN* 4/22/98).

Of course, Quinn's efforts on behalf of labor put him in tune with much
of his Democratic constituency, but his bipartisan style has also meant that
Quinn has had an interesting relationship with the national Republican
Party. Quinn has generally compiled a record supportive of Republican
themes, supporting balanced budgets, welfare reform, and congressional
term limits (*PIA* 1998, 1050).[3]

He cast important votes on behalf of provisions of the Contract with
America and, in 1994, was part of a bipartisan working group drafting
legislation (passed in the 104th Congress) on a line item veto (*PIA* 1996,
960). He is not seen as pro-choice (*BN* 12/9/92) (he did not support
President Clinton's 1993 efforts to lift the "gag rule" in federally funded
family planning clinics [*PIA* 1994, 1106] or partial birth abortion [*PIA*
2000, 988]), and "without even trying," he never scored less than 80

percent on the Christian Coalition's scorecard in his first six years (*BN* 10/28/98).

Quinn has sometimes remained loyal to his party even voting against constituency on some important concerns in the first session of the 104th Congress. The most publicized of these involved controversy over the Low Income Home Energy Assistance Program (LIHEAP), providing funding to senior and poor citizens who need assistance with energy and heating bills, an obvious issue in the Buffalo area. Although Quinn had been a strong supporter of this program in the 103rd Congress, he voted to cut funding in the 104th. Though he explained his vote by noting the cuts wouldn't take effect until the following year (implying the decision might be reversed), and though he subsequently was a leader in efforts to preserve the program (*PIA* 2000, 987), his 1995 vote upset many constituents (*BN* 3/21/95).

In addition, according to a newspaper editorial from a dissatisfied constituent: "In the last month Quinn has voted against subsidies for Amtrak, against subsidies for the light rail system. He voted to end the Davis-Bacon Act. . . . Quinn in the budget cast his second vote in five weeks to kill the Low Income Home Energy Assistance Program" (*BN* 5/22/95). Afterward, he told the *Buffalo News:* "The easy vote for me would be to keep these programs going, but I don't think I got sent down here to do that. . . . My main concern is that we have to cut the deficit" (*BN* 5/22/95).

However, as he had done in the 1992 campaign, Quinn has also often avowed bipartisanship: "There's enough blame in Washington to go around for all the parties, including mine. . . . We have to stop wasting time on that." Quinn added that he will seek advice not only from fellow Republican Bill Paxon, but from Democrat John J. LaFalce as well (*BN* 11/4/92).

In fact, his party unity scores between 1993 and 1998 generally averaged just below eighty, reaching their low of sixty-eight in 1996 (*PIA* 2002, 729), and he expressed concern when Speaker Gingrich was under investigation for ethics violations (*BN* 12/30/96). Quinn consistently advocated for a stronger leadership role for moderate Republicans: "Before, it so often ended up being cast as us either being for or against the leadership . . . I would rather that we get involved in shaping the legislation" (*BN* 11/10/96).

Not surprisingly, Quinn has supported the bipartisan civility retreats held for members of Congress ("Representative Jack Quinn . . . said between events that there was an incalculable benefit to 'getting to know someone over a tuna fish sandwich and a Pepsi instead of a minimum wage agreement'" [*NYT* 3/21/99]).

As we have seen, "[h]e long has been willing to buck his party on high-profile issues" (*PIA* 2000, 987). His support for President Clinton has averaged around 49%, ranging from a low of 30% in 1998 to a fairly supportive 60% in 1994 and 57% in 1996 (*PIA* 2002, 729). As a freshman he was one of only forty Republicans to support The Family and Medical Leave Act (*PIA* 1994, 1106) and one of forty-six Republicans to support President Clinton's crime bills (*PIA* 1996, 960). "He opposed efforts to allow states to deny public education to illegal aliens" and voted against the repeal of the assault weapons ban (*PIA* 2000, 988). "In 1998, he was one of only nine Republicans to oppose the House GOP's annual budget resolution, which squeaked through by a 216–204 tally" (*PIA* 2000, 987).

In a very different vein, Quinn has also shown "sartorial independence":

> In June 1998, Quinn flew in for a House vote from Buffalo, where he had taken in a Buffalo Sabres hockey playoff game. As required, Quinn had on a jacket and tie. He also had on shorts and deck shoes without socks. "They said you need a tie and a coat, and I qualify," Quinn said.[4] (*PIA* 2000, 989)

Quinn's bipartisan style and willingness to deviate at important points from party have meant that he developed an interesting relationship with then-president Clinton. Beginning with his support of Clinton's 1994 crime/assault weapons ban legislation, the two politicians have had an important personal connection which has also had political consequences. Quinn found himself in the position of being a potential swing vote when Clinton was advocating his initial crime control legislation. Based on input from community leaders back home in Buffalo ("[Mayor] Masiello told Quinn he needed more 'flexibility' in Buffalo in the way federal crime-fighting aid is spent than was provided in the original version" [*BN* 8/22/94]), Quinn came to support an idea that several sources credit as being critical to the bill's passage: block grants rather than categorical grants for particular programs.

In this context, and despite the obvious fact that "first term congressmen from the opposition party ordinarily see a president when everyone else does—on TV" (*BN* 8/21/94), Quinn was involved in a top-level strategy meeting with Clinton, Vice President Gore, and other administration officials ("I learned you can't be bashful when you get a chance like that, so I spoke right up" [*BN* 8/22/94]).[5]

It was against this background of friendship (Quinn had gone on to watch Super Bowls with Clinton [*BN* 2/13/99] that the impeachment issue in late 1998 turned out to be one of the "most controversial vote[s] he is ever likely to cast" (*BN* 10/16/99). It is not particularly surprising, given this friendship and his Democratic constituency that Quinn initially spoke out against impeachment. As late as December 9, 1998, "Clinton called Quinn from Air Force One and Quinn gave no sign of wavering" (*Almanac* 2002, 1123). But, as he listened to the arguments of the Judiciary Committee Republicans, he did. (*Almanac* 2002, 1123) "It wasn't a single event. It was a gradual process. It was just a very difficult decision to make. My friendship with the president made it doubly difficult" (*Almanac* 2002, 1123).

Quinn also stressed that he has no regrets about his decision to vote for impeachment. Quinn said in December that he opposed impeachment when the only thing he saw was Independent Counsel Kenneth W. Starr's report—and its lurid details of the Clinton relationship. Quinn said he changed his mind as the House Judiciary Committee hearings revealed "clear evidence of perjury and obstruction of justice" in Clinton's attempts to cover up his adulterous affair (*BN* 2/13/99). "The more I learn about the serious details of perjury and obstruction of justice, the more I am concerned about the president's failure to tell the truth under oath. The issue is about principle, not politics" (*BN* 12/20/98).

Quinn also turned out to be an opinion leader for moderate Republicans on the impeachment votes. In fact:

> Several Republican moderates who were on the fence then declared their support for impeachment as well, even leading an unnamed White House aide to tell the *New York Daily News* how Clinton became the second president ever to be impeached: "Two words: Jack Quinn." (*PIA* 2000, 987)

Consequently, Quinn was left to heal the personal relationship and deal with electoral fallout:

> At last month's State of the Union address, Rep. Jack F. Quinn reached out to shake President Clinton's hand, only to see the president look him in the eye and walk away. . . . "Our relationship will never be the same, having gone through this," said Quinn. "I just want to make certain that he knows that this (impeachment) issue is separate and distinct from my desire that we work together for the good of my district and the country." (*BN* 2/13/99)

Discussion

The profile of Representative Quinn has documented one Congress member's efforts to remain true to a primary constituency while stretching out to promote the interests of a broader reelection coalition. Indeed, if these efforts were the only part of the story, they would be interesting in and of themselves. Thus, in his effort to hold his coalition together, Quinn has not only followed in the footsteps of his Democratic predecessor by engaging in a wide variety of traditional constituency services—appearing frequently in the district, helping individual constituents—and bringing grants to the area, but he has also initiated what would appear to be some fairly innovative constituent interactions, for instance, the labor Round Table and the emphasis on closing constituent casework. Thus, it would appear that this is an office that doesn't just talk the talk, but also walks the walk.

Quinn's profile, illustrating one congressman's style of reaching out to a broad reelection constituency, is made even more interesting given the atypical constituency Quinn represents. His style of representation takes on additional significance given that it places Quinn in a unique position within the national Republican Party.

Yet, due to his strong district roots, a local orientation, and a "nice guy" image, Rep. Quinn has been able to win and retain his congressional seat, satisfying his Republican base while reaching out to broader constituencies and creating unusual coalitions. He ranks high on scales supporting both liberal and conservative groups (with occasional exceptions, his support of the AFL-CIO averages in the middle sixties; his ADA scores average around thirty, ranging from fifteen to fifty; his CCUS (Chamber of Commerce of the United States) scores average around eighty (*PIA* 2000, 989; *PIA* 2002, 729); and his 1996 NFIB (National Federation of Independent Business) score was eighty-six) (*Almanac* 1998, 1181). Similarly, Quinn has been honored by many and varied groups. In addition to the recognition he received from labor, he has also received recognition from, for instance, the CCUS and 1999 Spirit of Enterprise Award for his strong support for pro-business policies and legislation in the 105th Congress" (PR 3/99), the National Association of Manufacturers (NAM) (PR 11/2/98), and "the New York Farm Bureau, honored Rep. Quinn" (Web bio). He also received "the prestigious AMVETS Silver Helmet Award for his work on behalf of our nation's veterans" and "the golden spike award from railroad groups" (Web bio).

What does all this add to our understanding of the local-national connection? First and foremost, Quinn's profile suggests that even a fairly locally oriented representative occasionally finds himself in the national spotlight, for instance, the minimum wage and impeachment controversies. In addition, his profile reiterates the sometimes complex interconnections between local and national politics. In the cases of his work on behalf of veterans or railroads, he has "taken" local interests to Washington, contributed to national policy and claimed credit back in the district. His profile also illustrates the importance of the institutional opportunities afforded by the structure of Congress; even junior members are in a position to get noticed by presidents of the opposite party, and even in an era of important party cohesion, congressional party leadership sometimes perceives incentives to placate alternative views, in this case allowing moderate Republicans to force a minimum wage vote. So, often, Quinn's efforts in the local and national political arenas exhibited a very positive interconnection. On the other hand, varied contextual pressures, including a constituency of the opposite party, a declining regional economy, and a more conservative and stronger national party, at times led Quinn to emphasize his political independence, sometimes at the expense of his stature in Washington.

So, as they alternatively present opportunities and constraints, the relationships between national factors (electoral tides, debates on issues, the structure of Congress) have a fairly complex relationship to the local.

Despite Quinn's success in building unusual coalitions, it is this complexity that leads to a consideration as to the downsides of this type of home style. Obviously, in attempting to portray himself as a moderate, Quinn (and other members like him) runs the dual risks that his record will seem inconsistent to some and that it will simply alienate others—recall the quote at the beginning of this profile likening Quinn to the "Teflon" character of President Ronald Reagan. In attempting to satisfy a wide variety of voices across the political spectrum, Quinn faces the risk of angering some groups (*BN* 1/4/95; 4/30/94; 6/7/96).

And though Quinn in the main has forestalled strong challengers, the balancing of constituencies necessary to hold his district provides an ever-present reminder of his precarious electoral position. Though he avoided electoral difficulty in 1998 and 2000, his impeachment stand profoundly angered segments of his otherwise solid labor support ("We thought he was a friend of ours said a labor official" [*Almanac* 2002, 1123]. Even more, in the context of his controversial votes in the 104th Congress and the efforts of labor unions in an unsuccessful effort to help regain a

Democratic majority in the House in 1996 ([*BN* 9/11/96]), Democrats came closest to defeating Quinn. Francis Pordum, a well-respected state legislator, garnered some labor endorsements which had formerly gone to Quinn: Not surprisingly, Pordum attempted to link Quinn to Speaker Gingrich and the national Republican Party: "Jack Quinn voted with Newt Gingrich 89 percent of the time, and 96 percent of the time during the crucial first 100 days when they dealt with the Contract with America. . . . You can't run away from your record" (*BN* 10/23/96).

Responding that he believes in balanced budgets if not always the specifics of Republican plans to achieve them, Quinn highlighted his perception of his independence from party. "The voters in Buffalo understood and have ample opportunity to know, I vote independently. . . . We have a pretty independent record, and we reminded the voters of that" (*PIA* 2000, 987).

In the end, Quinn highlighted his local accomplishments, his bipartisanship, and, as before, his nice guy image (a constituent even told him: "Oh! You're even better looking than you are on television!" [*BN* 10/30/96]). Therefore, the 1996 election nicely sums up the opportunities and constraints inherent in a home style that involves "having your cake and eating it too," a home style also influenced in any number of ways by the larger national context.

Maurice Hinchey: Issue Activist at Home in his District

Regarding the Cherryhill-Sawkill road waterworks: Muriel Witticker, the battler, first gets the board of health to test water from wells. They are found to be contaminated. Ho! Hum. She then contacts Congressman Hinchey, who then conducts his own water well testing. This also shows contamination. Hinchey then has the Ulster town board fill out applications for grants and loans. The board fills them out, incorrectly. Hinchey then has his aide Allison Lee show the Town Board how to fill out applications. He is then able to help obtain all federal funds.
—*Kingston Daily Freeman* 7/28/97

It was fitting that the 25th anniversary celebration of the Woodstock music festival was held in Hinchey's district, in his hometown of Saugerties, for he remains firmly entrenched in the Democratic Party's liberal wing, a throwback to the 1960s. He has never scored less than a 95 percent voting rating for the Liberal Americans for Democratic Action, and he is a member of the Progressive Caucus, the furthest left of the Hill's policy groups.
—*PIA* 2000

The two descriptions quoted above definitely provide a good flavor for the multipronged nature of Rep. Hinchey's home style. Thus, the rather amusing efforts of Hinchey and his staff to obtain federal money for the cleanup of a contaminated well clearly show that Hinchey engages in many of the same service-oriented activities as does Rep. Quinn. In fact, the twists and turns of the story, even including the efforts of Hinchey's staff to perform independent tests on the well (how many Congress members are known for their well testing skills?), demonstrate that in many ways he is as proactive as Quinn in engaging in these sorts of activities.

But, the second description has a very different character. While it may make Hinchey appear to be a bit more extreme than he actually is—as a long-time state legislator with strong constituency roots, he focuses on the needs of his economically struggling area and works much of the time on fairly mainstream issues—the quote nevertheless highlights the most important thread of this profile: Hinchey's focus on a liberal primary constituency.

In a heterogeneous district where it might be politically safer to shy away from issue positions, he not only appears to enjoy speaking out but even more remains loyal to his version of "progressive" ideas. Thus, as we shall see, in the face of notably varying partisan and national tides, Hinchey clearly augments constituency activities with a strong focus on issues.

As a consequence, even more so than Quinn, national as well as local factors have figured into district politics. Indeed, at some level, in a district as close and diverse as Hinchey's, one might begin an analysis with the clear expectation that local politics would be of primary importance. What role could national factors play in the life of a congressperson representing a rather "ordinary" if not downright "obscure" mid–New York congressional district (have outsiders really heard of Saugerties or Ulster County?)? However, in addition to Hinchey's strong issue focus, indicative of modern politics, it is in fact the important ways in which national factors have mattered that make this profile particularly interesting.

Background

As Hinchey's background actually debunks stereotypes that only citizens raised in "advantaged" surroundings have the opportunity to rise to a top-level political career, the "particularly interesting" character of this profile begins with Hinchey's background.

While born on the lower west side of Manhattan (www . . . hinchey) in 1938 (*PIA* 2000, 977), Hinchey moved upstate as a child to the small town of Saugerties (*PIA* 2000). Growing up in a working-class home (*PIA* 2002, 720), instead of heading to college directly after high school, Hinchey served in the Navy for three years (1956–1959) (*PIA* 2002, 977), "serving in the Pacific on the destroyer U.S.S. Marshal" (www . . . hinchey). (He reminds his constituents that he received an honorable discharge [*PIA* 2002, 720]). "Further, Maurice Hinchey still remembers the experience of working alongside his father as a heavy equipment operator at a local cement plant," and he helped put himself through college working as a night-shift toll collector on the New York State Thruway (*PIA* 2002, 720). "He went on to earn a master's degree at New Paltz and did advanced graduate work in public administration and economics at the State University of New York at Albany" (Web bio).

Yet, at the same time, Hinchey's family had some political roots (*PIA* 2002, 721). "Hinchey's parents had thus been active in local party politics, his father having been a Democratic Party chair in Saugerties (*TU* 9/12/92) and his wife having worked as a long- time newscaster" (*TU* 9/12/92). So, "after his graduation from college, he was encouraged to get involved in behind-the-scenes political activities while starting a career in education" (*PIA* 2002, 721). "An environmental fight in the 1970s over the development of a huge power plant on the Hudson River was the primary impetus for Hinchey's entry into electoral politics" (*PIA* 2002, 720), and he made an unsuccessful run for state assembly in 1972 (*PIA* 2002, 721). Two years later, in the aftermath of Watergate and the resignation of Republican President Richard Nixon, circumstances were more on Hinchey's side. So, though "Maurice Hinchey of Ulster County undertook a quest that—at any other time—would have been deemed laughably quixotic: a run for the state Assembly, as a Democrat in an Ulster county district which had only sent one Democrat to Congress since the Civil War," the tide was in the Democratic direction:

> But 1974 was not an ordinary year . . . and it produced extraordinary electoral results across the nation, state and even Ulster County . . . fielding a team of dynamic young idealists to run in traditionally Republican districts. (*TU* 10/10/99)

In contrast to Quinn, from the start, Hinchey had the particular support of groups within a primary constituency—Democrats, environmentalists, and other "idealists."

How was he able to turn this somewhat unusual 1974 victory into not only a long (eighteen years) but distinguished career in the state legislature and ultimately into a career in the U.S. Congress? How did the amateur environmental activist become someone who could later run for higher legislative office, touting his record as a professional politician?

For starters, it was easy for Hinchey, the environmentalist, to hold the loyalty of core supporters. He became chairman of the Environmental Conservation Committee in 1978. "Under his leadership, the committee conducted a successful investigation into the causes of 'Love Canal,' one of the nation's first major toxic dumpsites, and developed landmark environmental legislation including the nation's first law to control acid rain" (www . . . hinchey).[6]

As his Web site touts his numerous accomplishments as a state legislator, he clearly wants constituents to be aware of his activism:

> During his tenure in Albany, he was responsible for the development of the statewide system of Urban Cultural Parks (now called Heritage Areas) including those in Kingston and Binghamton. He is the author of the 1991 act that created the Hudson River Valley Greenway, and later as a congressman, he wrote the federal legislation that established the Hudson River Valley American Heritage Area (which extends from Yonkers to Waterford). (*TU* 10/10/96).

Also, interestingly, "Hinchey led an investigation [1982–1992] into organized crime's control of the waste-hauling industry that led to the conviction of more than 20 criminal figures" (Web bio).

In addition to strengthening core support, Hinchey also showed himself to be an able politician with the skills to satisfy a broader reelection constituency. In fact, a record of his travels throughout the district as a state legislator generated some controversy in this regard. In order to do errands and, more importantly, to keep in touch with constituents, he apparently often drove a "meandering" route from his Saugerties home to his state legislative duties in Albany. In turn, when reimbursement time came around, critics claimed he was not entitled to the extra mileage (*IJ* 11/4/94). In addition, he "was proud of" passing what would appear to be a very large number (six hundred) of bills during his tenure in office (*Almanac* 2002, 1112) and of his service on key committees in the Assembly (Web bio). He was even mentioned as a candidate for lieutenant governor (*TU* 4/29/86) and later for governor (*TU* 4/10/97).

So, in 1992, with the surprise announcement of the retirement of his long-time friend and nine-term incumbent Democratic Congressman Matthew McHugh (*TU* 7/10/92), Hinchey had a difficult decision to make:

> I've got a safe seat here in Ulster County, relatively safe anyway. Even as a Democrat in a Republican district I get re-elected by about a 2-to-1 margin, usually. I've got the influence that goes with 18 years of experience in Albany, so I can get things done. I admit my closest friends urged me not to run. Making this decision was painful, physically painful. (*TU* 8/23/92)

It is beyond the scope of this project, focused as it is on home style, to elaborate on the extensive details of each of Hinchey's controversial and generally close (at least before 1998) elections—his 1996 opponent, Sue Wittig, though a political amateur, was an articulate conservative disagreeing with virtually all of Hinchey's positions, and in 1998 Randal Terry, founder of Operation Rescue, not only ran in the Republican primary but also in the general election on the Right-to-Life line. But the following illustrations, taken mostly from 1992 and 1994, nicely illustrate the impact national factors had on an otherwise local race.

Without doubt, local factors mattered. "Hinchey's nine terms in the state Legislature had made him enormously popular in his heavily Republican assembly district, where he won re-election by strong margins" (*PIA* 1996, 949).

And Hinchey is a vigorous campaigner adept at highlighting constituent needs: "They stopped at the farmer's market, the Friends of the Tompkins County Public Book Sale and the Ithaca Commons. 'I think Matt's [McHugh] done a great job for Ithaca in congress. . . . Everyone in Ithaca respects Matt, and he says so many good things about Maurice'" (*IJ* 9/22/92). He phone banked every registered Democrat to achieve a narrow victory in the 1992 primary (*PIA* 1994, 1094), touted his accomplishments as a state legislator, and, later, reminded constituents of the federal largess he had brought to the area.

Further, in a recession-hit area, Hinchey consistently focuses on the basics. "Every campaign is always about the economy. . . . If you don't have a good strong economy, if people aren't working. . . . They don't have the luxury of being concerned about other issues" (*Binghamton Press & Sun-Bulletin* 7/25/00).

However, the close partisan balance in the 26th, Hinchey's penchant for speaking out ("People know how I stand on the issues. I don't try to hide anything. . . . People appreciate that" [*KDF* 11/4/98]), and the partisan nature of the times brought the district to the attention of the national parties. Especially early on, Hinchey's elections were not exactly easy victories reaffirming the popularity of a safe incumbent. Rather, his races have consistently received national attention, and "Hinchey knows he's a target. And he revels in it" (*TU* 10/30/94).

> [The 1992 and 1994 general election] contest became a microcosm of the presidential race, matching populist Democrat Hinchey against a conservative Republican [Broome County legislator and moving company owner Bob Moppert]. . . . While Moppert preached a get-the-government-off-our-backs brand of business-led economic fundamentalism, Hinchey countered with Clinton-style calls for an activist federal government and investment in infrastructure. (*PIA* 1998, 1094)

In contrast to the liberal record Hinchey had developed as a state legislator, Moppert was a conservative Republican seeking to lower taxes and limit the role of the federal government. Thus, Moppert and Hinchey strongly disagreed on most key issues including the economy (Hinchey wanted government intervention; Moppert did not), abortion (Hinchey wanted government support; Moppert opposed Medicaid funding), and term limits (Hinchey opposed; Moppert supported) (*KDF* 11/1/92). He "called for national health insurance, a repeal of the Reagan-Bush tax cuts for the rich and corporations, and 'reindustrializing America'" (*Almanac* 2000, 1169) and he took a shot at Republican talk about family values:

> What some people mean by family values, is that they want to put their values on our families. The real family values are freedom of choice, equal opportunity, equal pay for equal work, child care, family leave, the right to a decent education, the right to a decent job. (*KDF* 11/1/92)

"In 1994, while Hinchey roundly criticized The Contract with America calling it 'deplorably wrong. It would seek to balance the budget on the backs of the most vulnerable people of our society'" (*IJ* 11/3/94), Moppert had presented one of its items (*PIA* 1996, 949).

Even more, in 1994, national partisan elements were ratcheted up. As one political scientist described the partisan atmosphere: "The district itself is irrelevant the race is all that matters," said Richard Fox, a Union College political science professor. . . . "It's happening all over," said Fox. "What's going on this year is unprecedented campaigning by Gingrich and other members. There use to be an old rule: You don't campaign against a sitting member." (*TU* 10/30/94).

Thus, a campaign highlight was a Gingrich fundraiser where the Republican leader described the "dark and bloody planet" that would result if the Democrats were to retain power (*TU* 10/30/94) and the national Republican Party made a $60,000 contribution (*PIA* 1996, 949).

So, Hinchey's strategy was two-pronged. He could reaffirm his own record and the accomplishments of the Democratic Party. President Clinton, Vice President Gore (actually, Hinchey acknowledged being in frequent contact with the vice president on issues related to the environment and emerging technologies [*TU* 9/24/94]), and other figures associated with Democratic causes campaigned on his behalf. "The political stars are coming out all along the Hudson River Valley and the Southern Tier"[7] (*TU* 10/30/94).

In addition, he could remind his broader reelection constituency: "I was successful before because people accept my honesty and candor. . . . Even if we don't agree, people see me as someone who has thought things through and is speaking for himself independently, unlike my opponent in this race, who is merely mouthing the logic provided by Newt Gingrich" (*TU* 10/30/94).

In the end, "In a contest that was not only partisan but geographic . . . Hinchey carried Ulster and Moppert carried the Binghamton area; Ithaca and Tompkins County decided it, going for Hinchey by 30 points" (*Almanac* 1996, 969–70).[8] In 1994, the results were even closer, with Hinchey winning by only 366 votes (*PIA* 1996, 949), a margin that increased to 1,233 votes once absentee ballots were counted (*PIA* 1996, 949). Subsequently, Hinchey had it a bit easier, winning in 1996 with 55 percent of the vote, and with 62 percent in 1998 and 2000 (*PIA* 2002, 720).

One final note: The 2000 election featured yet another Hinchey-Moppert rematch: "I haven't seen Bob in four years, five years, or so. I'm anxious to see him again," Hinchey said. "He's been in hibernation. He's had this sort of no-show job over there that the state gave him [former Pataki administration regional economic development director] and he's been staying low, and, you know, sleeping well. It's time for him to come out. . . . They don't catch on quickly. . . . You have to beat them over the head time and time again in order for them to get the message. And we'll be happy to do it again in the year 2000" (*PS* 7/25/00).

Home Style

Needless to say, freshman-elect Hinchey was pretty excited about going to Congress in 1992: "'Anyone who has come from the modest background I have to be a representative in the U.S. Congress is what this country is all about,' an emotional Hinchey said. . . . 'It proves anyone can do anything if they work hard enough'" (*KDF* 11/4/92). "With deep gratitude . . . I go to Washington determined to make a positive difference. I pledge to stand up for our rights in Congress and do all I can to make sure government is fighting on our side for change" (*KDF* 11/13/92). And, as was true of Quinn, the "positive difference" Hinchey hoped to make would begin in the constituency. "Maurice knows the county inside and out; it will be easy for him to represent Ulster County," said former Rep. Matthew McHugh (*KDF* 11/5/92).

Thus, as a member of Congress, Hinchey has opened offices in four of the district's population centers (Kingston, Binghamton, Ithaca, Monticello) (www . . . hinchey). Like Representative Quinn, he has interacted with constituents at town meetings, party fundraisers, student classrooms, and campaign events (*KDF* 11/3/94).

- Hinchey To Host All-Day Women's Health Conference (PR 4/24/98)
- Hinchey Tours Tornado Damage In Binghamton (PR 6/2/98)
- Hinchey Visits Pt. Ewen Library; Calls on FCC to Continue Internet Funding (PR 7/2/98)
- Hinchey Visits Magnet Schools (PR 9/9/98)

Too, Hinchey has nominated the New York State Citizens Coalition for Children to receive the 2000 Angel in Adoption award (*IJ* 10/13/00) and has supported the work of local AmeriCorps volunteers (*KDF* 7/15/97).

As he has promised in his campaigns, Hinchey has made the economic "security of working families across the Hudson Valley, Catskill Mountains and Southern tier his top priority" (www.hincheyforcongress.org). "As he said, I believe I was elected to bring back manufacturing jobs to New York State and elsewhere across the country" (*KDF* 11/11/92). Thus, "There's an exciting new community development program in New York's 26th Congressional District—the Rural Economic Area Partnership (REAP) Zone program" (www . . . hinchey).

In addition to numerous federal grants he has helped secure for the district ("Cornell University Awarded $1.1 Million To Help Disabled With

Information Technology" [PR 9/20/01]; "Lockheed Martin Awarded $149 Million Contract Modification" [PR 8/20/01]), Hinchey has also advocated for the diverse needs of groups across the region, lobbying for federal funds for apple growers threatened with foreign competition (AP 6/19/01), supporting "the St. Regis Mohawks' plan to build what is billed as the nation's largest casino about two hours from the Capital Region" (TU 4/7/00), and working for the completion of the upgrade of the Southern Tier Expressway to a federal interstate (I-86). He even wrote a letter to the New York Times advocating for the increased use of Stewart International Airport as an alternative to the more well-known metropolitan airports (NYT 4/14/01).

Hinchey also takes considerable pride in ongoing efforts to boost the economy and environment of the Hudson River so prominent in his district. As a state legislator, he had sponsored the Hudson River Valley Greenway legislation (TU 6/4/00). As a member of Congress, it is not surprising that one of the first bills he introduced was a proposal creating the Hudson River Valley American Heritage Area (which extends from Yonkers to Waterford) (TU 10/10/96). "The Hudson River is among 14 waterways that President Clinton will officially designate as American Heritage Rivers, a distinction that will pave the way to more federal dollars to protect its waters and develop its shore" (TU 7/28/98). Because of its importance to the district, Hinchey even "postponed a flight from Albany to Washington Monday afternoon—an hour before Gore made the official announcement—to announce the news himself at Rondout Creek, a Hudson tributary in Kingston"[9] (TU 7/28/98).

However, consistent with his campaigns, there can be a partisan/ideological side to Hinchey's district-oriented activity. He clearly situates himself within the traditions of the Democratic Party, even giving something of a history lesson as to his version of the party's founding. Participating at a ceremony marking the 220th anniversary of New York State's constitution and George Clinton, the first governor,

> Hinchey . . . told of Jefferson and Madison traveling up the Hudson River on a 'botanical exploration' in 1791. "They also were scouting out politics, looking to strike alliances for a party that would provide a counterweight to the Federalists," said Hinchey. . . . Hinchey said Jefferson and Madison met in Albany with Clinton and Aaron Burr to form the Democrats.[10] (KDF 4/20/97)

As a state legislator, he attended an anti-KKK rally to protest Ku Klux Klan activity in the area (*TU* 10/5/92), and he was actually arrested for marching in protest of President Reagan's Nicaraguan policy (*TU* 6/27/86). As a member of Congress, he has appeared at rallies co-sponsored by the liberal Hunger Action Network and at SUNY New Paltz College in support of abortion and woman's rights (*KDF* 11/3/94).

More recently, Hinchey has expressed his support for the needs of seniors in a very partisan though personal way: "U.S. Rep. Maurice Hinchey, D-Saugerties, who spoke to the group of New Yorkers as they boarded the bus, is supporting a bill in Congress that would require drug companies to charge everyone the same prices charged to Veterans Hospitals, which is a substantial discount. 'We need a system of national health insurance so that the government can negotiate with drug companies'" (*TU* 6/6/00).

And, he has not hesitated to let Democratic audiences know his views as to the 1994 Republican Revolution: "Hinchey is Slated To Discuss The Contract with America and the Rise of Right-Wing Politics" (*TU* 10/18/95).

More recently, in a protracted controversy of a very different order, Hinchey has been a key player in "[t]he decades-long debate over dredging PCBs from the Hudson" (*TU* 2/1/01). While it is beyond the scope of this project to describe the extent or depth of the controversy, the background is that the General Electric Company (legally [*TU* 6/22/00]) "released the now-banned polychlorinated biphenyls from 1947 to 1976 at its Fort Edward and Hudson Falls plants" (*TU* 5/12/00), and, in an unquestionably controversial decision, the Environmental Protection Agency proposed dredging as a mechanism to clean the Hudson.

Needless to say, this decision involves political, economic, and even scientific considerations (www.nodredging.com; *TU* 8/2/01; *NYT* 8/1/01). Mostly, of course, the controversy has pitted the General Electric Company against local communities, as GE contributed significant money to friendly candidates, ran controversial TV spots, and produced a Web site to promote its viewpoint (*DN* 6/13/00; *TU* 2/1/01).

Consistent with his environmental activism, over the course of this notably protracted debate, Rep. Hinchey has taken an unambiguously pro-dredging stand. He has been among those who point up the health risks of the current state of the Hudson and has been notably critical of both GE's efforts to block a cleanup (PR 8/4/99) and the EPA for delaying the start of dredging ("Delay, Delay, Delay: that's all we have been getting from the EPA when it comes to cleaning up the Hudson" [PR 3/9/98]). Thus, he has attended rallies (*TU*

8/21/99; TU 4/6/01), written to appropriate officials (*TU* 5/12/00), and worked in Washington to oppose delaying legislation (*DN* 6/13/00).

But, despite this partisan side, Hinchey can still have fun with constituents—Hinchey "tried to slip into a pair of borrowed waders while still wearing western boots" to celebrate the opening of trout season (*TU* 4/4/95).

The bottom line to all this constituency activity may have been summed up in the following description of a Hinchey walk to the voting booth in his home Ulster County:

> Everyone seemed to know Hinchey, greeting him by his first name, wishing him luck, shaking hands, slapping him on the back, calling across the parking lot. . . . A white haired woman was sitting at a folding chair near the table where election inspectors were checking registrations . . . Hinchey walked over, stuck out his hand and leaned forward. She knew him, but wasn't particularly interested in politics at that moment. "They're going to do that horrible festival thing again," Irma . . . said to Hinchey, who seemed surprised at her apparent opposition.
>
> "It didn't seem too bad," he said as Irma frowned.
>
> "It's all about money, drugs, rock and roll," Irma said, shaking her head.
>
> "It's about music." Hinchey replied. "That's the kind of music kids like." He disputed the drug use.
>
> "There were kids sliding in the mud with no clothes on." Hinchey assured her festival participants were muddy but not naked. (*KDF* 11/4/98)[11]

They never found out how she voted.

Washington Activity. As the following descriptions make clear, the distinctive features of Hinchey's activity within Congress have to do with his staunch partisanship and his belief that government intervention improves people's lives. Although he additionally focuses on more mainstream concerns, on balance, his work places him squarely within the camp of an easily definable primary constituency. Consider: "Hinchey's voting record reads as the diary of a faithful Democrat and reliable supporter of the Clinton administration on most initiatives. During the 103rd Congress, he supported the President's budget and deficit-reduction plan, the 'motor voter' registration bill and a measure requiring a five-day waiting period for handgun purchases. He also opposed a ban on federal funding of abortions" (*PIA* 1996, 949), and has voted to permit partial birth abortions (*PIA* 2000, 977).

Within this partisan context, "Hinchey's top priorities have been ensuring the economic security of working families, strengthening our education system and protecting the environment" (www . . . hinchey). Thus, recalling his graduate economics training, he has been a member of the Banking and Finance Committee, the House Senate Joint Economic Committee, and the Appropriations Committee since 1999. He has also been a co-chair of the Economic Renewal Task Force of the Democratic Caucus (Web bio) and regional representative on the Democratic Study Group Executive Committee.[12]

"He believes that the best ways to bring jobs to the area are through targeted federal grants and loans to jump-start the economy, investments in infrastructure and worker training, and tax cuts for businesses looking to develop and expand"(www.hincheyforcongress.org). As he explains his view in no uncertain terms: "The disparity in income between those at the top and those at the bottom of the ladder is a cancer that will ultimately sap the vitality of our economic system, exacerbating the social problems that are already plaguing our society" (*PIA* 2000, 978). "You can't feed a family on $5.15 an hour . . . a minimum wage that allows a parent to feed her children is a real family value" (*PIA* 2000, 976).[13]

In a different vein, Hinchey secured a seat on the Resources Committee (1993–1998), and he has retained his environmental activism. "Environmental policies remain Hinchey's principle concern outside of Appropriations, and it is on those issues that he is most likely to become embroiled in partisan disputes" (*PIA* 2002, 720). As his campaign material describes it,

> Hinchey has led numerous successful efforts in Congress to protect and improve our national parks and to preserve publicly owned wilderness. He is the sponsor of the America's Red Rocks Wilderness Act, which would protect 9.1 million acres of Utah's publicly owned red rock canyon lands from degradation. In 1999, 168 of his congressional colleagues join his successful effort to convince the Clinton Administration to protect the remaining roadless areas of our national forests, including the pristine Tongass National Forest in Alaska. As a member of the House Interior Appropriations Subcommittee, Hinchey has been a leader in blocking the passage of damaging riders to appropriations legislation that would allow oil drilling and mining in environmentally sensitive areas. (www.hincheyforcongress.org)

The story of "The America's Red Rock Wilderness Act" referred to above provides an illustration of the partisan controversy inherent in environmental issues as well as Hinchey's persistence. In his view, "the bill would protect some of the nation's most spectacular rock-scapes and rare and fragile lands" (PR 4/26/01), and Hinchey has introduced versions of the bill in every Congress since 1993.

> But even as he introduces it, Hinchey knows its chances of passage. "Not in this Congress," he said. "But this is a bill that is important to Utah and to the nation. We're keeping the issue alive and we're building support for it here in the Congress and around the country." (AP 4/26/01)

Obviously, those favoring development were not thrilled with these proposals. Nor were officials from Utah who viewed Hinchey's efforts as those of an out-of-stater meddling in western affairs (*Sierra,* September/October 1995). Utah Republican Representative Christopher Cannon went so far as to come to New York and protest Hinchey's activities within the 26th district (*TU* 4/21/97), and "Utah Republican Rep. James Hansen, who has sparred with Hinchey each time he has proposed the wilderness bill, said the bill's prospects were always slim and this year they're even slimmer. 'George Bush is in the White House, I'm chairman of the (House) Resources Committee, and Mo Hinchey is still from New York,' Hansen said. 'This bill is going nowhere'" (AP 4/26/01).

On a different note, Hinchey praised recommendations of the Environmental Protection Agency to reduce the use of MTBE additives in gasoline (PR 7/27/99), and, as his campaign material highlights, "Hinchey led the bipartisan effort in the House in November 1997 that urged Secretary Glickman to revise the draft Tongass Land Management Plan" (PR 4/14/99). More recently, "Hinchey Grills Energy Secretary Spencer Abraham, interior subcommittee appropriations. Hinchey also criticized budget proposals for 2002 for ignoring energy efficiency" (PR 5/3/01).

Thus, "Hinchey has been selected by the Sierra Club as an environmental 'hero' in each of his terms of Congress. He has also earned a 98% lifetime rating from the League of Conservation Voters. Three times, the LCV chose Hinchey as one of only eight members of the House and Senate on its Earth List. These eight legislators are considered the 'very best' of the candidates LCV endorses" (www.hincheyforcongress.org).

Hinchey expresses strong opinions in other areas as well. Partly as a result of the many colleges and universities throughout his district, and partly growing out of his own struggles as a first-generation college graduate,[14] Hinchey has been a longtime advocate of easier access to education: "Congressman Maurice Hinchey firmly believes that education and job training pave the way to a brighter future for all Americans. Improving our schools and providing access to higher education have been top priorities throughout his life in public service," (www.hincheyforcongress.org). "If we failed at everything else, but educated the next generation, we would have succeeded" (*KDF* 10/17/96). "When children go to school and find that the paint on the walls is peeling, their textbooks are obsolete and their classrooms are overcrowded, they often reach the logical conclusion that no one cares about them" (www.hincheyforcongress.org).

Thus, Hinchey has co-sponsored the National Service Act (allowing repayment of college loans through community service), the Scholarship Exemption Act, and the Employer Educational Assistance Exclusion Act (which allows tax breaks for education).[15] "He voted to make college more affordable by providing tuition tax credits, increased Pell grants, and HOPE scholarships. He has worked for higher standards in public schools, investments in school facilities, smaller class sizes and better access to technology" (www.hincheyforcongress.org). As he eloquently describes it: "It's important that everyone who is able and wants a college education should have access to higher education, we can't afford to lose those minds."[16]

On health care, Hinchey advocated: "We need to have the courage and foresight that our predecessors in the House had when they passed social security, when they passed the GI bill, and when they passed Medicare" (*PIA* 1996, 949). "He supported a Democratic plan to regulate managed health care organizations ('When you're sick, you want a doctor not an accountant making decisions about your care. . . . This common-sense legislation will guarantee consumer choice and access to emergency services and specialists. It will help protect consumers and restore their confidence in the health care system')" (*PIA* 2000, 977), and "Hinchey has been a strong advocate for fairer prescription drug pricing" ("Hinchey Releases Results of Prescription Drug Investigation; finds Price Discrimination Against Senior Citizens") (PR 9/30/98). In short, "we still need universal health care" (Web op. ed. 7/3/01).

Hinchey has also stood up for consumer concerns including the right of information privacy, for example, "Hinchey Blasts Republicans for Blocking Vote on Driver's License Amendment; Pledges to Introduce New Legislation" to prohibit states from "disclosing or selling" information (PR 6/23/99; Web op. ed. 6/2/00; PR 7/29/99).

Finally, the congressman has even weighed in on some foreign policy concerns: "My View: U.S. must commit to helping Israelis and Syrians" (Web op. ed. 1/21/00):

> Hinchey today continues his meetings with leaders of Middle East Nations in an effort to assist in re-establishing the peace process in that region. Hinchey has been traveling in the Middle East since Saturday on a fact finding mission sponsored by the Center for Middle East Peace and Economic Cooperation. (Web op. ed. 1/21/00)

And, "Hinchey Meets with Netanyahu, Reviews U.S. Troops Stationed in the Persian Gulf" (PR 2/17/99).

In addition, he advocated (in a provision of the Intelligence Authorization Act of 1999) that the CIA release information about the dictatorship and human rights abuses of Chilean leader Pinochet, whose regime came to power in the aftermath of overthrowing a democratically elected government (PR 11/9/99). He traveled to Poland "as part of the U.S. delegation attending the sixth annual session of the parliamentary assembly of the Organization for Security and Cooperation in Europe [of fifty-three countries]. . . . This meeting is an excellent opportunity to ensure that America's security needs are respected and that America's strong belief in human rights and environmental protection are shared throughout Europe" (KDF 7/6/97), and "Hinchey led a fight in the Agriculture Appropriations subcommittee to allow U.S. humanitarian aid against sanctioned countries last fall. . . . 'Millions starve in Cuba, North Korea, Iraq and other sanctioned nations,' Hinchey said. 'We are not punishing their dictators by withholding food and medicine, we are punishing innocent civilians'" (TU 2/16/00). (Along with Rep. McNulty, he also participated in a fact-finding trip to Cuba [TU 2/16/00]).

In all these areas, as we have seen, Hinchey has been described as a strong partisan and a "reliable" liberal. In 1997, he ranked ninth in party unity (Almanac 2000, 1169). He received a 99 percent career rating from the AFL-CIO and never less than a 95 percent rating from the Americans for Democratic Action[17] (PIA 2002, 720). A member of the Democratic whip organization, he unhesitatingly presents himself to constituents as a representative loyal to his party (PIA 2002).

- Hinchey, Democrats Unveil Patients Bill of Rights Act: Legislation to protect citizens receiving health care from managed care organizations (PR 3/31/98)
- Impeachment "Punishes the Country Not the President": Impeachment is a grave matter with grave consequences (Web op. ed. 12/15/98)
- Efforts to pass Northeastern Dairy Compact Thwarted by Republican Leadership (PR 9/28/99)
- Bush Squanders Budget Surplus, Hinchey Charges (PR 9/5/01)

Yet, it should also be clear that Hinchey is not the kind of staunch Democrat who refuses to work with Republicans. "I'm a moderate kind of guy" (*KDF* 10/15/96). And even after the Republican victory in 1994, he added, "I will be looking for opportunities to work with them on things that benefit the country and benefit the district" (*KDF* 11/2/94).

Thus, Hinchey "often teams with fellow upstate New York lawmakers" such as Houghton, for "funding to upgrade the southern tier's principal east-west highway to interstate status," and Rep. Walsh, on behalf of apple growers (*PIA* 2002, 720). On the lighter side, Hinchey, described as a "devout" New York Yankees baseball fan, even made a World Series bet with Georgia Republican representative Johnny Isakson (Atlanta Braves; they occupy neighboring offices) (PR 11/10/99).

In addition, he sometimes deviates from party when he casts roll call votes, voting against NAFTA and against the final version of President Clinton's welfare reform plan (*PIA* 2000, 977). Though he did vote for the five-day waiting period that was part of the Brady bill, unlike many traditional Democrats he has tended to support gun owner's rights. A member of the congressional sportsmen's caucus, "he was the only New York Democrat voting in 1996 to repeal the ban on certain semi-automatic assault-style weapons and the only New York Democrat to vote against the ban in the first place in the 103rd Congress" (*PIA* 2000, 978).[18]

Discussion

This profile has thus highlighted, against the backdrop of modern national politics, Rep. Hinchey's efforts to balance the interests of both his reelection and primary constituencies.

As we have seen, Hinchey has long-standing district connections. Like Quinn, he reaches out to constituents, providing services, working for jobs, bringing federal grants and projects to the district, and using constituent input as material for national legislation. "My job was to make sure my people got a fair shake" (*KDF* 10/21/96). Hinchey thus reminds us of the type of politician described by Fenno in the 1970s. How does a smart politician cultivate a heterogeneous constituency? Hinchey's profile reiterates the importance of developing personal connections, highlighting the local and cultivating constituent trust. As is equally obvious from this profile, because of the nature of his own personal experiences and because of his loyalty to primary constituents, Hinchey also unequivocally espouses a strong commitment to particular issue interests. As is shown by his concern for the environment, espousal of national health insurance and women's/civil rights, he has unhesitatingly chosen to handle the reelection/primary constituency dilemma posed at the beginning of this chapter by weighing in toward the primary constituency end.

More generally, it is also clear that Hinchey has integrated extra-district factors in his home style. The economic downturns experienced by his constituents place his district in the context of broader trends impacting large portions of the northeast. In addition, national and partisan factors impacted his election contests, and he is clearly committed to the national issue positions he takes. As the sometimes very partisan press releases on his Web site demonstrate, in many ways he has localized the national and in turn, he also sometimes nationalizes the local.

Indeed, though this profile is, at bottom, an illustration of one politician's successful attempts to represent a politically complex district, one is struck by the interconnections between the local and the national. Hinchey seeks federal help to better the local area while at the same time translating concerns about local jobs into votes for higher minimum wages or work on congressional committees concerned with the economy. In fact, in this profile, it seems misleading to separate out what is local from what is national. Thus, Hinchey works on economic and environmental concerns at all levels of government, exhibits party loyalty at home and in Washington and, referring back to the story of getting federal money to decontaminate the local well (top profile), he uses the tools available to achieve the job at hand.

In short, this profile demonstrates that though the worlds of the 26th district and Washington have their differences, there are also many interconnections between the local and the national.

Conclusion

It has been the purpose of this chapter to reexamine Fenno's bulls-eye model in the more national context of the 1990s. As we have seen, starting with the fact that they both represent economically troubled areas, there are many similarities between the activities of Reps. Quinn and Hinchey—both represent districts atypical of their party's mainstream, both are very much rooted within the culture of their communities, and both are certainly proactive when it comes to cultivating constituency connections.

But, of course, beyond those similarities, these representatives have made notably different representational choices, as we have seen, with

Quinn attempting to develop a broad-based reelection constituency and Hinchey never shying away from primary constituents. What factors explain these similarities and differences? As was true for the other case studies, it is an interesting interaction between constituency and background factors that matters here. Obviously, the two geographic/reelection constituencies set the boundaries for representational choices. Faced with serious economic hardships in their districts, both legislators devote large proportions of their efforts to revitalization. It makes sense that two smart politicians would emphasize the ways they have brought in federal money to boost the status of the local area or to benefit individual constituents. And, of course, from a political perspective, such reelection-oriented strategies also make sense. A focus on constituency connections and services can only help a legislator in the electorally difficult position of representing an opposite-party district or, even more, a politically diverse area.

But, his focus on labor concerns notwithstanding, Quinn has been willing to build cross-party coalitions, finding ways to keep his feet in many camps, while Hinchey places himself squarely within the ideological and partisan orientations of a primary constituency. As Republican Quinn represents a Democratic district, his predilection for coalition building could at least in part stem from constituency concerns. But background factors play a role as well. Recall that at various points in his life, Quinn was fairly apolitical—it took his uncle's sending him a voter registration form to get him to vote, and his first political experience was on a bipartisan Hamburg town board dealing with local concerns. In contrast, Hinchey had grown up in a staunchly Democratic family, had become politically involved himself as a result of an environmental controversy, and early on was elected to a partisan state assembly, his first election coming in the Democratic post-Watergate election of 1974. All this being said and, of course, granting that politicians can change with the times, it would appear as though the early political styles and precongressional careers of these legislators have notably marked their later in-office behavior.

As we have asked in other chapters, what do these profiles teach about the local-national distinction? First off, as we have seen, though the stories of these two politicians are at bottom locally oriented, these politicians have clearly had to take national factors into account. Because of the strong labor presence in his district, Quinn was driven to take a national role on issues including the minimum wage, and, of course, in part because of the Democratic nature of the district, he has had to steer clear of many national Republican policies. The national issue (minimum wage) has provided him with some opportunities, but national/partisan factors have also placed Quinn in awkward positions. Finally, it could be said that national factors shaped a piece of his home style, reinforcing constituency and background factors pushing Quinn toward independence and bipartisanship.

In contrast to Quinn, consistent with his emphasis on a primary constituency and his dedication to specific issue positions, Hinchey has interconnected the local and national. National factors have clearly impacted the politics of electoral campaigns in the 26th. As a consequence of these campaigns, his own background, and his loyalty to a primary constituency, Hinchey draws strong and, for the most part, positive connections between the local and the national.

He focuses on particular issues—the economy, the environment, and education—at all levels of government. He lets his constituents and his Washington colleagues know he is loyal to his Democratic Party. Indeed, as we have seen, reading his profile it can be easy to lose sight of the local-national connection. He does what he has to do, addressing the federal economy in his congressional committee work and, because he espouses government intervention, doing everything he can to bring federal projects to the 26th. Similarly, at home he may work to boost the status of the Hudson River while in Washington he will extend that environmental work to focus on preserving wilderness land across the country. He knows he is in Congress to represent constituents at home, but it is his partisanship/ideology that helps him connect forces inside and outside the district.

On balance, national factors have probably disadvantaged Quinn and forced him to distance himself from party (though in a Democratic district, those disadvantages may not be seriously detrimental). These same national factors may have had a more mixed effect for Hinchey. Modern campaign strategies of the national parties have meant that he has had a series of close elections, perhaps closer than might have been the case when politics had more local focus. But, more importantly, national factors have probably helped. Hinchey's ability to link local problems of the Clinton-Democratic agenda has been a plus for him, helping him cement the support of the primary constituency he needs to maintain. Thus, for both politicians, national factors matter. Even in profiles where the thrust is fundamentally local, the impact of national factors can be seen, providing additional evidence for local and national interconnections.

Chapter 7

CONCLUDING PERSPECTIVES

Hello and welcome to the Web site of the First Congressional District of Arizona. I am grateful for the opportunity to represent your Rural Arizona values in the 108th Congress. . . . An entirely rural district, the represented areas do not include any of the urban neighborhoods of Phoenix or Tucson.

View this message in Spanish.

View this message in Navajo.

—Rick Renzi, R-Arizona, http://www.house.gov/renzi/

Because of the hard work and strong support from people across the 5th District, I will go to Washington to support President Bush and help rebuild our economy.

—Jeb Hensarling, R-Texas, http://www.jebforcongress.org

A devoted son raised in the family business . . . A field artillery Captain who served his country in the U.S. Army . . . A loving Dad married to his high school sweetheart for sixteen years and going strong . . . We now have a Republican President . . . a real conservative chief executive . . . and a man of true character and integrity in the Oval Office.

And thank God for it.

—J. Gresham Barrett, R-South Carolina, http://www.barrettforcongress.com

As Fenno so convincingly demonstrated in the 1970s, "home style" and the presentation of self to local constituents are surprisingly important to the representational process. In the 1970s, access, extrapolicy concerns, and the development of trust were central to the representational linkage, so home styles were predominantly local. Yet, in turn, what do home styles look like in an era of new and nationalizing forces in politics? How do members of Congress translate the increased partisanship of the Washington world, the rise of interest groups, their own more national attitudes, and even voter desires for a more national focus into their district activity?

What aspects of home style have remained constant over time, and what elements might have changed?

Through four case study chapters, each highlighting an aspect of modern politics, this project sought to describe some home styles in a more nationalized Congress and to explain variations in those presentational styles. As we have seen, some of these legislators have chosen to be more national or partisan than others (chapters 3 and 4), while others, for varying reasons, have elected to represent different balances between reelection and primary constituencies. Consequently, the title of this book, *Dilemmas of Representation,* was purposely selected to reflect the alternative representational choices made by today's legislators, to set the local-national focus of this book in the context of broader questions about representation, and to engage the reader to consider, from a normative perspective, which representational styles are "best" or "most appropriate."

It is the goal of this concluding chapter to reiterate and highlight the themes and arguments developed throughout these case studies. As should be clear from the profiles, in addition to the localism predominant in Fenno's work, the argument to be developed in this chapter will be that, indeed, national forces and factors have played a role in the shaping of some current home styles. Members today are not only more likely to include some national elements in their home styles, but the modern political environment appears to provide many legislators with enough opportunities and leeway that they can find creative ways to integrate local and national politics.

To fully appreciate these conclusions, let's develop the argument by beginning with what appears to be constant since the 1970s:

The Importance of Local Politics

In the 1970s, Fenno, through his discussions of the bulls-eye model and of the central role of a member's career in and around the district, highlighted the importance of the local. Twenty or more years later, the literature described throughout this book has taken on a more national focus. The first generalization to highlight, then, is that at a political time where so much emphasis has been placed on the national, it is quite remarkable to appreciate the central role played by local factors. In many respects, Fenno's model has certainly proved resilient in the face of changing times.

Thus, it would be an understatement to say, after reading these profiles, that localism, access, constituency service, and trust are paramount in the home styles of many of these representatives and important for most. As the large number of examples throughout this book indicate, the legislators described here spend considerable time in their districts, go home often, and keep their staffs busy engaging in tremendous amounts of constituency activities. In this regard, the number of press accounts of members interacting with constituents is particularly striking.

So, the examples described throughout this work have included all manner of stories, from funny (Engel's offer to plunge a constituent's toilet, Maloney's efforts to settle a dispute about a loose bird) to moving (Engel's efforts to locate a son missing in Cyprus, Houghton's granting a dying child a trip to a crucial football game, or McNulty's praise for a heroic South Pole rescue conducted by National Guard Units in his district). More, the stories reflect ordinary interactions between legislators traversing their districts and engaging in normal political activities. In addition, members work for important district economic interests (preservation of military bases, labor concerns), and several see it as one of their most important functions as a member of Congress to stick closely to their perceptions of district interests.

Increasingly, of course, members are able to extend their communication capabilities via the Internet (Adler, Gent, and Overmeyer 1998). I will use these Web sites to provide a final reiteration of the importance of local politics. Thus, Table 7.1 highlights a wide variety of features describing legislator-constituent connections. So, looking down the checklist in the table, the large number of "Y"s demonstrates the local connection members wish to emphasize. All advertise constituent services, and virtually all provide the other basics: constituency maps, a written description of the district, and links to local activities and governments. Most go farther, including photos and some indication of their roots and ties to the area.

Indeed, all ten legislators include in their Web bios a local connection situating themselves in their geographic constituency ("Congresswoman Carolyn B. Maloney, a Democrat, represents the 14th district in New York City. Her district contains many of the city's most historic and well-known neighborhoods"), and they emphasize their commitment to the area ("In Congress, Representative Velazquez has been a vocal advocate for a district that has been faced with a variety of challenges [housing, labor, education, health care]") and remind constituents of the ways their Washington work reflects the character of their districts ("In addition to his committee roles, Rep. Quinn also serves as Chairman of the Executive Committee of the Congressional Steel Caucus, co-chair of the Northeast-Midwest Congressional Coalition, and co-chair of the House Republican Working Group on Labor" [Web bios]).

Local Roots

But, the profiles also demonstrate perhaps an even more profound point. The constituent-representative connection would appear to be even deeper. Accessibility to constituents in and of itself is not the only way members can "stay local." In a more national time, it might be easy to underestimate the depth of the roots that connect many members to their districts. So, at one level, it is one thing to intellectually understand that most legislators must have had prior political experiences in and connections with their local areas in order to stand a chance of gaining office. It is another thing to fully appreciate the dimensions of these roots:

- McNulty became an Eagle Scout in the Boy Scouts of America on July 15, 1960, at the age of twelve. (Web bio)
- Hinchey then enrolled in the State University of New York at New Paltz and put himself through college working as a night-shift toll collector on the New York State Thruway. (Web bio)
- Carolyn Maloney, originally from North Carolina, came to Manhattan as a young adult, loved it and just stayed. (Web bio)

Implicit in these descriptions (and these are indicative of virtually all ten members), of course, is that these representatives encountered most of their significant life experiences in and around the constituents they would later represent. Most grew up in the local areas, worked in the districts, and developed all manner of personal connections prior to a political career. Thus, if political scholars depict legislator-constituent representational linkages through a combination of constituency opinion and a legislator's own attitudes (Kingdon 1989; Miller and Stokes 1963), these profiles certainly demonstrate the plausibility of the attitudinal link.

As a point for future speculation, it is worth noting that the nature of the roots these individuals share with their constituents differs. Some members

TABLE 7.1 Analysis of Local and National References on Legislator Web Sites

	Maloney	Houghton	McHugh	Kelly	McNulty	McCarthy	Engel	Velazquez	Quinn	Hinchey
Word Count (Bio)	1681	596	1072	494	673	747	360	424	910	610
Para Count (Bio)	17	11	11	10	10	14	7	7	13	7
Local										
Welcome to Constituents	Y	Y	N	Y	N	Y	Y	N	Y	Y
District Map	Y	N	Y	Y	Y	N	N	N	N	Y
District Description*	2	2	5	5	5	5	2	2	4	5
Constituency Service	Y	Y	Y	Y	Y	Y	Y	Y	Y	Y
Local Links	Y	Y	Y	Y	Y	Y	Y	Y	Y	Y
Photos with "Locals"	Y	Y	N	N	N	Y	Y	Y	Y	N
Local Roots	Y	Y	Y	Y	Y	Y	Y	Y	Y	Y
National										
National Links	Y	Y	Y	Y	Y	Y	Y	Y	N	Y
Congressional Procedure	Y	Y	Y	Y	Y	Y	Y	Y	Y	Y
Committees	Y	Y	N	Y	Y	N	Y	Y	Y	Y
Bills	Y	N	Y	N	N	Y	N	Y	Y	Y
Issues	Y	N	Y	N	N	Y	Y	N	N	Y
Party	Y	Y	Y	N	N	N	Y	Y	Y	Y
Photos with National Figures	Y	Y	N	N	N	Y	Y	Y	Y	N

*Web sites were classified as to the extensiveness of the descriptions of the representatives' constiuencies, Least Thorough = 1, Most Thorough = 5

(Reps. Quinn, a former teacher, and McCarthy, a nurse) appear to share many life experiences with their "average" constituent.

Others (Reps. McNulty, son to a political family, and Houghton, the former CEO) may reflect the underlying values of their communities quite nicely; yet each in a different way is a bit apart from the "average" constituent. As we have seen, these pairs of legislators have been equally able to develop constituency connections, but they have forged those identifications in somewhat different ways.

In sum, though, what is so striking from these profiles is that, in an era where it might be acceptable to minimize local connections, it appears that, if anything, these members go out of their way to reinforce their identifications with the local.

National Elements Matter Too

However, the raison-d'être for this project stemmed from the argument that, for all the reasons laid out in chapters 1 and 2 (including increasing national-level partisanship, changing recruitment patterns, potentially altered voter attitudes), politics has become more nationalized.

The question was raised in chapter 2: Can home styles be national? In the extreme case, the answer, at least judging from these ten members, appears to be, no. To the extent that "going national" implies leaving behind the local, none of these ten members exhibit solely national home styles.

However, if we ask instead whether home styles can include strong national elements, the answer is an unequivocal, yes. For instance, the home styles of two of the three representatives considered in chapter 3 (the chapter directly confronting the local-national connection) clearly demonstrate this. In addition to engaging in a wide variety of local activities, both Reps. Maloney and Houghton exhibited a strong national focus, including the former's strong issue interests and the latter's moderate partisanship. More generally, virtually all the profiles described throughout this work demonstrate the importance of at least some national connections. Many members (Kelly, McCarthy) focused on major national issues, developed important party or other national connections (Kelly, Velazquez) or linked home and Washington activities fairly closely (McCarthy, Hinchey). The fortunes of several (Houghton, Kelly, McNulty) were impacted by electoral events and circumstances, and in many instances, it was simply difficult to separate local from national politics.

Further, it is important to appreciate that even representatives whose style reflects a predominantly local character engage in some national activity and are impacted by national forces. Rep. Quinn has been active on labor and railroad concerns, McHugh focuses on military interests, and McNulty works within his party's leadership structure and engages in considerable international travel.

Table 7.1 reiterates the "national" material found throughout these profiles by highlighting the national activities listed on member Web sites. Just as members want their constituents to know about their local activity, the checklist of Web site information relating to members' national efforts shows a lot of "Y"s. On their Web sites, members include links to other federal government agencies, to their congressional committees, and to information about congressional rules and procedures. These legislators advertise their committee work, link to bills they sponsored, and often highlight their national issue positions. In addition, about half of the Web sites include photos of the member of Congress with important national figures and proclaim the legislator's party identification. So, national themes, events, and circumstances have certainly characterized these profiles.

Partisanship

Breaking down the "national" a bit more precisely, we can return to a related question: In contrast to Fenno's findings from the 1970s, can home styles of members of Congress a few decades later be partisan? In other words, how have today's members incorporated the national efforts at increasingly responsible parties into their home districts?

Can home styles be partisan? Judging from these case studies, the answer is yes. Just as these profiles demonstrate considerable "national" material, they also illustrate important "party" themes. Based on these profiles, most of these legislators remain loyal to party, sharing a fundamental agreement with many of their party's positions and certainly exhibiting strong emotional bonds with their own party. Many participate in the House leadership structure, and a few place partisanship front and center as part of their home styles.

In addition, these profiles document instances of national party involvement in local elections. National figures have consistently campaigned for these House members, the national parties contributed strategic money, especially in close contests, and some members have been particularly targeted by the opposition party.

Moreover, the simple fact of majority or minority party status loomed in the background of a surprising number of these home styles. At one level, it is obvious that majority party status matters to a host of organizational and policy features of Congress. On the other hand, recent scholarly attention to responsible parties obscures this basic fact of congressional life. On attaining majority status, several Republicans were quick to point out to constituents that such status would allow them to find new ways to help their districts—even the locally oriented Rep. McHugh benefited with the opportunity to chair a subcommittee (on postal affairs). In turn, several Democrats (Rep. McNulty, for one) struggled to keep valued committee positions after the shift in party control or simply worked harder to generate campaign funds.

Yet, phrasing questions about partisanship somewhat differently also allows us to understand the limitations of partisan politics. In addition to asking whether home styles can be partisan, it is also useful to ask a somewhat more complex question: How important is partisanship relative to other elements of home style? If we put the question this way, the answer becomes more qualified. In fact, given the strong partisan changes that have characterized national politics over the last decades, one might actually be impressed with the lack of partisanship apparent across the home styles described here. For instance, one of the main points of chapter 4 (on parties) highlighted the variability in partisan styles even in an era of strong responsible parties. Rep. Kelly certainly jumped on the responsible party bandwagon of the 1990s, but McNulty exhibited a more balanced approach to party, and McCarthy successfully developed a steadfastly nonpartisan style. So, while we might expect partisanship to dominate these presentations of self, and while we certainly find considerable party loyalty and allegiance, we find perhaps more variability in partisan responses and behaviors than might have been anticipated.

Thus, it is equally important to add that in answering the question, "Can members of congress be partisan?" legislators are sometimes faced with conflicts among party, constituency, and their own personal attitudes. Judging from these profiles, when faced with such conflicts, national party, over the long run generally loses. So, though Rep. Kelly based her initial campaign in large part on the basis of her support for the Contract with America and served as a spokesperson for the freshman class of Republicans of the 104th Congress, two years later, in the face of a Republican backlash in her relatively ideologically moderate constituency, she had to do some backtracking, highlighting her moderate politics and her service to constituents. Similarly, in part because of his solidly Democratic constituency, Republican Rep. Quinn has often been forced to downplay his partisanship, and on the Democratic side, Rep. McNulty has occasionally had to balance the liberal stands of the national Democratic Party against the needs of his moderate to conservative Democratic constituency.

Not only do legislators face party-constituency conflicts, but sometimes party also conflicts with their own strongly held beliefs. Thus, Rep. Houghton, the former CEO, has for decades advocated for the importance of moderate politics, and Rep. Kelly came to Congress with something of her own issue agenda (including women's concerns and a pro-choice stand). It is important to reiterate that in the face of an out-and-out conflict, national party appears again to lose.

Finally, despite the modern emphasis on strong partisanship, the literature on American political parties more generally stresses the many different meanings and dimensions to partisanship. Modern scholarship has highlighted our increasingly responsible national party system. However, the profiles presented here also reiterate themes discussed in older party scholarship; there is more to "party" than issue stands, intraparty agreement, or a national focus. Reps. Kelly and Maloney have cultivated national party networks and acted as media spokespeople. Rep. Hinchey links "Democrat" to his association with liberal causes, Velazquez's ties to the Democratic Party can be traced to her association with Latino advocacy, and for McNulty, "party" likely evokes identification with family and a long-standing political machine.

In short, though these profiles provide examples of strong partisanship in home styles, they also demonstrate the multifaceted conceptualization of party that has characterized modern American politics. So, at the same time that there are important partisan elements in some of these home styles, the profiles throughout this book also demonstrate some of the limits and tradeoffs to a fully responsible party system.

The Role of Women and Minorities

Certainly, one of the biggest changes occurring across the nation since the 1970s is the more diverse nature of congressional electorates, and consequently of congressional membership. As we have seen, participation in electoral politics has broadened opportunities for formerly underrepresented groups. Due to an increasingly diverse population, legal mandates toward majority-minority districts, and broader sociopolitical trends, women, African Americans, Latinos, and other minorities have become a growing force in American politics (chapter 5).

In this book, these changes have been examined in two ways. Chapter 5 considered alternative styles of representing two multiracial, multiethnic congressional districts (New York's 12th and 17th). As we have seen, the home styles of the two legislators representing these areas have exhibited notable differences. In her efforts to empower individual constituents and to speak out on behalf of Latino concerns, Rep. Velazquez represents the 12th district as an advocate for the Latino community (Canon 1999, 4).

In contrast, Eliot Engel represents his perhaps even more diverse constituency in rather traditional and practical ways (the politics of commonality). Thus, Engel deals with difference not so much by making general statements about empowerment or equality but by simply treating all constituents as equal and attempting to deal with their diverse concerns through constituency service and emphasizing partisan ties.

Based on the Engel/Velazquez comparison, we can speculate that minority legislators in general might be more likely than white males (should they be elected) to represent minority districts on the basis of the politics of difference. Stereotypically, women and minority legislators such as Velazquez, because of their prepolitical experiences, their group identifications, or their "insider" status within their constituencies, might view themselves as political outsiders advocating for the needs and concerns of underrepresented groups, while white males may feel a need to prove themselves to such constituents, and a commonality approach could prove safer.

This speculation resonates with a more general finding. Our sample included four women and six men. Consistent with scholarship from the women and politics literature (Margolies-Mezvinsky 1994; Thomas 1994), we have found that women are more likely than men to place women's concerns on their political agenda. A prime case of this is Maloney, who has served as chair of the Congressional Caucus on Women's Issues, has been a prime sponsor of the Equal Rights Amendment, and has been a consistent advocate for issues of concern to women and families. Similarly, Rep. Kelly has been a strong pro-choice advocate, and consistent with her interests in health issues, she has made women's health an important part of her agenda. McCarthy in turn has been active promoting breast cancer research and issues of concern to widows, and Velazquez certainly stands out as the first Puerto Rican female member of Congress. Several of the male legislators (Hinchey, McNulty, and Engel) have certainly been supportive of the concerns of women; however, their activity level was notably lower in this area.

At the same time, in addition to their work on behalf of women, it is worth reiterating that all the women members in our sample have been active in other policy arenas: Maloney on government reform, Kelly on veterans and small business, McCarthy on gun violence and education, and Velazquez on Latino concerns. None of these representatives have made women's issues their sole focus. Rather, their efforts on behalf of women have been part of a larger issue agenda.

Finally, as another point for future speculation, it is worth noting that these women share other commonalities. Women's groups appear to be a part of the primary constituencies of all four female legislators. Thus, in addition to other impacts, simply having more women in Congress has the potential to broaden the nature of a representative's core supporters. Also, in an even more speculative mode, all four women would appear to share a focus on issues. They had ideas about things they wanted to get done and policy changes they wished to make. Further research would need to be conducted to determine the extent to which this pattern is truly attributable to gender or whether the conditions under which these women came to office, their party affiliation, or the constituencies they represent are more important factors in producing this result.

Explaining Variation: The Impact of Constituency, Legislator Backgrounds, and the National Political Climate

As we have seen and as Fenno certainly found, a good deal of complexity and diversity characterizes these profiles. It is clear that some legislators have chosen to be more national or partisan than others. What factors explain this variation?

From a qualitative perspective, the case studies have demonstrated the importance of constituency characteristics and member backgrounds in explaining this variation. For purposes of understanding these impacts in a more systematic way, I have recapitulated, for each of the ten legislators, information pertaining to their home styles, constituencies, and background characteristics (Table 7.2), and I have presented cross-tabulations relating these factors to characteristics of a legislator's home style (Table 7.3). As the analysis is based on ten cases, it is, of course, meant only as suggestive of potential generalizations.

To create these tables, I have first classified legislator home styles on national/local and partisan/less partisan continua, interestingly, a somewhat difficult task given the complexity of the information in the profiles. How does one simplify the vast amount of material covered throughout this work? For purposes of these tables, a categorization as "national" meant that a representative focused on issues having implications beyond the boundaries of the district or associated himself/herself with national groups or parties. Home styles were designated primarily as "local" (McHugh, McNulty, Quinn) if the predominant pattern in a representative's behavior demonstrated constituency service or an emphasis on issues primarily of concern to the local district.[1] Similarly, a designation as "partisan" means that party played a significant role in a legislator's home style, but this deserves some explanation. Some legislators (Maloney, Kelly) as we have seen, placed partisanship front and center in their presentations of self. Others (McHugh) were less vocal. However, as the loyalty of these latter members was strong, and as their districts were solidly comprised of

TABLE 7.2 Summary of Home Styles, Constituency Characteristics, and Legislator Backgrounds*

Name	Party	National Home Style	Partisan Home Style	Urban	College Educated	Median Income	Electoral Safety	Downstate	National Background
Maloney	Dem	Y	Y	H	H	H	S	Y	Y
Houghton	Rep	Y	N	L	L	L	S	N	Y
McHugh	Rep	N	Y	L	L	L	S	N	N
Kelly	Rep	Y	Y	M	H	H	N	Y	Y
McNulty	Dem	N	Y	H	M	M	S	N	N
McCarthy	Dem	Y	N	H	M	H	N	Y	Y
Engel	Dem	M	Y	H	L	M	S	Y	N
Velazquez	Dem	Y	Y	H	L	L	S	Y	Y
Quinn	Rep	N	N	H	L	M	S	N	N
Hinchey	Dem	M	Y	M	M	M	N	N	N

*Variables classified as follows: L = Low, M = Medium, H = High

National home style: wholly or partly national (M)

Urban: 80% or greater

Education: Districts divided in thirds according to percent college educated.

Income: Districts divided into thirds according to median income.

Electoral safety: safe = average winning % greater than 60.

constituents of one party, it is clear that partisanship was both unquestioned and expected from these legislators[2].

Before examining Table 7.3, it is also useful to set out some expectations. It seems fair to hypothesize that representatives from urban, well-educated, or well-off areas would choose to "go national." Stereotypically, residents of urban areas might be expected to exhibit a more diverse range of concerns, highly informed constituents might obviously be expected to attend to a wider variety of issues or national events, and individuals living in better-off areas might have less need for government services (Yanakis 1981)—all conditions pushing their representatives in more national directions. Similarly, to the extent that electoral freedom drives the choice to go national or to stay local, we might expect a higher proportion of representatives from safe rather than marginal districts to make the "national" leap. (More will be said below about the additional independent variables in the table.)

In addition, what kinds of districts might elect very partisan members to Congress? Certainly, while we might expect members who represent solidly one-party areas to have the freedom to be more partisan than other

TABLE 7.3 Types of Home Styles by Constituency Factors and Legislator
Backgrounds*

Characteristic	Percent Reps with National Home Styles	Percent Reps with Partisan Home Styles	N
Urban/Rural			
Urban	67%**	67%	6
Rural/Partly Urban	75%	75%	4
Education, Percent College			
High	80%	80%	5
Low	60%	60%	5
Income			
High	100%	67%	3
Middle	50%	75%	4
Low	66%	67%	3
Upstate/Downstate			
Upstate	40%	60%	5
Downstate	100%	80%	5
Party			
Democrat	83%	83%	6
Republican	50%	50%	4
Electoral Safety			
Safe	56%	70%	7
Not Safe	100%	67%	3
Legislator Background			
National	100%	67%	6
Local	100%	25%	4

*Variables classified as follows:

National home style: wholly or partly national.

Urban, as classified by *PIA*

Education: Districts divided in half at the 20% mark.

Income: Districts divided into thirds according to median income.

**Percentages reflect the percentage of legislators with either a national or partisan home style, e.g., 67% of legislators from urban districts have a national home style.

legislators, expectations are less clear for the other independent variables. Why would members from urban, well-educated, or well-off districts be more or less partisan than other members?

Looking across Table 7.3, how well are these expectations met? Perhaps the most important point is that national and partisan home styles can emanate from legislators representing constituents in a great variety of congressional districts. That is, though there are associations between some constituency characteristics (see below) and home styles, the development of a "national" or "partisan" home style is not exclusively related to any single geographic or demographic condition. In the modern era, some members of Congress go "national."

Table 7.3 does, however, display some patterns, and suggests some generalizations worthy of testing by future research. As expected, judging from these ten members, there is a tendency for nationally oriented home styles to be associated with representatives from districts with more highly educated and more well-off constituents. However, at least in these data, there is no connection with district urbanness, and the upstate/downstate differences shown here certainly seem more a function of New York State geography than of any generalizable feature about politics.

Consistent with expectations, though higher-income districts in this sample elect congresspeople with more partisan home styles, no general pattern between district demographics and partisanship emerges.

Some findings run contrary to expectation, particularly those pertaining to electoral safety. Seven of the ten representatives here have won election with an average victory margin upward of 60 percent, while three have experienced closer elections. Findings from this sample demonstrate no relationship between victory margin and the nature of home styles; victory margin has no impact on the partisan character of a home style (70 percent of legislators from "safe" districts were classified as having partisan home styles, compared to 67 percent of those from more marginal districts), and congresspeople representing more competitive districts are actually more likely to adopt national rather than local home styles (100 percent to 70 percent). In these data, it happens that electoral safety appears somewhat correlated with constituent education, so two of the representatives (Kelly, McCarthy) whose election margins are closer, also represent well-educated constituents, and three of the seven districts where members are electorally safe represent less well-educated constituencies. The findings thus might be explained by the education–victory margin correlation. On the other hand, for most of these legislators, characteristics of home style (e.g., the level of partisanship) appear to be a stable aspect of their lives, so more than the electoral competitiveness of an area seems relevant.

One final point is important. The finding that Democrats have more national and partisan home styles than Republicans is clearly a function of New York State politics. Recall New York's tradition of liberal Republicanism (chapter 2). Given that there is so much "nationally" oriented material found throughout these profiles, might we not expect even more evidence for such styles had other states or regions of the country been chosen as the focus of analysis?

In sum, Table 7.3 shows some relationships between characteristics of geographic constituencies and home styles. The profiles more generally also demonstrate linkages between features of member reelection and primary constituencies with presentations of self. In fact, for the most part, considered holistically, Congress members appear to be acting very much within the boundaries set by their electorates. For example, Rep. Maloney, whose home style is national, issue-oriented, and partisan, is clearly acting within the constraints of her urban, very metropolitan and solidly Democratic constituency. For Rep. Velazquez, representing her Latino district places her in the center of some national and even international controversies. Wouldn't it be difficult to represent either of these districts without regard to national concerns? Considering more upstate constituencies, wouldn't it be fairly close to electoral suicide for legislators such as Reps. Hinchey and Quinn to ignore the serious economic downturns facing their constituents or for Rep. McHugh to downplay the interests of Fort Drum or dairy farmers?

Thus, with one important caveat, the linkages Fenno found between constituency characteristics and home styles are quite evident in these profiles. The caveat involves the very nature of Fenno's bulls-eye model, a model so influential because it was intended to capture the complexity inherent in a legislator's local constituency. What may have changed since the 1970s is not so much the influence of the concentric circles as the type of constituents comprising each circle. Given current politics, national as well as local groups and individuals—the parties, nationally oriented interest groups, out-of-district campaign contributions—may form a part of both the reelection and primary constituencies to a greater degree than thirty years ago. Though these profiles make clear that the local comes first, the circles of the bulls-eye model today seem to include national as well as local elements. Put another way, when considering the bulls-eye model, the local and the national seem more interconnected at each level.

So, just as constituency factors shaped home styles in the 1970s, they set important constraints on legislators today. This said, perhaps an even more striking conclusion of this study has to do with the role of Fenno's other independent variable, legislator backgrounds. Within the constraints set by constituencies, the many ways in which members can place their own stamp on their activities is actually quite striking. An extensive literature on recruitment clearly highlights the importance of background characteristics, prepolitical experiences and personality traits influencing a member's in-office behavior (Fowler 1993). Fenno (1996) begins *Senators on the Campaign Trail* with a discussion of the importance of the prepolitical careers of several senators. Dan Quayle's strong desire to be an "effective senator" developed out of a need to make up for a (to say the least) slow start on an adult professional career. In contrast, John Glenn, the astronaut and American hero, had no particular need to demonstrate effectiveness but had considerable difficulty transitioning from a nonpolitical to a political role. These and other examples clearly suggest that a member's roots, background, and attitudes can and do, either in direct or indirect ways, impact his/her political behavior.

And, as should be clear by now, personal factors played a considerable role in explaining the actions of the congresspeople examined throughout this book. To begin, consider some of the limits of constituency factors as determinants of home style. For example, the two mid-state Democrats in our sample are Reps. Hinchey and McNulty. While McNulty by any stretch of the imagination represents a safely Democratic constituency, Hinchey's district is an almost even partisan mix, and his elections have been close. If constituency characteristics were the only contributor to partisan home styles, we would expect that Rep. McNulty would be the loyal Democrat and that Hinchey would find ways to cross party lines. If anything, the reverse is true. Hinchey has remained staunchly Democratic, and McNulty's voting record has shifted somewhat with changing partisan times.

Relatedly, as Reps. Houghton and McHugh represent demographically similar and safe Republican constituencies, McHugh's local focus versus Houghton's national orientation cannot be explained solely by district factors.[3]

More directly, we have seen that a representative's personality and interests have an important influence on the character of his/her home style. The profiles make clear, to an extent greater than expected, the importance of member backgrounds. Thus, Rep. Sue Kelly has been a behind-the-scenes Republican activist, McNulty was socialized from his earliest days into the traditions of a strong Democratic political machine, and Hinchey has been a longtime environmental advocate. More generally, we find any number of examples in this study where members take the lead on concerns important to them and legislators' own attitudes, beliefs, and experiences impact their behaviors.

Thus, constituency constraints notwithstanding, members have enough leeway to place their own stamp on their actions, to emphasize some concerns rather than others or to highlight certain activities as they go about the business of interacting with constituents. Rep. Maloney is making a choice to highlight her activities on behalf of women as part of her home style; her male predecessor shared her values but chose to focus on other arenas. Rep. Houghton is highlighting bipartisanship in a constituency that certainly would accept a more partisan style, and Rep. McCarthy is, of course, advocating an end to gun violence in the face of a constituency divided on the question.

Of course, in more instances than not, member goals are congruent with the needs of the districts they represent, for example, Rep. Quinn's support for labor in a highly unionized area or Kelly's focus on health issues in her relatively well-off and suburban constituency. While other members do face constituency-background conflicts (McCarthy's gun violence position, Hinchey's Democratic loyalty in a divided constituency), the impact of member backgrounds is nonetheless quite striking.

The last columns of Table 7.2 nicely summarize the point. I classified legislators as to whether or not they had some "national" experiences as part of their pre-congressional career. As can be seen from the table, fully six could point to such a connection, whereas four could not. The striking finding is that a virtually perfect relationship exists between prior background and local-national home styles. In this sample, fully 100 percent of representatives with some national experience as part of their background also developed home styles incorporating some national elements, and 100 percent of the legislators with little national experience, for the most part, stayed local. While this degree of correspondence may be too much to expect in a larger sample, it certainly makes the point quite nicely: member backgrounds, along with constituency factors, impact the character of home styles.

In addition, the underlying premise of this book, that sociopolitical times have changed, suggests that scholars need to attend to the impact of a third broad explanatory variable: the national political climate. In the 1970s, home styles were predominantly local. Judging from the profiles in this book, today some home styles reflect a more mixed bag of local and national elements. Thus, just as constituency characteristics condition what members of Congress do, so too are legislators impacted by events and circumstances beyond the boundaries of their constituencies—electoral forces, including the 1992 Year of the Woman or the 1994 Contract with

America, have ramifications for home styles in local districts. The degree of national-level partisanship forces legislators to make choices when presenting themselves to the folks back home, providing opportunities for some representatives and challenges for others. Whatever the issues are confronting the political agenda (witness the impact of September 11 as a unifying force) must in some way enter into debates not only in Washington but also in 435 local areas. Though the impact of these forces on each local district can vary, current political trends certainly appear to have contributed to more national elements in local home styles, so the national climate needs to be added to the list of explanations for variation in the district-oriented behavior of legislators.

Assessing the Local-National Interconnection

A final point remains. In addition to reiterating the local and national elements in some current home styles, a central finding of this study reflects the strong and generally positive interconnections between the local and the national. Some legislators (e.g., McHugh's support for dairy farmers, Quinn's work on behalf of labor) bring local concerns to the Washington arena and choose to use their Washington activity to highlight constituent interests. Others "nationalize" the "local"—they arrive in Congress with a mission to protect some local interest (e.g., McHugh's efforts on behalf of Fort Drum) but in the course of their Washington careers and/or because of factors including committee assignments or changes in the national issue agenda, they are led to broaden their expertise, adding a more national focus. In turn, still others do the reverse, "localizing" the "national." Thus, in the face of a rash of arson attempts at African American churches across the country, Rep. Engel sponsored prevention meetings in his multiracial Bronx district; Rep. Velazquez consistently makes sure her Latino and Asian constituents are informed about changes in immigration policy; while other representatives consistently hold town meetings letting constituents know about their Washington activity.

Some representatives link home and Washington more directly: "Her [Kelly] career is a model of community and national service" or "His [McNulty] record includes extensive legislative and executive service at the local, state and national levels" (Web bios). Other representatives choose to focus on issues/activities that "work" in both arenas or even blur the local-national connection altogether, simply doing their jobs; for instance,

Rep. Velazquez is a Latino advocate, Hinchey works for an improved economy and environment at home and in Washington, and Houghton highlights national connections along with local values. One wonders: Are these legislators really separating out what they are doing and thinking in Washington from what they are doing and thinking at home?

However, as we have seen, of course, some legislators have an easier time than others linking the local and the national. For some (liberal Democrats from New York City, for instance, or conservative Republicans from conservative upstate areas), there is simply more congruence between constituent pressures, the legislator's own background, as well as the direction of national political forces. All factors point in similar directions, enhancing member opportunities to forge positive local-national connections.

Alternatively, as we have also seen, some representatives are faced with a more difficult strategic situation. In the modern political era it is the moderate Republicans, for example, Houghton and Quinn (and to a lesser extent more conservative Democrats, e.g., McNulty) who struggle to balance the potential for negative repercussions at home of national forces.

On balance, however, the most important point to emphasize reiterates the surprising degree of local-national interconnections found throughout these profiles. For some purposes, as some theories predict, the Washington and home environments may characterize two different worlds, and yet, those worlds often interconnect.

Conclusion

What does all this mean for the study of representation? Are these findings about local and national elements in home styles a fluke of a New York State focus, or are they generalizable to other areas of the nation or even to future politics? New York State as a point of study may have some limitations—as we have seen, there exists an abundance of relatively liberal Republicans compared to the rest of the country. Yet, its districts, as we have also seen, vary along a wide variety of dimensions (urban/rural, homogeneous/heterogeneous), and representatives certainly exhibit a range of home styles.

As it turns out, perhaps the liberal Republican tradition of New York State isn't, after all, so much a limitation. Aren't findings of positive local-national connections even more striking given such a tradition? Put another way, shouldn't these descriptions highlighting local-national linkages be even more likely to hold in other areas of the nation with a better fit between partisanship and constituency, such as the South and parts of the West or Midwest? In a slightly different context, wouldn't some of the descriptions of national elements in home styles be even more likely after the horrific but nationalizing events of 9/11 and the more global economy of the modern day?

Preliminary hints as to the potential generalizability of these findings, as well as a look into at least the near future, can be gleaned from the excerpts at the top of this chapter, taken from the Web sites of three Republican freshmen elected to the U.S. House of Representatives in the 2002 congressional races. As did the headlines from the Web sites of Reps. Maloney and Quinn that introduced chapter 1 of this book, the excerpts presented here offer at least a glimpse into the thinking of some of the newest members of Congress.

As has been the case with the New Yorkers profiled throughout this work, all three representatives highlight the local. Hensarling thanks his constituents for their hard work, Barrett acknowledges his ties to the area, and most colorfully, Renzi proclaims, "I am grateful for the opportunity to represent your Rural Arizona values in the 108th Congress," and, amusingly to an outsider, he clarifies: "an entirely rural district, the represented areas do not include any of the urban neighborhoods of Phoenix or Tucson."

However, as in the case of the New Yorkers, two of these three representatives interconnect local and national concerns. Hensarling speaks of working with President Bush to better "our economy"; and make no mistake, Barrett will be bringing the world of Washington to his South Carolina district: "We now have a Republican President . . . a real conservative chief executive . . . and a man of true character and integrity in the Oval Office. And thank God for it."

Even Renzi, after highlighting the importance of rural values, goes on to let his constituents know that they can click on his Web site in Navajo or Spanish. Thus, as was true of the New Yorkers, even Renzi may develop a vehicle (perhaps Native American affairs or border concerns) from which to integrate local and national concerns.

These three freshmen of the 108th Congress, representing diverse regions of the nation, provide an indication of the generalizability of the findings depicted throughout this book.

Thus, to conclude and reiterate: it is a fundamental fact of American politics that home styles are both local and diverse. Nevertheless, many representatives also add national elements to their presentations of self, find varied ways to connect the local and the national and sometimes appear to so integrate the two arenas as to blur geographic distinctions.

Should we encourage one type of home style over another? Are some ways of presenting oneself to constituents more "desirable" than others? As the *Dilemmas of Representation* title of this book suggests, normative answers to these questions must be left to the reader, but those answers must also take into account a consideration of a balance of local and national elements.

All in all, as we have just passed the millennium and as technology and global interconnections advance at astounding rates, perhaps we should not be so surprised that the "local" and the "national" interconnection appears more like a two-way street than the dead-end road suggested by much literature. As current trends continue, we should expect more of this legislative behavior as we head into the future of the American democracy.

POSTSCRIPT

Using data drawn primarily from the 1990s, this project has examined the impact of local and national factors in an age of increasing partisanship and nationalization. During that time, most of the representatives studied here dealt with at least some national forces in their home styles, and most were able to link local and national factors in fairly positive ways. In writing a postscript to update the material for this book, several strategies presented themselves. Since it is case study methodology that has been employed here, it is naturally tempting to seek to write a descriptive update highlighting as many current activities of these representatives, who, as we have illustrated, present themselves as an interesting cast of characters. It is also tempting to focus on factors that create the possibility for change in home styles—including redistricting, the increasing seniority of these members, the partisanship surrounding the 2000 election, and of course the switch toward a more foreign policy–oriented agenda post-9/11.[1]

To simplify the job and to reiterate the focus on the main theme of this project, the continuing interconnections between local and national politics, I have limited the material covered in this postscript to two interrelated sections. With particular reference to the local-national distinction, the first section below updates, with some variation, the essential stability of the home styles of these representatives. In light of that stability, the second section focuses on the activities of these legislators surrounding the events in the aftermath of September 11, 2001. How would we expect these legislators to respond? Given the magnitude and immediacy of the disaster, particularly in New York, examining the responses of these legislators to an important new component of the national political agenda sheds unique light on the local-national connection. One might expect the responses of these representatives, both from within and outside of New York City, quite appropriately to focus solely on local efforts. The fact that, consistent with their already developed home styles, many additionally nationalized the issues provides interesting evidence for the continuing positive-sum connections between local and national politics. Finally, the foreign policy focus inherent in the events of September 11, along with the increasing globalization of society and politics more generally, reiterates the potential for continued local-national-international political linkages.

Update: Home Style Stability

Due to electoral stability as well as to the predilections of these legislators to put their own stamp on their activities (chapter 7), it is not surprising to report overall continuity in the broad contours of their home styles. To be sure, as these members accrued electoral safety and congressional seniority, there were slight modifications in legislator behavior. For instance, perhaps learning from her close election in 1996, Rep. Sue Kelly appears now to do a better job integrating local and national politics. Recall that her profile (chapter 4) was titled "Balancing Constituent Interests, Issues, and Party." Elements of this balancing act remain—some view her political moderation as a reason for her failure to obtain a full committee chairmanship from more conservative party leaders in 2001 and sometimes her voting record (following her party's leadership to vote against a minimum wage increase and campaign finance reform [*Almanac* 2004])—probably goes against constituency preferences. Yet, when she reminds constituents—"Kelly Says Final 2005 Job Numbers Are Positive Sign of Economic Growth" in the Hudson Valley and the nation at large (PR 1/6/06)—Kelly demonstrates that she has learned how to keep herself safe in the district, in the process showing she does a good job linking local and national politics.[2]

In turn, for Rep. McHugh, a combination of the changed political agenda following September 11 as well as his increasing seniority within the majority party allowed him to incorporate additional national elements into his home style. As was demonstrated toward the end of his profile, the accrual of seniority helped him develop expertise and a national reputation on aspects of postal reform and concerns of the armed forces. In the context of the post-9/11 climate, his position on Armed Services takes on obvious additional political significance. He can tell constituents he has "asked Defense Secretary Donald Rumsfeld to investigate charges of misconduct by National Guard commanders who reportedly had inflated reports of their troop strength . . . [and] he raised concerns about the adverse reaction of some Fort Bragg soldiers to an anti-malaria drug linked to aggression and suicides" (*Almanac* 2004, 1166). In an interesting procedural aside, Rep. McHugh also used this seniority to assist Reps. Maloney and King (R-NY) in their post-9/11 efforts to improve retirement credit for national guardspeople who had served in disaster zones after September 11 by assisting in adding provisions to the National Defense Authorization Act (PR 5/25/05). Thus, without detracting from his local focus, he can additionally present himself to constituents highlighting his expertise, letting them know that he is a "senior member" on several key committees and "a leader in the country's policy on national defense" recently appointed to the Permanent Select Committee on Intelligence (Web bio).

Finally, also by virtue of seniority (this time within the minority party), Velazquez enhanced her national focus by augmenting her efforts in at least a partially new direction. Her seniority within the institution of Congress helped her add another first to her illustrious career, becoming the first Hispanic woman to serve as ranking member of a full House committee, Small Business. She "has used her post on the Small Business committee as a bully pulpit to badger the federal government to do more business with small firms, especially those owned by minorities and women . . . a number of other House committees outrank Small Business in terms of prestige and clout, but Velazquez has worked hard to make the panel relevant" (*PIA* 2004, 704), using the position to promote the particular problems of small business owners and making it an annual event to issue a "report card" as to how the government is doing with respect to contracting with small businesses, sometimes giving low grades (*PIA* 2004, 704). As an indication of the importance of this assignment, each and every press release on Velazquez's Web site, under her name, has the following designation: "Representing New York's 12th Congressional District—Brooklyn, Manhattan, Queens Ranking Democratic Member, House Small Business Committee."[3]

But, despite these modifications, it is also worth updating that representatives' priorities in terms of the local-national balance highlighted in this book have remained fairly stable. There is considerable continuity in their interests and home styles. Thus, while all these representatives have retained their local focus, the representatives portrayed throughout these profiles as having an additional national orientation have also retained such a focus. McCarthy continues to include gun violence as one of her top priorities (displayed on her home page is a link to "gun safety issues," and she has sponsored legislation including a reauthorization of the assault weapons ban). Maloney focuses on national issues, including women's rights (e.g., a reintroduction of the Equal Rights Amendment), and highlights strong partisanship. Hinchey emphasizes the views of his liberal Democratic primary constituency (he voted against supporting the war in Iraq), and Engel combines constituency service with interests in a variety of domestic and foreign policy areas (he labeled the passage of "a sanctions bill targeting Syria" as "one of my greatest legislative victories" [*PIA* 2006, 729]).

In addition, because party loyalty poses more of a conflict for some legislators than others, the partisan variation associated with the representatives studied here also persists. As was described in their profiles, several remain loyal partisans:

- Hinchey Slams Republicans For Putting Politics Above Patient Safety (PR 5/25/05)
- Engel: Bush's Awful Energy Policy Ripping off New Yorkers at the Gas Pump (PR 4/18/05)
- Media Advisory: Velazquez Campaigns Through Florida with Hispanic Leaders for Senator Kerry (PR 9/20/04)

In contrast, as we have seen, some legislators have a more complex relationship to party. On the Democratic side, Reps. McNulty and McCarthy remain willing to cross party lines or to advocate nonpartisanship altogether. While McNulty has by now advanced within Congress to Minority At-Large Whip (Web bio), and more interestingly, while otherwise nonpartisan McCarthy has been appointed to leadership positions within her party and has even officially registered as a Democrat (April 2003) (*PIA* 2006), as indicated throughout their profiles, both sometimes nevertheless remain outside their party's mainstream either in terms of policy positions or style.

On the Republican side, for Reps. Quinn and Houghton, the conflicts between national party positions and constituency (Quinn) and/or a representative's own beliefs (Houghton) described throughout these profiles have been reiterated in notably interesting ways. Quinn's position as a Republican from a labor-oriented district continued to complicate his relationship to the national party and to occasionally place this fundamentally locally oriented representative in the national spotlight. Sometimes, Quinn's labor connections were advantageous. For example, in an interesting political sidebar, under pressure to extend the set of citizens eligible for unemployment insurance after 9/11, according to reports, "House GOPers insisted that Rep. Jack Quinn . . . move the bill–not Rep. Jerrold

Nadler (D-Manhattan), a Democrat who wrote the legislation with [Sen.] Clinton" (*NYP* 3/19/02). Thus, it was the exigencies of party politics that allowed Quinn to play a role in a highly visible piece of legislation.

On the other hand, sometimes Quinn has been faced with conflict. Despite his strong record of support for labor interests (recall his profile and see *PIA* 2004), as he did in the case of the impeachment controversy, he has chosen party over constituency. Despite early support, he ultimately voted with Republican Party leadership against federalization of airport screeners (*Boston Globe* 10/27/01; *Almanac* 2004, 1176). A year later, in the context of debates about the creation of the Department of Homeland Security, Quinn broke with labor to follow his party's lead. After an intense meeting with the president, "Bush got Quinn to help smooth the way with other House moderates for a provision that would change, some say eliminate, century-old job security rights of up to 50,000 federal employees destined to be transferred into the new Homeland Security Department" (*BN* 8/11/02). According to Quinn, "'I owe you big time,' the president said" (*BN* 8/11/02)[4].

In turn, as was described in his profile, Houghton continued to buck the party line on behalf of his perception of political moderation. Most dramatically, he was one of only six House Republicans to vote against the use of force resolution supportive of President Bush's Iraq war efforts (*PIA* 2004), and he (unsuccessfully) sought to mount competition to Rep. Tom Delay's ascension to majority leader (*Almanac* 2004, 1182). As he explains, clearly stating his position toward his connection to his party, "'I would like to make sure the Republican Party is centered,' Houghton said Tuesday. 'We veered too much to the right. We've always had this problem. The Democrats tend to veer to the left, the Republicans tend to veer to the right, and the center of both parties is constantly, constantly trying to pull us back'" (*BN* 4/8/04).

In the face of this partisan context, it is important to note that both Reps. Quinn and Houghton announced their retirements in 2004. Though it is probable that age and perhaps other personal factors were more relevant for Houghton than dissatisfaction with a partisan Congress ("'I don't want to be known as 'Strom' Houghton,' he said, referring to former South Carolina Sen. Strom Thurmond, who died last year at age 100 just a few months after retiring" [*BN* 4/7/04]), partisanship likely figured more prominently in the case of Quinn. While personal factors were relevant (*BN* 4/27/04; 12/27/04), several sources also link his decision to his difficult place in the institution, speculating about threatened sanctions for his moderate behavior (*BN* 4/27/04; 4/30/04) as well as his decreasing prospects for leadership among House Republicans (*BN* 12/27/04). Quinn himself admitted he was "weary of the sharp partisan divide in Congress, which has made consensus builders an increasingly rare commodity (*BN* 12/27/04). . . . 'I think Jack just got tired of trying to be a moderate Republican—you can't do that around here anymore,' said Charles Moneypenny of the Transport Workers Union"[5] (*BN* 12/27/04).

The successors (Republican John R. "Randy" Kuhl and Brian Higgins, incidentally a Democrat) to Houghton and Quinn demonstrate the potential for continung local-national linkages. Both Houghton and Quinn were replaced by members of the New York State Assembly moving up the political ranks. As both have strong roots and ties to their districts (Web bios), and as it is easy to find examples of constituency services on their Web sites, both exhibit strong local orientations. Yet both representatives, even this early in their careers, are also connecting the local and the national:

- Congressman Higgins Returns from Irish Peace Talks and Announces Gerry Adams Visit to Buffalo (PR 1/20/06)
- Kuhl Keeps Commitment to Fiscal Responsibility: Votes for the Deficit Reduction Act (PR 11/17/05)

In sum, despite some changes, we see considerable stability in the home styles of the representatives profiled for this project and in the local-national balance characterizing those home styles.

The Local-National Balance and Agenda Change

The increased emphasis on foreign affairs post-September 11 of course highlights the interconnections between local and national politics for these representatives. Because these events had such a particular and immediate impact on New York City and State, an examination of the responses of the legislators under study here provides a unique perspective, first off with an analysis of the events themselves, and also enhances our understanding of local and national linkages. It is not surprising that these representatives were forced to think locally—those from New York City needed state and federal help with horrendous cleanup efforts, and those from other parts of the state faced challenges in light of uncharted constituent concerns. If ever there was a time when representatives would be likely to think locally, surely that would hold for New Yorkers post-9/11.

As the following account of a partial listing of the activities of these legislators will demonstrate, though consistent with the themes of this book,
these representatives additionally retained their national (and sometimes
even their partisan) focus, again demonstrating the local-national connections they are able to make. The discussion ends with some speculations
about which types of legislators might be most likely to "go national"
when faced with these kinds of crisis circumstances.

There were, clearly, symbolic gestures in the face of the severity of the
attacks:

- Velazquez: 1. H.CON.RES.424: Commending the patriotic contributions of the roofing professionals who replaced, at no cost to the Federal Government, the section of the Pentagon's slate roof that was de-
  stroyed as a result of the terrorist attacks against the United States that
  occurred on September 11, 2001
- McHugh Urges Americans to Start Traveling (PR 11/29/01)
- McNulty, Congress Aid Victims' Families, Promote Patriotic Initiatives
  (PR 9/13/01)

And clearly, constituency services of all types were needed to an unprecedented degree:

- Kelly, Engel, Lowey to NRC: Any Failures of Indian Point Emergency
  Sirens Are Unacceptable (Kelly, PR 1/25/05) (part of ongoing effort to
  secure the safety of the Indian Point nuclear reactor)
- Engel Calls on House Leadership to Pass Unemployment Benefits for
  Victims of Sept. 11 (PR 3/5/02)
- Velazquez Introduces "Phoenix Fund" for Terrorist Disaster Victim Re-
  covery (PR 9/20/01)
- McCarthy Calls on Congress to Let New York Keep 9/11 Aid (PR
  06/17/05)

Most notably, of course, New York City needed money for cleanup
and revitalization. "Today, New York's health care system, our educational system, our police and firemen and nearly every other city function
is hurting. There is going to be a 15% across-the-board-cut for New York
City services." He emphasized, "[t]he World Trade Center is still smoking, and the crisis in New York is still burning" (Engel PR 11/28/01). And
today, almost five years later, Maloney's Web site poignantly describes,

"The September 11th terrorist attacks on the World Trade Center continue to have serious and lasting impacts on New York and its residents" ("long-term health problems," "extensive job loss," "extreme difficulty making mortgage and rental payments or keeping a small business going") (Web bio).

Regardless of the need, the provision of aid to New York City quickly took on partisan overtones, and some of the most partisan representatives profiled in this book led the charge.[6] "The President promised New York $20 billion dollars in aid. Unfortunately, the President and the Republican leadership in Congress have failed to come through with this much needed money. For countless reasons, New York needs this money to rebuild after the attack on the World Trade Center," said Rep. Engel (PR 11/28/01). "The President has promised to fund homeland security, but he isn't putting his money where his mouth is" (Engel, PR 3/19/03).

Maloney also criticized the federal response: "When the initial pledge made by the President somehow wrongly became a ceiling, rather than a floor for what the federal government would be willing to provide, many of the specific recovery needs in New York became neglected or treated partially" (Maloney Web site special section)

Consequently, one of the functions of the New York congressional delegation (city and statewide) became advocacy for the needs of the city. As Maloney explained, consistent with the getting-involved style that characterized her profile, "My top priority since 9/11 has been to strengthen the federal response in each area of the recovery and to ensure that adequate federal aid is provided to the city for each specific need that emerged from the disaster" (Maloney Web site special section). Thus, she "was the first to complain that President Bush was reneging on his promise of $20 billion in federal funds to help rebuild New York City (*PIA* 2004, 708), she is the only one of these representatives to include on her Web site an extensive section, "Special Update on the 9/11 Recovery: Working for New York's Fair Share," to monitor ongoing recovery efforts, New York's needs, and the federal government's response, and, indicative of her priorities, fully seven of the paragraphs on the current version of her Web site biography include reference to September 11 or broader issues of national security.

Nor was she alone. McCarthy sponsored legislation which would require money confiscated from terrorist groups to be used to help pay for the cleanup (Engel PR 11/7/01). With input from Governor Pataki and President Bush, Houghton (though not from NYC, as we have seen very interested in affairs outside his district) proposed legislation, subsequently enacted, making Lower Manhattan a "liberty zone" "with 5 billion in tax breaks and incentives available to businesses rebuilding" (PR 11/29/01; 4/7/02; Web bio).

In all these efforts, it was Rep. Velazquez who, in addition to her other efforts, remembered to include the minority perspective (PR 3/8/02; 3/23/05), and consistent with her own personal experiences and a home style emphasizing human connections, McCarthy has even provided ongoing grief counseling to families (*PIA* 2006, 703).

Given the extent of the agenda change, it is not surprising that legislators outside New York City also had to respond to new concerns within their own districts. Those with defense plants in their areas could more easily advocate for district interests:

- McHugh Announces Third Brigade to be Added at Drum (PR 5/10/04)
- McNulty, Perry, Announce Funds for Local Firm to Develop Portable Power Systems for Soldiers (PR 5/17/ 05)
- Hinchey, Boehlert Announce Final House Approval of Funding For Lockheed Martin Marine One Helicopter (PR 12/19/05)

Other legislators faced new challenges. Because of the close proximity of their districts to Canada, McHugh was pleased about upgrades in border patrols (*PIA* 2004, 272), and Quinn was also happy that plans to search each and every car traveling across the border were scrapped (*Almanac* 2004, 1177). Hinchey released an "EMERGENCY PREPAREDNESS REPORT based on a survey of local municipalities" (PR 6/25/02), and, interestingly, consistent with his "bridge-builder" affinities, Rep. Houghton particularly reached out to the (what must be a very small) Muslim community in his district: "6:00 P.M.: Meeting with Muslim, Sikh and Hindu Community at the Econo Lodge in Painted Post" (PR 9/27/01); "2:15 P.M.: Visit to Olean Mosque" (PR 9/28/01).

In addition to these local efforts, and considering the nature of the disaster, while the local focus could have been all-consuming for these representatives, many framed issues and events in a national and sometimes partisan perspective. Hinchey followed up his survey with efforts to increase funding for local emergency preparedness (PR 9/9/02) and with a bill sponsored for the purpose of offering a federal income tax credit to volunteer firefighters and emergency medical responders. Houghton sponsored "a bill to discourage trade in 'conflict diamonds,' which are used to finance illegal causes, such as the Al Qaeda terror network" (*Almanac* 2004, 1182) and later

created the Congressional French Caucus (PR 10/22/03) to improve relations with France relative to policy differences on the war in Iraq.[7] Interestingly, by arguing that a "Homeland Security Bill Ignores Threat Posed by
Pre-9/11 Gun Laws" (PR 5/18/05), McCarthy hoped both to strengthen
those laws and to ensure terrorist suspects could be dissuaded by their provisions.[8] Engel "announced that he is taking a lead role in the Homeland Security Task Force and will serve as the task force's vice chairman . . . will
fight for greater federal spending and challenge the administration's record
on all issues affecting homeland security" (PR 6/6/03).

Finally, in an interesting confluence of the local and the national, Maloney and Rep. Christopher Shays (R-CT) formed the bipartisan 9/11 Commission Congressional Caucus. "Beginning in July 2004 and working
closely with family members of 9/11 victims on the Family Steering Committee (Web bio), Maloney and Shays attempted to pass a bipartisan security reform bill in the House," and subsequently were active participants in
the ultimately successful effort to approve many 9/11 Commission recommendations. Interestingly, "Maloney's Caucus continues to press for the
enactment of additional commission recommendations, and Maloney is
the author of a proposal to reorganize Congress for better oversight of
Homeland Security and Intelligence, one of the commission's chief concerns" (Web bio).

As they provide a final reiteration of major themes of this project, a
couple of points about this national involvement prove particularly interesting. While it is generally true that the legislators described throughout
these profiles as having more nationally oriented home styles were most
likely to "go national" with respect to 9/11, it is also true that the magnitude of the crisis (or, more cynically, the political credit associated with participation) assured that virtually all these legislators could be connected in
some way with crisis-related activities. In a word, everyone got involved.
Thus, as we have seen throughout this book, even locally oriented legislators occasionally take (or find themselves placed in) the national spotlight.
Because of subcommittee chairmanships, Rep. Quinn could preside over
hearings on railroad security (*Boston Globe* 5/6/04), Kelly continues her
work in Congress to "bolster worldwide efforts to shut down terrorist
funding networks by passing legislation through the Financial Services
Committee" (PR 11/16/05), and McHugh has worked "to Reimburse State
and Local Governments for Costs Associated with Illegal Alien Incarcera-
tion" (PR 6/16/03). Because of his unique place within the Republican
Party, Quinn found his votes on key homeland security issues particularly

difficult. And sometimes, legislators might come up with relevant proposals: "Along with Senator Clinton, Rep. McNulty Proposes Homeland Security Block Grants—Plan Would Guide $3.5 Billion Directly to Local Municipalities & States, Over $200 Million to New York State and Provide Discretion for its Use" (3/21/02).

At the same time, some speculation is in order. Why did some legislators become more nationally involved than others? Put differently, can we predict from legislator home styles their reactions to a sudden and dramatic event? Throughout the pages of this book, we have described a set of legislators who have developed specific and successful ways of presenting themselves to constituents. How do they respond when confronted with changed circumstances of varying degrees of novelty? At least in the case of these entrenched incumbents and their response to a national shock (which quickly returned to politics as usual), it is striking that their actions (for example, the national focus of Maloney or Houghton versus the more local perspective of McNulty, the partisan view of Engel versus the more moderate Houghton or McCarthy) for the most part fit into their already developed home styles. The specifics of their reactions differ, but the broader concept of home style certainly provides a framework within which to understand the actions of these members of Congress.

Variation notwithstanding, what, in addition to an interesting descriptive update, has the material covered in this postscript added to an understanding of the local-national linkage? The discussion of the stability and continuity of home styles reiterates that local-national interconnections were not a fluke of the 1990s, and the brief look at some Congress members' responses in the immediate aftermath of September 11, in conjunction with a description of the stability of the local and national elements in their home styles, provides a uniquely local perspective on a key national event. In addition, it is very much in keeping with the themes of this book that, in accord with their obvious efforts to rebuild from the devastation, it was not a stretch for most of these representatives to also go national, incorporating broader perspectives in their extensive local activities. Given both the ongoing war on terrorism but also trends towards significantly increased globalization, the combination of local and national politics, which has characterized the profiles of this book, should certainly be expected to continue.

NOTES

Chapter 1. Introduction

1. Thus, the use of the word "dilemma" in the title is meant to highlight the advantages and disadvantages inherent in alternative presentations of self. It is not necessarily intended to imply that individual legislators are making conscious choices or facing personal "dilemmas" as to how to connect with constituents, though for some, these decisions may be more difficult than for others.

Chapter 2. Overview of Theoretical and Methodological Concerns

1. Source: http://quickfacts.census.gov/qfd/states/36000.html.
2. Sources: http://www.csmonitor.com/durable/1998/01/06/us/us.4.html; http://news.bbc.co.uk/hi/english/special_report/1998/09/98/us_midterms/newsid_204000/204483.stm.
3. Source: http://clinton.senate.gov/Brochureopening.html.

Chapter 3. Rethinking the Local-National Debate

1. Source: http://www.whitehouse.gov/history/firstladies/hc42.html.
2. http://www.cnn.com/2000/ALLPOLITICS/stories/10/22/clinton.endorse.
3. In truth, Maloney's economic status has also been estimated in the three to five million dollar range (PIA 1994, 1060).
4. Unfortunately, a civilian trial also found Berenson guilty. Thereafter, Maloney (and others) requested the Peruvian president to grant clemency (PIA 1994).
5. She followed up with hearings monitoring enforcement (PIA 1994).
6. Maloney has continued to advocate breastfeeding, proposing tax incentives and workplace antidiscrimination legislation (PR 3/8/00).
7. Specifically, she wanted amendments lowering social security taxes (Newsday 5/26/93). While Maloney received considerable criticism from some constituent groups, others viewed her vote as a "profile in courage" (Newsday 6/5/93).

8. The census was a good issue for Maloney not only in terms of partisanship but also because many feel that the use of statistical sampling would be of particular benefit to urban areas including, New York City in terms of congressional representation and, of equal importance, federal funding formulas (*PIA* 2000; *PIA* 2002).

9. The Mexican trip proved so successful that it resulted in contracts for at least one company (BN 10/12/94) and earned Houghton the notice of President Clinton and other relevant officials, as the undersecretary of commerce and international trade echoed Houghton's enthusiasm for the district, commenting upon the district's selection as one of six cities to participate in a pilot project encouraging export assistance. "We would like to do more things in this district in a prototype way. This is a great place to expand our efforts" (*BN* 5/20/95).

10. Later, he capitalized on the Nicaraguan connection to ensure that New York State wine was the official American wine at a Nicaraguan presidential inauguration (*Almanac* 1988, 870).

11. His concerns included disagreement with the emphasis on harsher penalties as the route to crime prevention, worrying that tax cuts would produce higher deficits, and advocating for not placing limits on the number of American troops under United Nations control (*Almanac* 1988).

12. Houghton disagrees with other mainstream Republican positions as well. Though he believes in the importance of balanced budgets, he doesn't think that a constitutional amendment is the only way to produce such a result (*PIA* 1992, 962). He was one of three Republicans in 1993 who refused to promise no new taxes (*Almanac* 1994), one of eleven in 1995 to vote against the initial GOP tax cut proposals (*PIA* 1998), and one of seventeen to vote against a constitutional amendment prohibiting flag burning (*PIA* 1992, 1080). He is generally pro-choice, is often a supporter of gay rights (*PIA* 1996) ("Whether or not you agree with the concept of gay rights, who are we to be judgmental?" [*PIA* 2000, 962]), and though a card-carrying member of the NRA, he has advocated for more restrictive gun legislation (PR 6/18/99).

13. How did McHugh spend the funds? What is campaign money spent on in a rural and dispersed district? In part, his expenses consisted of forty-three thousand dollars on radio and TV ads, twenty-five thousand on advocacy mailings, three thousand on palm cards and bumper stickers, and three hundred eight-eight dollars in pencils (*1992 House Races*).

14. In fact, between one-quarter and one-half of the press releases on his Web site for 1999 and 2000 contain announcements of federal grants awarded to the 24th district.

15. At the same time McHugh stated, "There will be problems in transition, but people won't walk away from the truly needy" (*WDT* 8/2/96).

Chapter 4. National Parties, Individual Choices

1. For scholarly disagreement as to the extent of the changes described in this chapter, see Green (2002).

2. Source: http://www.Jeffords.senate.gov/declaration_of_independence.html.

3. As of 2001, this contract was, however, under review, as the Bush administration assessed the utility of specific weapons systems in the Post–cold war
era (*TU* 4/24/01).

4. Actually, a record exists of his co-sponsorship but not his sponsorship of this
legislation.

5. Indeed, as part of his committee work, he was initially slated to be on a plane
with Representative Mickey Leland in 1989. Subsequently, the plane
crashed, killing all aboard (*TU* 8/9/89).

6. Actually, these figures appear somewhat in dispute, as one source cites the
party ratio as three-to-one Republican (*Newsday* 10/31/00).

7. Interestingly, Frisa defended his controversial 1995 vote against banning assault weapons that so angered McCarthy: "Shortly after he voted to repeal
the assault-weapons ban, Frisa introduced a bill creating a ban that he said
would be stronger than the one in place. 'I stood up to get rid of a bad law,'
Frisa has said" (*New Orleans Times Picayune* 7/21/96).

8. Also the site of Charles Lindbergh's takeoff for his historic transatlantic
flight (*PIA* 2000, 921).

9. Subsequently, "Carolyn continues her efforts to reduce gun violence through
legislation to enforce existing gun laws, research smart gun technology and
close the gun show loophole. Carolyn also remains an outspoken advocate
for victims of crime, and travels extensively to educate Americans on ways to
reduce gun violence" (Web bio).

10. Schumer said he wasn't bothered by it, adding that it says more about
D'Amato than McCarthy. "My guess is he knew it would be good for him to
do that," he said (*Newsday* 5/25/97).

11. Actually, the one endorsement that she gave was to a local candidate associated with her son's school. Ironically, because it was a primary and she is a
registered Republican, she could not vote for the candidate she endorsed
(*Newsday* 8/29/01).

Chapter 5. The Local-National Connection and the Representa-
tion of Minorities

1. In fact, the 12th includes most of Manhattan's famed Chinatown.

2. Source: Bronx Tourism Council http://ilovethebronx.com.

3. Because of the vindictiveness of the contest and the surprising closeness of
Engel's subsequent victory margin, at the time, the race proved a real
shocker. While the details would be a side track from the main focus of
this profile, the issues raised in the primary contest notably reiterate the
themes highlighted here—arguments as to the importance of the role of racial representation and the utility of emphasizing constituency service perhaps at the expense of policy considerations. In addition, the race highlighted factional politics (*DN* 9/10/00; *NPR* 9/3/00) and some unusual
charges that Seabrook had divorced his wife without actually informing

her of the proceedings (*DN* 9/13/00, *NYP* 9/6/00).See also *Crain's New York Business* (7/24/00).

4. Solarz also had been implicated in a congressional bank scandal, having made 743 overdrafts on the House Bank (*Almanac* 1994).

5. Subsequently, Velazquez filed a lawsuit against St. Clare's hospital for ten million dollars to "send a message to all institutions which maintain patients' confidential files, and also to redress the wrongs done to me" (*TU* 5/14/94).

6. In conjunction with a congressional delegation and other advocacy groups, Velazquez also led a group of Congresspeople to sign a brief to the Supreme Court seeking to block Arizona's English-only law (*DN* 7/26/96).

7. Hurricane damage carries personal meaning for Velazquez. When a 1998 hurricane hit her hometown, Velazquez described the incident: "There was no communication. I kept trying until I was finally able to talk to my mother it was around 11 PM. After that there was no communication again" (*DN* 9/23/98).

8. After the inadvertent killing of a civilian security guard, protests called for the closing of Viequez, which has been used for U.S. military training, including the dropping of live bombs.

9. Of equal concern to Velazquez in the case of NAFTA was the fact that President Clinton engaged in so much "deal making" to ensure final passage. "If you see some of the dealings going on here it makes you question the dignity of this institution" (*Newsday* 11/18/93).

10. In addition, it is worth noting that Velazquez also espoused her partisan side at the local level, expressing dissatisfaction with Republican mayor Giuliani (*Newsday* 1/1/95), supporting other local Democrats (*NYT* 8/18/93), and sometimes becoming involved in factional politics (*NYT* 2/9/98; *DN* 3/1/98).

Chapter 6. Balancing Constituencies: Fenno's Bulls-eye Model in the 1990s

1. Source: http://www.state.ny.us/governor/press/year99/sept20_99.htm.

2. On occasion, Quinn got involved on issues not particularly related to constituency concerns; interestingly, "In 1997, he helped garner 160 House signatures on a petition urging Clinton to override Pentagon objections and join a Canadian-sponsored effort to sign a treaty that would ban the use of land mines" (*PIA* 2000, 988).

3. He didn't pledge to accept term limits for himself (*PIA* 1994, 1106).

4. An aide to Speaker Gingrich even wrote a letter to Quinn's mother requesting she help him improve his dress (*WP* 6/24/98).

5. Quinn was involved in other aspects of the bill's passage, helping the president "count noses" (*BN* 8/22/94) and defending the legislation against the criticisms of sportsmen by "pointing out that the bill contains provisions expressly exempting 670 types of hunting and sporting firearms as well as antique firearms" (*BN* 5/3/94).

6. He presided over controversial hearings on the Love Canal, winning plaudits for holding hearings at times affected residents could attend (*BN* 8/1/98).

7. Capitalizing on national connections, Hinchey also ran some fairly creative ads. Observe one constituent's description: "I loved the Robert Redford radio ads Hinchey ran with the usual campfire guitars being plucked softly in the background, the environmentally dedicated actor told us why we should send Hinchey back to Congress, mentioning his own name twice" (*KDF* 11/2/98).

8. Hinchey even acknowledged that had liberal Ithaca been redistricted out of the 26th, he might not have attempted a 1992 run (*KDF* 11/9/94).

9. The designation involved considerable partisan politics. Republicans actually sued President Clinton in an effort to kill heritage designations. In addition, the Hudson didn't make an initial cut of ten rivers but was added when the list was expanded to fourteen (*TU* 7/28/98). The designation appears to have paid off: "Economic development aid totaling $40 million will be available to 10 counties along the Hudson River, federal officials said Monday" (*AP* 4/11/00).

10. Clinton was vice president under both Jefferson and Madison, and the first VP to die in office, in 1812.

11. Hinchey was a supporter of Woodstock '94, and his wife did public relations for the promoters (*KDF* 11/4/98).

12. Source: http://www.nydems.org/elected/hinchey.html.

13. These strong beliefs have gotten him into some unusual situations. Early in his career, he took the unusual step of criticizing a popular President Clinton for what he saw as going back on campaign pledges to generate more economic growth (*WP* 7/18/93). Also, "As a member of the Banking Committee, Hinchey has been a frequent critic of the Federal Reserve," expressing concern about "excessive increases in interest rates" (www.hincheyforcongress.org). As the economy worsened in the late 1990s, however, he became a strong advocate for lowering interest rates (PR 3/16/98, 1/31/01).

14. Source: http://www.ulster.net/~fomh/mhissues.htm#students.

15. Source: http://www.ulster.net/~fomh/mhissues.htm.

16. Ibid.

17. "Congressman Hinchey also serves as one of two Regional Whips for New York State and as a Whip-at-Large, responsible for developing legislative strategy with the House Democratic leadership: He is also a member of the Democratic Caucus task forces on education and health care" (www . . . hinchey). "In the 106th Congress, he was on Democratic task forces on education and health" (PIA 2002, 720).

18. Hinchey was issued a summons at a Washington airport for carrying a handgun in a carry-on bag. He pleaded no contest to the charges but, interestingly, noted that he had carried the gun ever since his work as a state legislator investigating the role of organized crime in the garbage industry (*TU* 12/2/94).

Chapter 7. Concluding Perspectives

1. Note: Rep. Engel, who emphasizes service and who represents a district with many "international" interests was nevertheless classified as "moderately national" due to his strong foreign policy focus.
2. Despite the fact that partisanship played a central role in his profile, Rep. Houghton was classified as "not" partisan because he so steadfastly believes in moderate politics.
3. It is interesting to note that two former New York State representatives (Bill Paxon and the late Gerald Solomon) who represented equally rural and Republican areas both jumped on the national partisan bandwagon (Paxon headed the Republican Congressional Campaign Committee and Solomon chaired the House Rules Committee under the Gingrich speakership).

Postscript

1. Of all the changes occurring since the cutoff of data collection for this book, I have chosen to highlight responses to 9/11 because of their relevance to New York in particular and to local-national interconnections more generally. It is worth noting, however, with respect to the changes listed in the text, that despite an intense and controversial process, it was Rep. Engel who was most impacted by the redistricting of 2002. Though he retained a multiracial (50% White, 32% African American, and 18% Hispanic) and multiethnic district, he nevertheless gained more "White" constituents, alleviating at least some of the racial conflict that characterized his profile (*Almanac* 2004, 1148). The impact of seniority along with the continuing partisanship in Congress after the 2000 election will be touched on in the text.
2. As we have also seen toward the end of her profile, particularly with respect to her Washington activity, a learning curve may have occurred for McCarthy as well; she developed a better understanding of the give-and-take and compromise inherent in the legislative process (*Almanac* 2004).
3. Yet, using Canon's distinction about a politics of difference versus a politics of commonality, recall that in chapter 5, Velazquez's profile was contrasted with that of Rep. Engel. With her efforts on behalf of small business, which have the potential to aid citizens of all races and to offer equal opportunities and treatment for all, Velazquez may be moving in part toward a home style of commonality.
4. Quinn did, however, offer amendments that he said "puts labor representatives at the table from day one . . . and they preserve their right to appeal" (*BN* 8/11/02)
5. The job Quinn took after leaving Congress was "as president of Cassidy Associates, a gold-plated Washington lobbying firm" interestingly with historically Democratic associations (*BN* 11/14/04).

6. A full accounting of these events would also include many bipartisan efforts originating from both sides of the aisle.
7. His conflict diamonds bill was subsequently enacted into law (PR 4/28/03).
8. She unsuccessfully also used the context of a homeland security bill as a vehicle for proposing a reinstatement of the assault weapons ban, thus linking gun violence to concerns about terrorism (PR 5/18/05).

WORKS CITED

Abramson, Paul R., John H. Aldrich, and David W. Rohde. *Change and Continuity in the 1992 Elections*. Washington, DC: CQ Press, 1994.

———. *Change and Continuity in the 1996 Elections*. Washington, DC: CQ Press, 1998.

Adler, E. Scott, Chariti E. Gent, and Cary B. Overmeyer. "The Home Style Homepage: Legislator Use of the World Wide Web for Constituency Contact." *Legislative Studies Quarterly* 23 (1998): 585–95.

Aldrich, John H., and David W. Rohde. "The Logic of Conditional Party Government: Revisiting the Electoral Connection." *Congress Reconsidered*. Ed. Lawrence C. Dodd and Bruce Oppenheimer. Washington, DC: CQ Press, 2001. 269–92.

Ansolabehere, Stephen, James M. Snyder Jr., and Charles Stewart III. "The Effects of Party and Preferences on Congressional Roll-Call Voting." *Legislative Studies Quarterly* 26 (2001): 533–72.

Bader, John B. *Taking the Initiative: Leadership Agendas in Congress and "the Contract with America."* Washington, DC: Georgetown UP, 1996.

Bailey, Michael A., Clyde Wilcox, and Ronald A. Faucheux. *Campaigns and Elections: Contemporary Case Studies*. Washington, DC: CQ Press, 2000.

Barone, Michael, and Richard Cohen. *The Almanac of American Politics 2002*. Washington, DC: National Journal, 2001. See other volumes in the series 1988–2000.

Beck, Paul Allen. *Party Politics in America*, 8th ed. New York: Longman, 1997.

Berry, Jeffrey M. *The New Liberalism: The Rising Power of Citizen Groups*. Washington, DC: Brookings Institution Press, 1999.

Bibby, John F. "Party Networks: National-State Integration, Allied Groups, and Issue Activists." *The State of the Parties*. Ed. John C. Green and Daniel M. Shea. Lanham, MD: Rowman and Littlefield, 1999.

Brady, David W., and Kara Z. Buckley. "Coalitions and Policy in the U.S. Congress: Lessons from the 103rd and 104th Congresses." *The Parties Respond: Changes in American Parties and Campaigns*. Ed. L. Sandy Maisel. Boulder: Westview, 1998.

Bruck, Connie. "The Politics of Perception." *New Yorker*. October 9, 1999.

Canon, David T. *Race, Redistricting, and Representation: The Unintended Consequences of Black Majority Districts*. Chicago: U of Chicago P, 1999.

Canon, David T., Matthew M. Schousen, and Patrick J. Sellers. "The Supply Side Of Congressional Redistricting: Race and Strategic Politicians, 1972-1992." *Journal of Politics* 58 (1996): 846–62.

Carroll, Susan J. "Representing Women: Congresswomen's Perceptions of Their Representation Roles." *Women Transforming Congress*. Ed. Cindy Simon Rosenthal. Norman: U of Oklahoma P, 2002: 50–68.

Cohen, Richard E. *Washington at Work: Back Rooms and Clean Air.* Boston: Allyn and Bacon, 1995.

Congressional Districts in the 1990s: A Portrait of America. Washington, DC: CQ Press, 1993.

Davidson, Roger H., and Walter J. Oleszek. *Congress and Its Members.* Washington, DC: CQ Press, 2000.

———. *Congress and Its Members.* Washington, DC: CQ Press, 2002.

Ehrenhalt, Alan. *The United States of Ambition: Politicians, Power, and the Pursuit of Office* New York: Times Books, 1991.

Farley, Reynolds, and Walter R. Allen. *The Color Line and the Quality of Life in America.* New York: Russell Sage Foundation, 1987.

Fenno, Richard F., Jr. *Congressmen in Committees.* Boston: Little, Brown, 1973.

———. *Home Style: House Members in Their Districts.* New York: Harper Collins, 1978.

———. *Senators on the Campaign Trail: The Politics of Representation.* Norman: U of Oklahoma P, 1996.

———. *Congress at the Grassroots.* Chapel Hill: U of North Carolina P, 2000.

———. *Going Home: Black Representatives and Their Constituents.* Chicago: U of Chicago P, 2003.

Fiorina, Morris P. *Congress: Keystone of the Washington Establishment.* New Haven: Yale UP, 1977.

———. "Some Problems in Studying the Effects of Resource Allocation in Congressional Elections." *American Journal of Political Science* 25 (1981): 543–67.

———. "Keystone Reconsidered." *Congress Reconsidered.* Ed. Lawrence C. Dodd and Bruce I. Oppenheimer. Washington, DC: CQ Press, 2005. 159–79.

Fowler, Linda L. *Candidates, Congress, and the American Democracy.* Ann Arbor: U of Michigan P, 1993.

Fowler, Linda L., and Robert D. McClure. *Political Ambition: Who Decides to Run for Congress.* New Haven: Yale UP, 1989.

Friedman, Sally, and Christopher Witko. "Business Backgrounds and Congressional Decision-making." Paper presented at the American Political Science Association Annual Meeting, Washington, DC, 2005.

Gilligan, Carol. *In a Different Voice: Psychological Theory and Women's Development.* Cambridge: Harvard UP, 1982.

Gimpel, James G. *Fulfilling the Contract.* Boston: Allyn and Bacon, 1996.

Green, John C. "Still Functional After All These Years: Parties in the United States, 1960–2000." *Political Parties in Advanced Industrial Democracies.* Ed. Paul Webb, David Farrell, and Ian Holliday. New York: Oxford UP, 2002.

Hacker, Jacob S., and Paul Pierson. *Off Center: The Republican Revolution and the Erosion of American Democracy.* New Haven: Yale UP, 1995.

Hawkings, David, and Brian Nutting. *CQ's Politics in America 2004: the 108th Congress.* Washington, DC: CQ Press, 2003. See other volumes in the series 1996–2000.

Hero, Rodney E., and Caroline J. Tolbert. "Latinos and Substantive Representation in the U.S. House of Representatives: Direct, Indirect, or Non-existent?" *American Journal of Political Science* 39 (1995): 640–52.

Herrnson, Paul S. "Congress' Other Farm Team: Congressional Staff." *Polity* 27 (1994): 133–56.

———. "National Party Organizations at the Century's End." *The Parties Respond: Changes in American Parties and Campaigns.* Ed. L. Sandy Maisel. Boulder: Westview, 1998. 50–82.

Jacobson, Gary C. *The Politics of Congressional Elections.* Boston: Addison-Wesley, 2001.

Johannes, John R., and John C. McAdams. "The Congressional Incumbency Effect: Is It Casework, Policy Compatibility, or Something Else? An Examination of the 1978 Election." *American Journal of Political Science* 25 (1981): 512–42.

Johnson, Janet Buttolph, and Richard A. Joslyn. *Political Science Research Methods.* Washington, DC: CQ Press, 1995.

Kennedy, William J. *O Albany!: Improbable City of Political Wizards, Fearless Ethnics, Spectacular Aristocrats, Splendid Nobodies, and Underrated Scoundrels.* New York: Viking, 1985.

Kerr, Brinck, and Will Miller. "Latino Representation, It's Direct and Indirect (in Replications)." *American Journal of Political Science* 41(1997): 1066–71.

King, Gary, Robert O. Keohane, and Sidney Verba. *Designing Social Inquiry: Scientific Inference in Qualitative Research.* Princeton: Princeton UP, 1994.

Kingdon, John W. *Congressmen's Voting Decisions.* New York: Harper, 1989.

Koopman, Douglas L. *Hostile Takeover: The House Republicans Party, 1980–1995.* Lanham, MD: Rowman and Littlefield, 1996.

Lublin, David. *The Paradox of Representation: Racial Gerrymandering and Minority Interests in Congress.* Princeton: Princeton UP, 1997.

Madison, James. "Federalist No. 10." In Hamilton, Alexander, James Madison, and John Jay. *The Federalist Papers.* New York: Bantam Books, 1982.

Malbin, Michael J. *Unelected Representatives : Congressional Staff and the Future of Representative Government.* New York: Basic Books, 1980.

Mann, Thomas E., and Raymond E. Wolfinger. "Candidates and Parties in Congressional Elections." *The American Political Science Review* 74 (1980): 617–32.

Mansbridge, Jane. "The Many Faces of Representation." Kennedy School of Government Politics Research Group Working Paper, 1998.

———. "Should Blacks Represent Blacks and Women Represent Women? A Contingent 'Yes.'" *Journal of Politics* 61(1999): 628–57.

Margolies-Mezvinsky, Marjorie, with Barbara Feinman. *A Woman's Place: The Freshmen Women Who Changed the Face of Congress.* New York: Crown, 1994.

Matthews, Donald R. *U.S. Senators and Their World.* Chapel Hill: U of North Carolina P, 1960.

Mayhew, David R. *Congress: The Electoral Connection*. New Haven: Yale UP, 1974.

———. "Congressional Elections: The Case of the Vanishing Marginals." *Polity* 6 (1974): 296–317.

Michelin Green Guide, New York City online. Accessed at: http://www.globe corner.com/t/t7/3792.php.

Miller, Warren E., and Donald E. Stokes. "Constituency Influence in Congress." *The American Political Science Review* 57 (1963): 45–56.

Miroff, Bruce, Raymond Seidelman, and Todd Swanstrom. *Debating Democracy: A Reader in American Politics*. Boston: Houghton Mifflin, 1997.

———. *The Democratic Debate*. Boston: Houghton Mifflin, 1998.

Morris, Dwight, and Murielle E. Gamache. *Handbook of Campaign Spending: Money in the 1992 Congressional Races*. Washington, DC: CQ Press, 1994.

Parker, Glenn R. *Homeward Bound: Explaining Changes in Congressional Behavior*. Pittsburgh: U of Pittsburgh P, 1986.

———. *Characteristics of Congress: Patterns in Congressional Behavior*. Englewood Cliffs: Prentice-Hall, 1989.

Paulson, Arthur. *Realignment and Party Revival: Understanding American Electoral Politics at the Turn of the Twenty-First Century*. Westport: Praeger, 2000.

Peters, Ronald M. *The American Speakership: The Office in Historical Perspective*. Baltimore: Johns Hopkins UP, 1990.

Polsby, Nelson W. *How Congress Evolves: Social Bases of Institutional Change*. New York: Oxford UP, 2004.

Ragsdale, Lyn. "The Fiction of Congressional Elections as Presidential Events." *American Politics Quarterly* 8 (1980): 375–98.

Robinson, Michael J. "Three Faces of Congressional Media." *The New Congress*. Ed. Thomas E. Mann and Norman J. Ornstein. Washington, DC: American Enterprise Institute, 1981.

Rohde, David W. *Parties and Leaders in the Postreform House*. Chicago: U of Chicago P, 1991.

Schickler, Eric, and Kathryn Pearson. "The House Leadership in an Era of Partisan Warfare." *Congress Reconsidered*. Eds. Lawrence C. Dodd and Bruce I. Oppenheimer. Washington, DC: CQ Press, 2005. 207–25.

Schneier, Edward V. *New York Politics: A Tale of Two States*. Armonk: M. E. Sharpe, 2001.

Sharp, J. Michael. *Directory of Congressional Voting Scores and Interest Group Ratings*. 2nd ed.,Vol. 1. Washington, DC: CQ Press, 1997.

Sinclair, Barbara. "Evolution or Revolution? Policy-Oriented Congressional Parties in the 1990's." *The Parties Respond: Changes in American Parties and Campaigns*. Ed. L. Sandy Maisel. Boulder: Westview, 1998: 263–85.

———. "The Dream Fullfilled? Party Development in Congress, 1950–2000." In John C. Green and Paul S. Herrnson, eds. *Responsible Partisanship? The Evolution of American Political Parties since 1950*. Lawrence: UP of Kansas, 2002.

Smith, Steven S., and Eric D. Lawrence. "Party Control of Committees in the Republican Congress." *Congress Reconsidered*. Ed. Lawrence C. Dodd and Bruce I. Oppenheimer. Washington, DC: CQ Press, 1997: 163–92.

Storing, Herbert. *What the Anti-Federalists Were For*. Chicago: U of Chicago P, 1981.

Swain, Carol M. *Black Faces, Black Interests*. Cambridge: Harvard UP, 1995.

Szardwarski, Alan. "Shuttle Democracy: Contact Between Legislators and Constituents in the Contemporary U.S." Paper presented at Midwest Political Science Association, Chicago, Illinois, 1999.

Takeda, Okiyoshi. "The Representation of Asian Americans in the U.S. Politics System." *Representation of Minority Groups in the United States: Implications for the 21st Century*. Ed. Charles E. Menifield. Lanham, MD: Austin and Winfield, 2001.

Thomas, Sue. *How Women Legislate*. Oxford: Oxford UP, 1994.

———. "Why Gender Matters: The Perceptions of Women Officeholders." *Women and Politics* 17 (1997): 27–53.

Thurber, James A., ed. *The Battle for Congress: Consultants, Candidates, and Voters*. Washington, DC: Brookings Institution Press, 2001.

Uslaner, Eric M. *The Decline of Comity in Congress*. Ann Arbor: U of Michigan P, 1993.

Washington Alert, 103–105 Congress.

Weisberg, Herbert F., Eric S. Heberling, and Lisa M. Campoli. *Classics in Congressional Politics*. Boston: Addison-Wesley, 1999.

Whitby, Kenny J. *The Color of Representation: Congressional Behavior and Black Interests*. Ann Arbor: U of Michigan P, 1997.

Wilson, James Q. "Two Negro Politicians: An Interpretation." *Midwest Journal Of Political Science* 4 (1960): 346–69.

Yin, Robert K. *Case Study Research: Design and Methods*. Beverly Hills: Sage, 2003.

INDEX

104th congress, 7, 39, 66, 82, 86, 89, 90, 91, 96, 111, 113, 133, 134, 151, 153, 165, 190, 192, 193, 197, 224, 257

1994 elections, 11, 42, 50, 75, 82, 84, 87, 90, 91, 97, 100, 115, 123, 138

9/11, 2001, 234, 238, 239–240, 243, 244, 248

abortion, 16, 40, 75, 87, 90, 91, 98, 104, 112, 115, 119, 122, 123, 133, 134, 136, 166, 168, 207, 211, 212
  gag rule, 196
  partial birth abortion, 98, 133, 134, 136, 196, 212
  pro-choice, 91, 93, 97, 98, 137, 156, 196, 228, 230, 254
  pro-life, 68, 75, 91, 92, 97, 100, 182, 206
  Roe v. Wade, 40
Abramson, Paul R., 83
ADA presidential support scores, 200
Adler, E. Scott, 223
AFL-CIO, 92, 186, 196, 200, 216
Africa, 54, 57, 59, 114, 155
African-American, 25, 36, 57, 63, 119, 139, 141, 142, 145, 148, 152, 153, 156, 159, 172, 175, 184, 189, 229, 238, 258
AIDS , 96, 152, 156, 170
Albanian, 148, 154
Albany, 77, 102, 103, 104, 105, 106, 107, 113, 115, 204, 205, 206, 210

Albany democratic political machine, 102–106, 108, 114, 116, 119, 229, 236
Aldrich, John H., 82, 83
"all politics is local," 2, 13, 19
Amo Mobile, 55
Amtrak, 192, 193, 197
Ansolabehere, Stephen, 8
anti-federalist, 33
Appropriations Committee, 111, 213
Armed Services Committee, 73, 109, 110, 111, 243
Armenia, 113
Armey, Dick, 60, 131, 194
Army caucus, 73
Asian constituents, 168, 172, 238

Bader, John B., 7, 8, 84
balanced budget, 70, 75, 84, 138, 196, 202, 207, 228
Banking and Finance Committee, 169, 213
Barclay, Douglas, 67
Barrett, Gresham, 221, 240
Base Closure and Realignment Commission, 69
Beck, Paul Allen, 85
Becker, Gregory, 135–136
Berenson, Lori, 43, 253
Biaggi, Mario, 150, 151, 152, 159
Bibby, John F., 82, 84
Binghamton, 25, 182, 184, 185, 105, 208, 209
bipartisan, 11, 47, 86, 117, 130, 132, 133, 135, 136, 137, 176, 186, 187, 188, 196, 197, 198, 202, 214, 219, 220, 228, 237, 245, 251

bipartisan civility, 61, 197
Boxer, Barbara, 176, 178
breastfeeding, 44
Bronx, NY, 36, 144, 145, 148, 149, 150, 151, 152, 153, 156, 158, 159, 160, 174, 238
Brooklyn, NY, 36, 38, 41, 123, 144, 145, 163, 244
Broome County, 185, 207
Budget Committee, 58
Buffalo, NY, 1, 3, 21, 25, 180, 181, 182, 184, 187, 189, 191, 192, 193, 197, 198, 202
bulls-eye model, 3, 21, 22, 176, 178, 179, 222, 235
bullwinkle district, 145
Bush, George H. W., 40, 89, 141, 188, 189, 207
Bush, George W., 1, 31, 49, 75, 89, 114, 188, 192, 196, 214, 216, 236, 240, 245, 246, 249, 250

campaign finance, 6, 39, 47, 83, 243
campaign finance reform, 47, 243
Canada, 71, 181, 250
Canadian border, 35, 65, 195, 256
candidate recruitment, 2, 6, 7, 15, 84, 99, 129, 226, 236
candidate training, 6, 7, 84
Canon, David, T., 139, 142, 162, 173, 229
carpetbagger, 33, 91, 95, 102, 162, 163
Carroll, Susan J., 141
Carter, James, 139
case study, 9, 10, 13, 22, 30, 222, 242
Catholic, 119, 153, 155, 182 187, 191
census, 1, 2, 44, 48, 49, 165, 170
Chamorro, Violeta, 57
China, 73, 99, 168
Chinese constituents, 183
Christian right, 16, 115, 197
civil rights, 6, 15, 48, 58, 62, 63, 89, 113, 139, 141, 142, 150, 155
civilian marksmanship program, 44
civility retreat, 61, 197

Clay, William, 139, 142
Clinton, Bill, 35, 40, 41, 43, 48, 49, 61, 66, 71, 75, 76, 89, 113, 119, 120, 127, 134, 136, 149, 158, 160, 165, 166, 167, 170, 172, 185, 188, 189, 194, 196, 198, 208, 210, 212, 213, 217
    impeachment, 7, 16, 61, 63, 80, 89, 95, 134, 141, 158, 199, 201, 216, 246
Clinton, Hillary, 25, 26, 30, 32–35, 43, 95, 98,100, 111, 121, 165, 246, 252
Cohen, Richard E., 22
Cohoes, NY, 104, 109
college graduation, 52, 66, 87, 124, 148, 181, 214
Collins, Dick, 116
Colombia, 145, 165
common sense, 116, 117, 176, 215
commonality, 65, 142, 144, 157, 173, 174, 175, 180, 229, 230
conditional party government, 82
Congressional Caucus on Women's Issues, 46, 97, 130, 169, 230
Congressional Hispanic Caucus, 143
Congressional parties, 82, 97
Congressman A, 4
Congressman B, 4, 19
Congressman C, 34
Congressman D, 4, 15
Congressman E, 4
Congressman F, 15, 63, 142, 143
Congressman H, 34
Congressman O, 19
conservative coalition scores, 75, 166
conservative coalition, 27
conservative democrat, 239
Conservative Party, 113, 243
constituency
    balancing, 11, 18, 85, 100, 143, 178, 217, 222, 228
    constituency oriented, 9, 20, 152, 189
    constituency service, 11, 26, 98, 100, 117, 142, 149, 158, 179,

186, 189, 190, 200, 223, 229, 231, 245, 247, 248
geographic, 3, 5, 21, 22, 103, 119, 176, 178, 180, 182, 219, 223, 235
heterogeneous, 22, 90, 92, 103, 104, 115, 158, 180, 185, 203, 217, 239
home style, affecting, 9, 16, 21, 35, 44, 49, 78
homogenous, 52, 77, 82–83, 239
intimate constituency, 3, 21
primary, 3, 11, 15, 16, 21, 52, 62, 75, 108, 142, 143, 161, 171, 173, 176, 178, 186, 189, 195, 200, 203, 204, 212, 217–219, 220, 222, 230, 235, 245
reelection, 9, 11, 21, 105, 143, 148, 172, 176, 179, 189, 192, 195, 200, 205, 208, 217, 218, 219, 222, 235
Contract with America, 60, 82, 84, 91, 92, 93, 94, 101, 112, 117, 138, 196, 202, 207, 211, 228
Co-op City, 150, 159
Corning Glass Inc., 51, 52, 57, 53, 54, 55, 56
Corning, Edwin, 104
Corning, Erastus, II, 105, 106
crime, 96, 112, 127, 165, 169, 191, 198, 205
Cuba, 113, 155, 165, 216
Cuomo, Mario, 70, 106, 120, 123

D'Amato, Alfonse, 26, 109, 119, 133, 188
Davidson, Roger H., 6, 7, 8, 17, 20, 63, 82, 84, 97, 141
DeLay, Tom, 60, 246
Democratic Party, 2, 7, 25, 27, 32, 38, 39, 40, 43, 48, 49, 50, 62, 66, 83, 92, 102, 104, 105–108, 110, 111, 114, 116, 117, 119, 121, 123, 136, 137, 150, 151, 159, 202, 204, 208, 210, 220, 228, 229, 234, 236

Dingell, John, 128, 129
Dinkins, David, 39, 163
DioGuardi, Joseph, 91, 92, 93, 97, 100
discrimination, 29, 168
district focus, 4, 30
district orientation, 3, 4, 13, 22, 30, 107, 192, 210, 238
domestic violence, 5, 96, 98, 191
Dornan, Robert, 97
downstate, 27, 234
dredging, 211

Education and Workforce Committee, 129
Ehrenhalt, Alan, 6, 20
elderly. *See* seniors
election margins, 19, 41, 50, 66, 92, 101, 123, 136, 186, 206, 208, 232, 234
Energy and Commerce Committee, 155, 174
Engel, Eliot
background of, 149–151
education issues, 155, 156, 157, 159, 248
health care issues, 156, 159, 172, 248
home style of, 151–158
labor issues, 159
and presentation, 156
primary campaign of, 158, 159, 160
veterans issues, 152, 157
English only, 165, 166, 256 n6
Environmental Conservation Committee, 205
Equal Rights Amendment, 39, 46, 230, 245
ERA, see Equal Rights Amendment
Erie County, 182, 188, 195
ERR (Extremely Reasonable Republicans), 60
extra-district, 6, 12, 15, 218

Faith and Politics Institute, 58
Family and Medical Leave Act, 76, 112, 198

Family Steering Committee, 251
Farley, Reynolds, 141
Federal Election Commission (FEC), 47
Federalist No. 10, 32
Federalists, 32, 210
Feinstein, Diane, 176, 178
Fenno, Richard F., Jr., xi, 3–9, 11–13, 15–23, 29, 34, 35, 42, 49, 62–63, 78–79, 83, 130, 138, 141–143, 160, 174, 176, 178–179, 217, 227, 231, 235, 236
Financial Services Committee, 45, 251
Fiorina, Morris P., 5, 6, 7, 13, 19, 20, 42, 84, 190
fiscal responsibility, 75, 247
Fish, Hamilton, III, 89, 92, 93
Fish, Hamilton, Jr., 89, 90, 91, 92, 98, 99
Foreign Affairs, 155
foreign policy, 51, 59, 113, 114, 153, 154, 155, 160, 174, 215, 242, 243, 245, 247
Fort Drum, 66, 68, 69, 70, 73, 235, 238, 250
Founders, 2, 32, 78, 154
Fowler, Linda L., 7, 22, 84, 236
Frisa, Daniel, 119, 120, 121, 123, 136

GATT, 76
gay rights, 254 n 12
GE (General Electric), 104, 211
geographic constituency. *See* constituency
Gephardt, Richard, 120, 132, 196
Gilligan, Carol, 141
Gimpel, James G., 7, 8, 84
Gingrich, Newt, 16, 58, 70, 80, 82, 83, 95, 96, 97, 100, 101, 115, 132, 167, 197, 202, 208
Giuliani, Rudy, 92
globalization, 45, 240, 241, 243, 252
going national, 11, 65, 79, 226, 232, 248, 251, 252
Government Reform and Oversight Committee, 48, 73

Gore, Albert, 43, 89, 111, 119, 121, 149, 185, 195, 198, 208, 210
Gorski, Dennis, 187, 188
Greek, 35, 38, 41, 48, 152
Green Island, 105, 106, 108
Green, Bill, 38, 39, 40, 41
gun control, 120, 123, 127, 129, 131, 134, 135, 136, 166, 171, 212, 237
gun legislation, 43, 123, 125, 126–128, 133, 135, 251
gun violence, 122, 124, 125, 126, 127, 134, 135, 136, 230

Hacker, Jacob S., 84
Haiti, 155, 165
Hamburg, NY, 186, 187, 188, 189, 195, 219
Harvard, 26, 53, 90
Hastert, Dennis, 43, 59, 131
Hensarling, Jeb, 221, 240
Herrnson, Paul S., 6, 84
heterogeneous district, 22, 86, 90, 92, 103, 158, 180, 185, 203, 239
Higgins, Brian, 247
Hinchey, Maurice
    background of, 203–209
    economic issues, 206–207, 210, 213, 218, 220
    education issues, 204, 207, 213, 214, 215
    environmental issues, 184, 204–205, 208, 210–211, 213–214, 216–220, 236, 239
    and government waste, 205
    health care issues, 209, 211, 215, 216, 217
    home style of, 209–217
    and presentation, 216
    primary campaign of, 206
    veterans issues, 211
Hispanic, 143, 144, 173, 244, 245, 258. *See also* Latino
HIV. *See* AIDS
HMO reform, 96, 129

Home style
  and Fenno, 3, 5, 7, 9, 13, 62, 78
  local elements affecting, 35, 44,
    50, 55, 62, 87, 107, 116, 124,
    130, 149, 158, 160, 173, 179,
    223
  local-national connection, 175
  national elements affecting, 6, 10,
    15–16, 20, 35, 51, 63, 65, 78,
    87, 100, 137, 172, 174, 179,
    202, 218, 222
  and September 11, 242, 251
Homeland Security, Department of,
  246
Homeland security issues, 249, 251
home-Washington connection, 8, 21
homogeneous districts, 52, 53, 77, 82,
  239
Houghton, Amo
  background of, 53–55
  economic issues, 51, 58, 62
  education issues, 52, 57, 59
  home style of, 55–62
  and John Lewis, 57–58, 68, 139,
    142
  military issues, 57
  and presentation, 56, 63
  primary campaign of, 52
  racism, 57–58
  religion, 58, 62
House Appropriations Committee, 40,
  111, 213
House Senate Joint Economic Committee, 213
House Trails Caucus, 94
Hudson River, 87, 89, 94, 109, 182,
  184, 191, 204, 205, 210, 211,
  220

I-86, 57, 210
IBM, 53, 89, 182
incumbent advantage, 5, 180
incumbency, 5, 13, 19–20, 35, 38, 39,
  40, 41, 84, 85, 89, 107, 121,
  123, 136, 150, 159, 162, 188,
  192, 206, 207, 252

insider, 65, 68, 72, 86, 102, 107, 110,
  111, 114, 137, 138, 230
International Relations Committee,
  59, 73
Internet, 5, 23, 99, 126, 209, 223
intimate constituency. *See* constituency
Irish, 67, 104, 112, 119, 148, 155,
  182, 187, 247
Israel, 123, 154, 193
Italian, 38, 104, 119, 148, 155
Ithaca, 25, 184, 185, 206, 208, 209

Jackson, Jesse, 121, 167, 171
Jacobson, Gary C., 5, 7, 19, 84
Jeffords, James, 80, 85
Jewish, 104, 108, 118, 119, 148, 150,
  154, 155, 159, 171
Jewish, 104, 108, 118, 119, 148, 150,
  154, 155, 159
Johannes, John R., 190
John Quincy Adams Society, 59
Johnson, Janet Buttolph, 28
Joint Economic Committee, 45, 213
Judiciary Committee, 32, 89, 128,
  134, 199
Joslyn, Richard A., 28

Kelly, Sue
  background of, 90–93
  census, 90
  education issues, 93, 94, 234
  environmental issues, 89, 94, 98, 99
  health care issues, 91, 94, 96, 97,
    230, 237
  home style of, 93–100
  military issues, 99
  and presentation, 93, 95
  primary campaign of, 91, 92, 97
  veterans issues, 96, 99, 230
Kennedy, Robert F., 34
Kennedy, Robert F. Jr., 94
Kennedy, William J., 104, 106
Keohane, Robert O., 28
King, Gary, 28
King, Peter, 125, 129, 130, 133, 165,
  244

Kingdon, John W., 82, 224
Kingston, NY, 25, 181, 184, 205, 210
Klein, Richard, 100, 101
Kosovo, 154, 175
Kuhl, Randy, 247

labor issues, 66, 109, 110, 121, 150,
    155, 159, 186, 187, 189, 190,
    191, 194, 195, 196, 200, 201,
    202, 206, 219, 223, 224, 226,
    237, 238, 245, 246
  connections, 245
  orientation, 245
  roundtable, 191, 200
  unions, 66, 109, 110, 122, 150,
    159, 166, 186, 187, 189, 190,
    194, 195, 196, 200, 201, 202,
    219, 223
Latino, 25, 38, 119, 141, 144, 145,
    148, 159, 161, 162, 163, 164–
    165, 166, 167, 169, 171–175,
    229, 230, 235, 238, 239
Lawrence, Eric, D., 8
Lazio, Rick, 30, 32, 33, 34
legislative background, 16, 49, 78, 235
Leland, Mickey, 143
liberal republican, 18, 28, 39, 85, 234,
    239
Littleton, CO, 128
local component, 2, 19, 49, 55, 62
local concerns, 2, 33, 73, 79, 174,
    179, 187, 189, 219, 238
local elements, 34, 235
local factors, 3, 6, 19, 117, 174, 175,
    179, 203, 222, 223
local level, 11, 15, 17, 98, 179
local orientation, 13, 200, 247
local parties, 9, 103, 116, 174, 204
local perspective, 34, 252
local roots, 122, 224, 225
localism, 5, 10, 15, 29, 174, 222, 223
localize, 175, 218
local-national balance, 15, 224, 247
local-national connection, 10, 17, 19,
    21, 50, 175, 179, 201, 226,
    238, 239, 242, 248

local-national distinction, 11, 64, 103,
    142, 174, 219, 242
local-national interconnections, 35,
    238, 239, 252
local-national linkage, 9, 239, 247,
    252
Long Island, 36, 54, 117, 118, 119,
    120, 124, 126, 129
Low Income HEAP, 197
Lowey, Nita, 91, 248
Lublin, David, 141
Lundine, Stan, 53–55, 63

Madison, James, 32, 210
Madison, James, 32–33
Main Street Coalition, 60
majority leader, 131, 194, 246
majority-minority districts, 144, 162,
    164, 175, 229
Malbin, Michael J., xi, 22
Maloney, Carolyn
  background of, 38–41
  and census, 1, 2, 44, 48, 49
  constituency, 36–41
  economic issues, 45
  education issues, 38
  and government waste, 39, 45
  health care issues, 248
  home style of, 41–49
  military issues, 46
  and presentation, 35
  primary campaign of, 42, 43
Mandela, Nelson, 59, 155, 160
Manhattan, 36, 38, 41, 50, 78, 144,
    145, 204, 224, 244, 250
Mann, Thomas E., 5
Mansbridge, Jane, 143
marginal district, 232, 234
Margolies-Mezvinsky, Marjorie, 6, 39,
    40, 41, 161, 163, 230
marriage penalty, 93
Martin, David, O'B., 68–69
Mayhew, David R., 5, 34, 42
McAdams, John C., 190
McCarthy, Carolyn
  background of, 120–123

economic issues, 118, 126
education issues, 124, 126, 129,
    131, 135, 136, 230, 234
environmental issues, 122
health care issues, 124, 127, 129–
    130, 131, 134, 135
home style of, 123–135
and presentation, 131, 132, 138
primary campaign of, 115, 116, 121
veterans issues, 124, 130, 135, 137
McCarthy, Dennis, 120
McCarthy, Kevin, 120, 122
McClure, Robert D., 7, 22, 84
McGrath, Ray, 119, 123
McHugh, John
    background of, 67–68
    and census 74, 75
    dairy issues, 57, 66, 67, 70, 76, 77,
        78, 235, 238
    economic issues, 66
    education issues, 73
    environmental issues, 71
    home style of, 68–76
    labor unions, 66
    military issues, 66, 69, 72, 73, 77,
        78, 226, 243
    postal reform, 73–74, 78
    and presentation, 73, 74, 75
    primary campaign of, 68
    veterans issues, 72
McNulty, John, Jr., 105
McNulty, Michael
    background of, 105–107
    economic issues, 103–104, 108–
        109
    education issues, 104, 106, 108,
        112
    environmental issues, 113, 115
    health care issues, 104, 113
    home style of, 107–114
    labor issues, 109, 110, 122, 150,
        223
    military issues, 109, 110
    postal reform, 128
    and presentation, 103, 107
    veterans issues, 108

Medicare, 43, 75, 112, 129, 152, 156,
    157, 215
Mexico, 57, 113, 195
Middle East, 1, 216
Miller, Warren E., 224
Million Mom March, 127
minimum wage, 60, 127, 167, 194,
    195, 197, 201, 213, 218, 219,
    243
Minorities
    concentration, 148
    and district, 36, 142, 230
    running for congress, 6
Miroff, Bruce, xi, 85, 141
moderate republicans, 60, 61, 87, 197,
    199, 201, 239, 247
modern congress, 82
Mohawk Tribe, 69, 210
money laundering, 169
Moppert, Bob, 207–208
motor voter, 212
Moynihan, Patrick Daniel, 26, 34, 50,
    132
multiethnic, 11, 24, 141, 142, 144,
    150, 153, 155, 160–161, 173,
    174, 175, 229
multiethnic districts, 11, 141, 142,
    144, 153, 155, 159, 160, 173,
    175, 229
Murtha, John, 128
Muslim, 161, 250

Nadler, Gerald, 61, 246
NAFTA, 76, 195, 196, 217
Nassau County
    and Independence Party, 122
    and republican political machine,
        119, 122
national component, 7, 19, 30, 78
national context, 35, 137, 202, 218
National Endowment for the Arts, 61,
    99
national figures, 16, 35, 227
National focus, 3, 6, 8, 32, 44–49, 58,
    79, 221, 222, 226, 229, 238,
    244, 252

national issues, 3, 15, 16, 32, 77, 78, 86, 115, 116, 218, 219, 226, 227, 238, 244

national level, 8, 9, 13, 15, 16, 19, 20, 32, 33, 75, 82, 83, 84, 85, 86, 103, 164, 226, 238

National orientation, 236, 244

National partisanship, 11, 35, 86, 137, 207, 220

national perspective, 6, 15, 58, 63, 116

national stature, 56, 63, 64

national themes, 41, 227

National Women's Political Caucus, 41, 92

nationalization, 9, 18, 96, 242

Nationalize, 6, 16, 19, 34, 192, 218, 222, 226, 238, 243

national-local distinction, 65, 86

Nationally oriented, 15, 17, 234, 235, 251

Nazi war criminals, 47, 108, 154

New England Dairy Compact, 57, 70

New York State legislature 25–26, 39, 85, 106, 173, 185, 204, 205, 206, 219, 247

Nicaragua, 57, 62, 211

nonpartisan, *see* bipartisan

North Country, 25, 35, 65, 66, 68, 69, 71

Northern Ireland, 113, 130, 155

NOW (National Organization of Women), 41

Nowak, Henry, 185, 187, 189, 192

NRA (National Rifle Association), 128, 254 n12

O'Brien, Leo, 102, 107

O'Connell, Daniel, 104, 106

O'Connell, Ed, 106

Office of Technology Assessment, 61

Oleszek, Walter J., 6, 7, 8, 17, 20, 63, 82, 84, 97, 141

ombudsperson, 2, 5, 20, 29, 171, 190

O'Neill, Tip, 13, 83

out-of-district, 3, 6, 15, 235

outsider, 19, 23, 68, 77, 114, 162, 165, 182, 230

PACs (see Political Action Committees), 6, 15

Parker, Glenn R., 5

partisan, 2, 9, 11, 18, 43, 48, 65, 75, 77, 78, 84, 85, 95, 100, 107, 114, 117, 133, 137, 150, 157, 164, 166, 169, 178, 180, 185, 189, 203, 206–208, 210–213, 216, 218–220, 222, 227–229, 231–237, 245–250, 252

partisan home style, 233–234

partisanship, 2, 5, 9, 11, 15, 21, 26, 35, 49, 51, 59, 60, 78, 79, 80, 82, 84, 86, 105, 121, 138, 149, 158, 167, 179, 189, 212, 220–221, 226–229, 231–234, 238, 240, 242, 245, 246

party loyalist , 93, 95, 137

party loyalty, 60, 63, 70, 76, 82, 84, 91, 95, 100, 117, 136, 155, 157, 158, 216, 218, 228, 237, 245

party polarization, 6, 7, 82, 83, 115

party unity, 48, 60, 75, 82, 83, 84, 85, 95, 115, 136, 157, 166, 197, 216

party unity (scores), 48, 75, 95, 115, 157, 166, 197

party whip, 75, 93, 110, 111, 137, 138, 216, 245

Pataki, George, 93, 133, 208, 249

Paulson, Arthur, 83

Paxon, Bill, 92, 157, 188, 197

PCBs, 94, 191

Pell, Clairborne, 63

Permanent Select Committee on Intelligence, 244

Perot, Ross, 185, 188

personal factors, 24, 236, 246

Peters, Ronald M., 22

Pierrepont Manor, 66

Pierson, Paul, 84
Plattsburgh Air Force Base, 66, 69
Polish, 38, 182
political insider, 65, 68, 72, 86, 102, 107, 110–114, 137, 138, 230
politics of commonality, 11, 142, 174
politics of difference, 11, 142, 175, 230
Polsby, Nelson W., 6, 84
Post Office and Civil Service committee, 155
Post Office and Civil Service Commission, 155
Postal reform, 73
Poughkeepsie, NY, 87, 99, 100
precongressional careers, 45, 93, 95, 149, 219, 230, 236
presentational strategies, 1, 2, 3, 4, 9, 10, 11, 15, 16, 18, 23, 24, 32, 33, 34, 78, 221, 222, 242, 244
presentation style, 9, 15, 18, 32, 35, 222
primary campaign, 21, 42, 43, 52, 68, 91, 92, 97, 115, 116, 121, 158, 159, 160, 162, 164, 167, 175, 206
primary constituency. *See* constituency
Public Works and Transportation Committee, 187
Puerto Rican constituents and issues, 144, 145, 161–163, 165, 166, 167, 168, 171

Queens, NY, 36, 38, 41, 118, 144, 145, 169, 244
Quinn, Jack
    background of, 186–189
    economic issues, 180–182, 188, 201
    education issues, 184, 198
    environmental issues, 193
    home style of, 189–199
    labor issues, 186, 187, 189, 190, 194, 195, 196, 200–202, 219
    veterans issues, 190, 191, 192, 193, 200, 201

Ragsdale, Lyn, 5
railroads, 1, 2, 25, 118, 187, 191, 192, 193, 200, 226, 251
Reagan, Ronald, 40, 53, 83, 185, 201, 207, 211
redistricting, xiii, 139, 144, 145, 148, 162, 173, 242
redistricting
    in 1992, 36, 38, 49, 152, 155
    in 1999, 43
reelection constituency. *See* constituency
Renzi, Rick, 221, 240
representation
    Optimal/normative, best, quality of, 10, 22, 32, 179, 222
    Choices, 2, 79
    and minorities, 141–144, 154, 161, 172–175, 230
    Type, 33, 34, 86, 142, 143, 159, 160, 162
representational styles, 3, 11, 29, 34–35, 51, 79, 86, 102, 013, 142, 173, 174, 175, 178, 186, 218, 219, 221, 222
representational style, 3, 11, 29, 34, 51, 79, 102, 103, 142, 173, 174, 186, 222
Republican bandwagon, 9, 11, 44, 85, 93, 100, 102, 138
Republican Campaign Committee, 121
Republican Party, 2, 7, 18, 34, 43, 60, 61, 70, 75, 82, 84, 89, 92, 95, 97, 121, 123, 186, 188, 192, 194, 196, 200, 202, 208, 234, 246, 249, 251
Republican revolution, 16, 60, 80, 94, 100, 138, 167, 211
Republican "takeover," 73, 75, 77, 93, 102, 115
Resources Committee, 213–214
responsible party, 8, 9, 11, 77, 82, 84, 85, 86, 93, 100, 101, 102, 103, 115, 116, 117, 136, 137, 227, 228

Rohde, David W., 7, 8, 82, 83
Rossiter, Caleb, 64
Route 17, 57, 64
rural, 28–29, 35, 51, 57, 58, 65–66, 68, 71, 76, 78, 87, 104, 126, 184, 209, 239, 240

Saugerties, NY, 202, 204, 205
Schenectady, NY, 103, 104
Schickler, Eric, 84
Schneier, Edward V., 27
Schousen, Matthew, M, 162
Schumer, Charles, 25, 121, 123, 124, 127, 133
Seabrook, Larry, 159, 255
Seidelman, Raymond, 85, 141
Sellers, Patrick J., 162
Seneca Falls Convention, 97
seniors, 44, 45, 47, 99, 100, 122, 129, 130, 137, 170, 190, 197, 211, 215
seniority, 15, 28, 187, 242, 243, 244, 258 n1
Shays, Christopher, 47, 194, 251
Sinclair, Barbara, 7, 8, 82, 84, 85
Small Business Committee, 94, 126, 169, 175, 244
Smith, Christopher, 97
Smith, Steven S., 8
Snyder, James M., 8
soaking and poking, 22–23
social security, 75, 112, 151, 152, 156, 171, 190, 193, 215
sociopolitical changes, 7, 8, 16, 28, 89, 105, 141, 168, 175, 184, 229, 237
Solarz, Stephen, 162, 163, 164, 175
Solomon, Gerald, 70, 109, 115
Southern Tier, 52, 56, 57, 184, 208, 209, 217
State of the Union, 153, 158, 199
Stewart, Charles, III, 8
Stokes, Donald E., 224
Storing, Herbert, 32, 33
Stratton Air Force Base, 116
Stratton, Sam, 102, 105, 107, 108, 109

suburban, 29, 87, 103, 118, 119, 124, 126, 138, 187, 237, 239
surrogate representation, 143
Swain, Carol M., 141, 142, 143
Swanstrom, Todd, 85, 141
swing district, 87, 185

Takeda, Okiyoshi, 145
terrorism, 43, 57, 59, 250, 252
Terry, Randal, 206
Thomas, Sue, 141, 230
town meetings, 4, 57, 99, 124, 170, 190, 209, 238

Ulster County, 185, 203, 204, 206, 208, 209, 212
upstate, 27, 33, 35, 66, 102, 180, 185, 194, 217, 234, 235, 239
urban, 22, 25, 28, 38, 103, 126, 144, 148, 159, 175, 182, 185, 232, 233, 235, 239
Uslaner, Eric M., 7, 8

Velazquez, Nydia
    background of, 161–164
    census, 165, 170
    economic issues, 169
    education issues, 166, 169, 170, 223
    health care issues, 224
    home style of, 164–171
    labor issues, 166
    and presentation, 166, 167, 170
    primary campaign of, 162, 164, 167, 175
Verba, Sidney, 28
Veterans Affairs Committee, 193
veterans issues, 72, 96, 99, 108, 124, 130, 135, 137, 152, 157, 190, 191, 192, 193, 200, 201, 211, 230
Viequez, 166
Vietnam War, 6, 15, 64, 108

Washington activity, 16, 49, 58, 97, 179, 212, 238